Jane Fonda

Also by Bill Davidson

Bill Davidson

Jane Fonda

An Intimate Biography

DUTTON   NEW YORK

DUTTON

Published by the Penguin Group
Penguin Books USA Inc., 375 Hudson Street,
New York, New York, 10014, U.S.A.
Penguin Books Ltd, 27 Wrights Lane,
London W8 5TZ, England
Penguin Books Australia Ltd, Ringwood,
Victoria, Australia
Penguin Books Canada Ltd, 2801 John Street,
Markham, Ontario, Canada L3R 1B4
Penguin Books (N.Z.) Ltd, 182–190 Wairau Road,
Auckland 10, New Zealand

Penguin Books Ltd, Registered Offices:
Harmondsworth, Middlesex, England

First published by Dutton, an imprint of Penguin Books USA Inc.
Published simultaneously in Canada by Fitzhenry & Whiteside, Limited, Toronto

First American printing, June, 1990

1 3 5 7 9 10 8 6 4 2

Library of Congress Cataloging-in-Publication Data

Davidson, Bill, 1918–
Jane Fonda: an intimate biography
Bill Davidson. — 1st ed.
p.   cm.
"Jane Fonda's films": p.
ISBN 0-525-24888-9
1. Fonda, Jane, 1937– . 2. Motion picture actors and actresses—
United States—Biography. I. Title.
PN2287.F56D38   1990
791.43'028'092—dc20
[B]   89-25833
                                        CIP

Printed in the United States of America
Set in Garamond

DESIGNED BY STEVEN N. STATHAKIS

Grateful acknowledgment is made for permission to reprint excerpts from the following:

"Fonda and Hayden: High Priests Stumble," by Anne Taylor Fleming, which originally
appeared in The New York Times, March 1, 1989. Copyright © 1989 by The New
York Times Company. Reprinted by permission.

Leo Janos's article on Jane Fonda, which originally appeared in Cosmopolitan, January
1985. Reprinted by permission.

For Maralynne

Jane Fonda

PROLOGUE

It is difficult to be totally objective about Jane Fonda—as a biographer is supposed to be. Having looked at her life microscopically for two years, and having known both Jane and her illustrious father, Henry Fonda, I come away with a mélange of conflicting emotions.

First there is awe. Here is one of the great actresses of our generation, an astoundingly successful businesswoman in other fields, a role model for millions of young women throughout the world.

Then there is anger. How could she have done some of the dumb things she did? Few personalities in our time have been so controversial, incurring the unremitting wrath of one segment of the population, in one of the most tumultuous times in our history. And few have made as many mistakes in their personal lives.

I

But, above all, there is admiration. She rebounded from early childhood tragedy, from the effects of a cold and sometimes antagonistic father, from a possibly fatal disease, from a series of bad relationships with men, from a long-running feud with J. Edgar Hoover's FBI and other powerful agencies of the U.S. government.

She prevailed—even against the FBI. And she keeps prevailing—even over her own mistakes. Which is a way of saying that Jane Fonda—exasperating at times, inspiring at others—is a modern-day version of the mythical phoenix, rising constantly from the ashes.

The Freedom of Information Act is a wondrous thing. You request the FBI's files on Jane Fonda, for example, and after months of backing and filling, the Bureau finally sends you 763 pages—with a reminder that this act of Congress is one of the factors that distinguishes us from secrecy-prone totalitarians.

If you've never seen information dispensed by government agencies under this act (and few of us have), on the next page is one of the 763 pages in the FBI's Jane Fonda file as released to me:

The blacked-out portions presumably are the name of the FBI informant, followed by all the other agencies of government to which the informant's report was sent.

The report itself consists of six pages of verbatim remarks made by Miss Fonda and is a repetition of the typical 1970s

JANE FONDA
SECURITY MATTERS -
ANARCHIST

On June 19, 1970, a representative of the FBI was
in attendance at a rally held at 217 West First Street,
Los Angeles, in support of militant causes; specifically
in support of three inmates at Soledad Prison, Soledad,

- 4 -

protest rhetoric against racial discrimination and in favor of freedom of speech. She appeals for funds to support the defense of black inmates at Soledad Prison in California.

Yet, note the heading on this FBI file: JANE FONDA, ANARCHIST.

Miss Fonda has never shot anybody, or blown up anything, or tried to destroy the U.S. government (which is what anarchists do), but that's the way she was identified in many of these pages released to me by the FBI.

Despite the copious use of black ink, many secrets do slip through when you are sent as many as 763 pages. Human error can cause many pages to be included that perhaps the agency didn't want to be included, pages that can prove to be extremely embarrassing to the government.

On June 19, 1970, for example, Wesley G. Grapp, then agent in charge of the FBI office in Los Angeles, sent the following memo about Jane Fonda to FBI Director J. Edgar Hoover:

TO: DIRECTOR, FBI
FROM: SAC, LOS ANGELES
RE: COUNTERINTELLIGENCE
            PROGRAM
            BLACK NATIONALIST-HATE
            GROUPS
            RACIAL INTELLIGENCE
            BLACK PANTHER PARTY (BPP)

Re Los Angeles teletype to Bureau, 6/15/70, entitled "COMMITTEE UNITED FOR POLITICAL PRISONERS (CUPP), IS MISCELLANEOUS, THREAT AGAINST PRESIDENT NIXON".

Bureau authority is requested in sending the following letter from a fictitious person to Army Archerd, Hollywood "gossip" columnist for the "Daily Variety", who noted in his 6/11/70 column that JANE FONDA, noted film actress, was to be present at the 6/13/70 Black Panther Party fund raising function sponsored by CUPP in Los Angeles. It is felt that knowledge of FONDA'S involvement would cause her embarrassment and detract from her status with the general public.

"Dear Army,

I saw your article about Jane Fonda in "Daily Variety" last Thursday and happened to be present for Vadim's "Joan of Arc" performance for the Black Panthers Saturday night. I hadn't been confronted with this Panther phenomena before but we were searched upon entering Embassy Auditorium, encouraged in revival-like fashion to contribute to defend jailed Panther leaders and buy guns for "the coming revolution", and led by Jane and one of the Panther chaps in a "we will kill Richard Nixon, and any other M——F—— who stands in our way" refrain (which was shocking to say the least!). I think Jane has gotten in over her head as the whole atmosphere had the 1930's Munich beer-hall aura.

"I also think my curiosity about the Panthers has been satisfied.

"Regards
/a/ "Morris"

If approved, appropriate precautions will be taken to preclude the identity of the Bureau as the source of this operation.

As is evident in this memo, Grapp is asking permission of Director Hoover to concoct a phony letter about Jane Fonda, to be signed by a fictitious "Morris," which he would mail to *Daily Variety* columnist Army Archerd. "Morris" is to write that he went to a Black Panther rally, where he heard Miss

Fonda advocate the purchase of guns for "the coming revolution" and that he heard her exhorting the crowd to chant, "We will kill Richard Nixon and any other motherfucker who stands in our way." Since Mr. Hoover did not approve of foul language among his agents, "motherfucker" appears in the memo as M——F——.

One would expect Mr. Hoover to reject such a hare-brained and immoral scheme out of hand, but on June 25, Hoover sent the following memo to Grapp, slightly editing the "Morris" letter, authorizing him to send it, and warning that Grapp "insure that mailing cannot be traced to the Bureau."

TO: SAC, LOS ANGELES
FROM: DIRECTOR, FBI
        COUNTERINTELLIGENCE
        PROGRAM
        BLACK NATIONALIST-HATE
        GROUPS
        RACIAL INTELLIGENCE
        BLACK PANTHER PARTY

LAairtel 6/17/70.

You are authorized to prepare a letter as set forth in relet and mail to Army Archerd, the Hollywood "gossip" columnist. Insure that mailing cannot be traced to the Bureau.

NOTE:

Los Angeles proposed that a letter from a fictit. person be sent to Hollywood "gossip" columnist of the "Daily Variety" in connection with his column on 6/11/70 indicating Jane Fonda, noted film actress, would attend a Black Panther Party fund raising function on 6/13/70. The proposed letter states the writer attended the function and was searched upon entering, urged to contribute funds for jailed Panther leaders and to buy guns for "the coming

7

revolution." Also, that Jane and one of the Panthers led a refrain "We will kill Richard Nixon, and any other M——F—— who stands in our way." It can be expected that Fonda's involvement with the BPP cause could detract from her status with the general public if reported in a Hollywood "gossip" column.

This outrageous act by the director of the storied and once highly respected Federal Bureau of Investigation came to light in the 1975 U.S. Senate Church Committee hearings investigating wrongful FBI and CIA activities against U.S. citizens. To my knowledge, this is the first time the actual FBI "Morris" memos have ever been seen by the public.

What happened to the letter? It was mailed to columnist Archerd, but it never ran in *Daily Variety.*

Archerd told me, "I never use an item like that without trying to verify it. The only way I could verify it was through the guy who signed the letter, Morris. There was no return address so I threw the thing in the wastebasket. The only Morris I knew at that time was a cat who sold cat food in TV commercials."

So much for the skill of the FBI in those troubled Vietnam war protest years.

And so much for Jane Fonda as victim, which is only one of the many contradictory sides of this powerful, fascinating, memorable woman.

2

Jack Lemmon calls Jane Fonda "one of the three finest movie actresses in the world, the other two being Anne Bancroft and England's Maggie Smith."

After Miss Fonda's 1972 trip to Hanoi and her broadcasts on North Vietnam Radio, two congressmen, Fletcher Thompson and Richard Ichord, demanded that she be tried for treason. The *Manchester* (N.H.) *Union-Leader* editorially called for her to be shot. In a debate in the Maryland state legislature, there were suggestions that "she either be hanged or have her tongue cut out."

Jane's father, Henry Fonda, once said, "The problem with my daughter is that she lets her motor run too fast."

In 1984, *Fortune* featured an article about Jane as one of the nation's leading businesswomen (for her multimillion-dollar workout business, which includes tapes and books as well) and chided her for "becoming Big Business when her philosophies always had been *anti*–Big Business."

But at least six physical-fitness and physical–well-being mavens have accused Jane of stealing their ideas. Her old exercise teacher, Gilda Marx, says snidely, "Jane is an actress. Her profession is to copy what someone else has done." To date, none of these allegations have been tested or confirmed in court.

The late Abbie Hoffman, one of the best-known protest leaders in Jane's radical days, said, "Jumping Jane. Wow! Does she take things seriously." Then, referring to another protest leader, Jerry Rubin, the acerbic Hoffman added, "I always thought that Jerry and Jane should have mated. Then you could have had taut strong bodies with shallow minds—the perfect yuppie prototype, the Jerry Janes."

Yet, Donald Sutherland, who was with Jane through most of her radical period, has said, "She's one of the most intelligent women I have known."

To the political Republican right, Jane remains, to this day, a favorite target. Although she has long since joined the mainstream liberal wing of the Democratic Party, even a casual handshake with Jane at a public concert is enough for a candidate to be branded by a conservative opponent as "being a part of the kookie Jane Fonda left."

There still are bumper stickers that read: I'm Not Fonda Hanoi Jane. The same slogan still appears on signs at veterans' rallies and conventions, yet, strangely, not so much at Vietnam veterans' functions.

Even George Bush tried to use the negative Jane Fonda image in the 1988 presidential campaign. In attempting to associate Michael Dukakis with her, Bush said, in San Diego on September 4, "I will not be surprised if my opponent thinks a naval exercise is something you find in the *Jane Fonda Workout Book.*"

So how do you account for the fact that her workout tapes and books outsell all others; and that her recent films (with just one exception) have made millions and invariably end up on the list of top-grossing pictures for the year?

And how do you account for her inclusion in polls to find the most-admired women? In 1984, Gallup ranked her just behind Mother Teresa, Margaret Thatcher, and Nancy Reagan. In April 1985, Roper found that in a poll of eighteen- to twenty-four-year-olds, Jane Fonda was number one among women, and number three (behind Ronald Reagan and Clint Eastwood) when most-admired men and women were combined.

It's a puzzlement, as Yul Brynner said in his role in *The King and I.* And Jane Fonda is a lady of contradictions, which is why there are so many conflicting opinions about her.

I have my own theories about why people either love or hate her.

First, the love factors:

For one thing, she enjoys a lasting residual benefit from the deep affection and respect that the public held for her father, Henry Fonda. Henry never offended anyone, and his work in films and on the stage was almost universally praised. Unlike his daughter, he rarely took public stands on controversial issues—even when, as Jane says, "He got so mad at Joe McCarthy during the Army-McCarthy hearings that I saw him kick in the television screen." The public on the whole doesn't know that Jane was estranged from her father for much of her life. She admits that it was only in their one picture together, *On Golden Pond,* shortly after which Henry died, "that we were able to say to one another, through our characters in the film, 'I love you.' " To those who knew the circumstances, it was one of the most touching onscreen moments in the recent history of film—comparable to Spencer Tracy's farewell with love to Katharine Hepburn in *Guess Who's Coming to Dinner.*

A second reason for many people's admiration of Jane is her resiliency. It was Robert Redford who first said, "She's like a phoenix who keeps rising from the ashes." Some of the ashes have been of her own making (as when she was practically blackballed from the movie industry during and after her activist period); some have not. Deep emotional scars were left in a twelve-year-old child whose mother committed suicide in a particularly horrible way, leaving Jane to suffer twenty-three years of a debilitating and life-threatening type of emotional/physical disease, bulimia, over which she eventually triumphed at the age of thirty-six. She suffered paternal neglect as a youngster, struggled to acclimate herself to a succession of stepmothers, and she was used by a succession of men early in her career. She went through a period she now loathes in which her main movie role was that of the empty-headed "sex-kitten" (even doing one famous striptease on-screen in *Barbarella*). But after breaking away from her first husband, French director Roger Vadim, she resurrected her career with the fine American film *They Shoot Horses, Don't They?* Somehow, part of the public seems to have sensed all these struggles, creating a residue of warmth for Jane that exists to this day.

This seems to be particularly true of women. Asked why they consider her the most-admired woman in America, many of them told me her stardom and business success are only *partial* reasons for their idolatry. They say things like: "She fights back," "She takes men on at their own game," "She's had a tough life and overcame a lot of stuff," and "I like the way she doesn't get thrown by the hard knocks she had to take, which is why she's my role model." I heard these reactions from women in all categories of life—from my cleaning lady to TV network executives.

The third quotient in the love–Jane Fonda category is, I believe, the unique quality of the roles she has chosen for herself, especially since she founded her own production company (now called Fonda Films) in 1977. She is almost always sympathetic—the psychiatrist trying to help a troubled young novitiate in a convent in *Agnes of God*; the TV reporter getting involved with an atomic-energy-plant engineer who is trying to avert a Chernobyl-like disaster in *The China Syndrome*; even the office worker joining with her colleagues, Lily Tomlin and Dolly Parton, to attain more respect for women from their tyrannical boss in the comedy *Nine to Five.* It would seem to be difficult to develop sympathy for an alcoholic actress, but Jane, with the help of her writers, managed to do that, too, in *The Morning After.* If you accept the old Louis B. Mayer axiom that moviegoers identify actors mostly with the characters they play on the screen (Ronald Reagan with Notre Dame football hero George Gipp, "the Gipper," for example), much of the public would seem to have accepted Miss Fonda, in recent years, as a tough, compassionate, right-thinking lady with all the correct instincts.

Not so for the *hate*–Jane Fonda segment of the population that has never forgiven her for what they consider to be her political transgressions. To them, she is *still* too activist, and at the very least, too liberal. Her estranged husband, Tom Hayden, now a respected California assemblyman but once a top radical himself, once advanced an interesting theory for the hate segment of the love-hate relationship. He said, "People saw Jane on the screen as this adorable, harmless little girl in her early days. I think a lot of men fell in love with that sex-kitten image. They had fantasies about her. But then, in her activist period, suddenly she was coming at them from a different direction. She was destroying their dreams. To this day, with the more substantial roles she's playing, some of them still want to punish her for destroying their dreams."

There are more complicated reasons, of course. Angela Lansbury, who worked with Jane in *In the Cool of the Day* in 1963, says, "It's a matter of power. Some people, especially men, are leery of very powerful women, which Jane is in the movie industry today." Proof of this is that when David Puttnam was forced to resign as the head of Columbia Pictures in 1987, the recurring nervous question I heard in the corridors of the studio's Burbank office building was, "Can we hold on to Bill Cosby? Will Fonda Films stay with us?" Both did, and the next Fonda film, *Old Gringo* with Jane and Gregory Peck, was slated to be the big Columbia Christmas blockbuster of 1988—a release date which, because of post-production problems, had to be advanced into 1989.

Fear, resentment, other intangible factors, have built up

a minority of Jane-haters (about 15 percent, according to polls commissioned by her). The haters came into dramatic conflict with the Jane-lovers in 1988 when she was scheduled to begin filming a picture in the mostly blue-collar town of Waterbury, Connecticut. Some local residents still call it the Battle of Waterbury.

It all began innocently enough when Metro-Goldwyn-Mayer (M-G-M)—*not* Fonda Films—bought a property then called *Union Street.* It was a simple, touching love story about a widow in a working-class town in New England who falls in love with a baker, whom she learns is totally illiterate and cannot read or write. The woman, Iris, then sets about educating the baker, Stanley, and in the process and through much travail, their love broadens and deepens. M-G-M hired the fine director Martin Ritt *(Norma Rae)* to direct a sensitive script written by Irving Ravetch and his wife, Harriet Frank, Jr. *(Hud, The Long Hot Summer, Norma Rae)*. The film's name was changed to *Stanley and Iris.* The script was sent to Jane Fonda and Robert De Niro, both of whom loved it and agreed to play the leads. They were both signed on as actors-for-hire. Fonda Films was not involved in the production. The subject matter was totally uncontroversial, but Jane was intrigued with the premise of a woman fighting illiteracy, a severe American problem.

‹ The opening salvo in the Battle of Waterbury came on Veterans Day 1987, when it became known that M-G-M was about to use several New England factory cities, among them Waterbury, for the *Stanley and Iris* locations, though the principal photography would be done in Toronto. Apparently infuriated by this news, a seventy-year-old World War II veteran and a former major general in the Connecticut National Guard named Gaetano Russo went into action. "It's very difficult for me to accept a traitor," Russo said in a letter to the conservative *Waterbury Republican* expressing what he called his "disatisfaction" with Fonda even appearing in the city for filming.

Saying that his letter to the editor had prompted a "deluge" of supportive phone calls, Russo then proceeded to print and sell hundreds of I'm Not Fonda Hanoi Jane bumper stickers. They began to appear in some numbers throughout the area. The local congressman, Republican John Rowland, threw in his support, and so did Waterbury Mayor Joseph Sanpietro, saying through an aide, "Waterbury is and always has been a very patriotic town. We honor Flag Day, we honor Veterans Day, we're out there in the rain, the snow, the sleet, marching. Everyone has their flags out in front of their businesses. This is a salt-of-the-earth, blue-collar, patriotic American town."

The anti-Fonda campaign began to take hold in nearby Holyoke and Chicopee, which also had been named as possible location sites for the film. Local press coverage was picked up by the national press and it looked as if this part of New England was girding for another war. In fact, Gaetano Russo, whose nickname is Guy, who had never been near Vietnam, promised a battle "the size of the Tet Offensive" if Jane Fonda came to town.

While all this was going on, Jane was in the remote deserts of northern Mexico making *Old Gringo,* and only vaguely aware of the flap. She has, however, a skilled public-relations expert, Stephen Rivers, a short, bearded executive on the staff of Fonda Films, who previously had had much experience in "spin control" (the calming down of flaps) as press secretary to Assemblyman Tom Hayden. "I really didn't take it too seriously," says Rivers. "I figured it was mostly the work of one right-wing guy, Russo, and one right-wing newspaper, the *Waterbury Republican.* But I decided I'd better get into action right away."

The first thing Rivers did was to get specific information about the extent of the problem. He hired the marketing research firm of Fairbank, Bregman, and Maullin to do a scientifically based public-opinion poll in Waterbury on December 12 and 13, 1987. It was a random sampling of 402 adults, age eighteen and older. The results were quite startling: 73 percent said that Jane Fonda should not be prevented from making a movie in their city; only 13 percent responded that she should be stopped. There was practically no difference between veterans' families (73 percent pro filming) and non-veterans' families (74 percent). Sixty-four percent of all respondents (including the veterans) said that "even though they may disagree with Jane Fonda on some inportant issues, she is still considered a loyal American." A subsequent follow-up poll in the area, with a larger sample (602), generally confirmed these results. An additional question was a head-on "Do you have a favorable or unfavorable opinion of Jane Fonda?" Fifty-eight percent said "favorable." It was almost dead even with a 59 percent "favorable" for Ronald Reagan, obtained in the same poll.

Armed with these statistics, which he, of course, released to the press nationwide, Rivers decided to go to Waterbury to take on Russo face-to-face. He brought with him letters of support for Jane from such personages as former House Speaker "Tip" O'Neill and Max Cleland, the severely disabled war veteran who was head of the Veterans Administration and now is Georgia's Secretary of State. He also arranged to bring in some pro-Fonda Vietnam veterans.

The battle was joined, and Russo and his cohorts turned out to be tough enemies. They held rallies; they promised boycotts and violent demonstrations if filming were to begin. In a hearing at Chicopee City Hall, one Steven Page said, "I will do everything in my power to stop her, even if it means facing arrest a hundred times a day." A legless vet, Clayton Hough, said, "Jane, don't come here. Go to Hanoi. Go wherever you want, but don't come here."

But Rivers's troops were there to counterattack. James Jackson, a Vietnam Green Beret and POW, got up and said, "I'm only saddened. Miss Fonda's a great artist and a fine lady. It's something that she admits was stupid. I lived in a cage as a POW and suffered. If I can find it in my heart to forgive, I don't see what anybody else can complain about."

It got to be a running skirmish—from Chicopee to Holyoke to Waterbury's Library Square. Russo's forces were outgunned. A man got up in the midst of an anti-Fonda veterans' rally and said he was Charles Liteky of Washington, D.C., adding that he was a holder of the Congressional Medal of Honor. (He had won the nation's highest military honor when, as a chaplain with the 12th Infantry in Bien Hoa Province in Vietnam, he rescued twenty wounded soldiers despite severe wounds to himself.) The awed crowd of vets fell silent as Liteky spoke. He said, "Of course, I was distressed by Jane Fonda's antiwar protests when I was in 'Nam, but then I began to feel betrayed by the politicians and businessmen who promoted that war. As far as letting Jane Fonda come here, why shouldn't she come? That's what I fought for."

But the most telling blow was struck by a *local* vet, Brian Powell. It was aimed directly at Guy Russo, who had started and promulgated the anti-Fonda flap. Said Powell, "Where was Guy Russo in 1970 when I applied for membership in the VFW on Bank Street and was rejected because they said Vietnam wasn't a real war? Guy Russo wasn't in Vietnam and he has no right to speak for us."

That was March 25, 1988. On the same day, M-G-M announced that filming would take place in Waterbury, despite any threat of continuing protests. Steve Rivers had pretty much won the battle.

On April 27, the Waterbury Board of Aldermen voted down, 11 to 2, a resolution denying any welcome "symbolic or otherwise" to Fonda.

On June 18, Fonda flew in to meet with twenty-six Vietnam vets at St. Michael's Episcopal Church in nearby Naugatuck. The press was barred, but Rev. John McColley, a Vietnam vet who moderated the session, said that the meeting went on for three and a half hours. "There was a lot of arguing and explaining," said McColley, "and some of the men even cried. Miss Fonda admitted she had romanticized the other side in the war and was wrong to do so. To my total amazement, she and all the men ended up good friends at the end of the session." One of the converts was Robert Genovese, commander of VFW Post 1946. He said, "There's no way you can take twenty-six angry veterans and snow them with an Academy Award performance. After all, a lot has changed for all of us in the last sixteen years." Jane said, "I think we learned a lot about each other. It was a very moving experience."

Filming began in Waterbury on July 25. Jane arrived by car from New York a couple of days earlier. She still looked wan and tired from the exhausting Mexican location for *Old Gringo.* She was, however, a little overweight around the middle from all the tortillas she had consumed, and she immediately asked director Martin Ritt to have his production manager line up a gym in which she could work out and a park in which she could jog. Ritt said fine, and Jane was whisked away to a private home that had been rented for her. There wasn't a picket in sight to mar her arrival.

There *were* pickets carrying their I'm Not Fonda Hanoi Jane signs when production began outside an old brick button factory on South Main Street, which had been converted into the bakery where Stanley (Robert De Niro) worked. The pickets numbered about twenty-five and were very vocal. About 11:00 A.M., when they became too raucous and tried to thrust their picket signs in camera range, the Waterbury police moved in and several of them were arrested on disorderly conduct charges, including Guy Russo. All were later released when they agreed not to try to interfere with production again. After that, things began to change.

Some of it could be attributed to pure economics and the lure of Hollywood magic in a town rarely, if ever, singled out for such show-business attention. M-G-M's casting people put out a call for 500 local extras and some 2,000 responded, snaking for blocks around the Mattatuck Museum, where the auditions were held. The extras received $50 a day for their efforts, mostly walking around, and if they were lucky, sitting in buses, et cetera, with Fonda and Robert De Niro.

The second component that forced the change in Waterbury's attitude may have been Steve Rivers's continuing "spin doctoring." On July 29, both Fonda and De Niro appeared at a fund-raising event in nearby Quassy Amusement Park for the benefit of handicapped children of vets who had been exposed to Agent Orange in Vietnam. A newly formed organization, Vets Who Care, sponsored the event. Some 2,500 local people attended the benefit, which raised $27,000. For an extra $15, a contributor could be photographed with both stars, and about 400 did so.

Similarly, some 200 people paid $50 each to attend a fund-raiser for the Literacy Volunteers of Waterbury at the Mattatuck Museum. Meeting Jane was the sole attraction of the event, which took in $10,000.

The third reason for the change in Waterbury's attitude was Jane herself. She ate in local restaurants, such as No Fish Today and the Westside Lobster House; she was gracious and friendly and signed autographs for all who asked—especially the children.

By August 8, the result of all this was startling. Only two dispirited pickets were visible outside a house on Sycamore Lane being used as Iris's home in the movie, and the pickets, glumly sitting on the grass, were obscured by more than a hundred fans watching the film action from behind ribboned police lines across the street.

On Grant Street, near City Hall, it was hard to believe that such a bitter battle had rent this community for nearly a year. Most of the people didn't seem to care one way or the other that film production was still under way. But there was still plenty of talk about Jane Fonda. Kim Washington gushed over the autograph she had received from Jane. Teacher Gina Pannone said, "She's a great role model." Louie Marques, the proprietor of the coffee shop Jimmy's Charcoal Kitchen, said, "I now think the movie was a good idea, bring good business to Waterbury." A twelve-year-old named Michael said, "This is the best thing that's happened since my baby brother was born."

Some of the veterans, like Frank Fabbri, were unplacated, saying, "Where are the men nowadays? When I was young,

Fonda would've been afraid to drive through town." But others had become ambivalent. Marine Vietnam vet Frank McCarthy said, "I still can't forgive her, but when she helps our Agent Orange campaign, I respect her. It's time to let it go, to try to channel all this energy into something positive."

And World War II vet Frank Germinaro, an extra in the film, said something that might have been unthinkable in Waterbury just six months earlier: "She had good intentions at heart—bringing peace to that part of the world, bringing our boys home."

One curious thing about the entire hassle was that all the scenes I saw being filmed in Waterbury were "exteriors"—the outsides of buildings and people walking in and out of them. With the main filming set for Toronto, the "exteriors" could have been shot anywhere that *looked* like New England; several peaceful factory towns in Northern California have long been used for the purpose. A star of Fonda's magnitude easily could have asked for the switch when trouble began brewing in Waterbury. But she didn't. She never ducks controversy.

Which is why she probably is the only movie star of today whose biography requires research—under the Freedom of Information Act—in the files of such government agencies as the FBI and the CIA.

3

To those who think of Jane Fonda with less than admiration, she is, of course, more the provocateur than the victim. Jack Lemmon recalls that when he worked with Jane and Michael Douglas in *The China Syndrome,* some of the scenes were done in a non-nuclear power plant, which, Lemmon says, "looks exactly like a nuclear plant in its inside control rooms."

Lemmon says, "There were a lot of hard hats from the plant standing around watching us, and because Michael and I had spoken out against the dangers of nuclear power, the hard hats kept yelling all kinds of terrible things at us: 'Commie,' 'Pinko,' 'Fag.' That, of course, was before Three Mile Island and Chernobyl, so they may have changed their tune by now. But the tune still is the same for Jane, who took by far the brunt of the abuse. She heard it then, and occasionally she still hears it today. That ugly refrain, 'Go back to Russia, you Commie cunt.'

"The great thing about Jane is that she crossed them up, as she frequently does. She *did* go back to Russia, but it was for a purpose that completely confused her opposition. She defied the Soviet government and slipped into the country to rescue a *dissident,* of all people."

So here we have the lady of contradictions—at her most contradictory. After having been accused of abetting the Communists in Vietnam, now she was taking on the Russians in the very heartland of Communism itself. And this was long before the advent of Mikhail Gorbachev and his reconciling *glasnost* philosophy.

The roots of Jane's Russian invasion go back many years—to about the same time, ironically, that she was filming *The China Syndrome* and was being assailed verbally by what she calls "that cottage industry of Fonda-haters in America." It was then that, through Tom Hayden, she met Benyamin Navon, the Israeli Consul in Los Angeles, and became concerned with the plight of Jews who wanted to leave the Soviet Union and were being prevented from doing so. When asked why she, the ultimate WASP, should have become so concerned about Soviet Jews, she replied, "It's a matter of human freedom. It's the same reason why thousands of white people got involved in Reverend Martin Luther King's marches in the South."

According to Stephen Rivers, Jane's involvement began to focus on a single individual in July 1980. "That summer," says Rivers, "she and Tom and their two children, Vanessa and Troy, went to Israel for a vacation. Like all tourists, they visited *Yad Vashem,* that horrifying memorial to the Holocaust. She came out shaken, like everyone does, and ended up in a small courtyard on the grounds of the memorial. A group of women was waiting to speak with Jane there. They called themselves IWIN, the acronym for Israeli Women for Ida Nudel. One of the women was Ida Nudel's sister, Elana Friedman."

Rivers continues: "Who was Ida Nudel? She was the only woman leader of the refusenik movement of dissident Jews in Russia. At the time, she was in a prison in Siberia, the only female in a barracks filled with Soviet criminal types, including murderers, rapists, and armed robbers. Jane asked for more information about Ida. She always gets touched first by her heart, and what she learned really touched her heart.

"Ida was a tiny woman, only four feet seven inches tall, but apparently dynamic in her beliefs, the kind of woman Jane always gets drawn to. Ida had applied for emigration in 1971 but was turned down by the Soviets on the grounds that she was an economist and knew too many state secrets. Actually, the only thing she was familiar with was hygiene practices, for which she was an accountant in the Ministry of Microbiotics— hardly a matter of national security."

In 1978, after years of frustrating appeals, Ida hung a sign from the balcony of her apartment, reading KGB, GIVE ME MY VISA. For this one act, she was arrested and tried for "hooliganism." Her sentence was four years at hard labor in the Siberian prison of Krivosheino. There was no mention of the fact that she had been a constant thorn in the side of Soviet officialdom. Known as "the Guardian Angel" of the refusenik movement, she had developed an incredible intelligence system and knew where every Jewish dissident was jailed. She smuggled food packages to them and wrote them letters that got through censorship, because she mingled meaningful Hebrew words in among the Russian sentences. The most famous dissident, Anatoly Sharansky, says, "She was incredible, the main contact between the prisoners and their families, in many cases their only source of hope and optimism."

When Jane Fonda heard all this, she became totally involved in the Free Ida Nudel campaign. There was no way to reach Ida, of course, but she corresponded with her through her sister, Elana, who had gotten out to Israel in 1972. Jane wrote reams of letters to congressmen to put pressure on the

Soviet government, and she bombarded Russian officialdom itself with letters—none of which were answered. Jane even ran in ten-kilometer races, carrying a Free Ida Nudel sign for the television cameras.

Finally, in 1984, Jane decided that she must embark on more direct action. By now, Ida had served her four-year prison term in Siberia but was living under close surveillance in the little town of Benderi, in Soviet Moldavia, near the Rumanian border. Ida's sister Elana told Jane, "If a celebrity of your stature could get inside Russia to visit Ida, that would give Ida a kind of protection from government harassment and might even make it easier for her to get out."

Jane says, "I wasn't sure if this would make any sense. Would they even let me in? And if they did and I couldn't even get to see Ida, what would be the purpose of the trip?"

Steve Rivers resolved her doubts. He said he'd go with her, and they would take with them a lawyer friend, Marshall Grossman, who was familiar with Soviet law. Rivers said to Jane, "Remember that some of your films are popular in Russia, and they especially remember *The Blue Bird*." (*The Blue Bird* was a 1975 joint Russian-American film starring Elizabeth Taylor, Ava Gardner, Fonda, and Cicely Tyson, filmed mainly in and around Moscow.)

Rivers says: "Jane said, 'Okay, let's give it a shot,' and Jane, Grossman, and I applied for visas with Anatoly Mishkoff, the Soviet Consul-General in San Francisco. Mishkoff is a pleasant enough fellow, but our request obviously pained him. He said, 'Please don't do this. It isn't going to help Nudel.' Jane said to Mishkoff, 'The simplest thing is to let Nudel out, and then I don't have to go.' That argument got nowhere, but a few weeks later we got the visas. Why? I don't know. With these guys, you never know why they do anything. There was no word of our wanting to visit Nudel, or even permission to go to Benderi. They gave us tourist visas, pure and simple—as if we just wanted to visit Moscow and see the vineyards around Kishinev, the capital of Moldavia."

They flew to Moscow on April 24, 1984. Steve Rivers says, "We had a few hours to spare. One of our contacts in the U.S. State Department had told us to make an appointment to see a man named Rudolf Kuznetzov, who was the head of the Soviet Emigration Agency. There was no time to make an appointment, so we just bulled our way into his office. The Soviets aren't used to that, so it caused quite a tussle in his reception room. Kuznetzov must have heard the noise because he finally came down and spoke with us in the foyer. At first he said he'd speak only with Jane but she said, 'I insist you speak with all three of us.' You know how she can be when she gets that fixed, determined look on her face, hair flapping. Kuznetzov looked rattled and said, 'Da.'

"We spoke with him for forty-five minutes and made no headway in the matter of Ida Nudel's release. But the meeting had a purpose. We caused a stir. And as we later found out, it was a stir that went all through the bureaucracy.

"We flew to Kishinev in the morning," Rivers continues. "We had visas to go to Kishinev but not to Benderi, where Ida lived. We tried to contact her but she was not allowed to have a phone. Ida's sister had told us to try to reach her through the phone of a friendly neighbor named Rueck. But we discovered that Rueck's phone had been disconnected by the authorities the day before. Totally discouraged, we were reduced to talking with our Intourist guides. I don't know whether they were aware of our mission, or just dumb. They kept trying to talk us into making a tour of 'this lovely wine country' with vineyard wine-tastings just as in the Napa Valley of California. Exhausted, Jane finally went up to her room to get some rest."

Rivers and Grossman were standing at the front desk in the Kishinev hotel, trying to get off another telegram to Nudel. Suddenly a voice behind them said in accented English, "Excuse me. Are you Steve Rivers and Marshall Grossman?" They looked down and, from having seen her photos, immediately recognized the tiny figure of Ida Nudel. There was much handshaking and kissing. Ida explained how, in her inexplicable ingenious ways, she had managed to take a bus from Benderi to the Kishinev airport despite her constant KGB surveillance; and then, having missed the Americans at the airport, she had come to the hotel where her mysterious intelligence sources had told her they'd be staying. Rivers said, "We've got to wake Jane up. Come upstairs with us to her room."

Jane says, "I heard this knocking on my door and I heard Steve say, 'You'd better come out here.' I threw on some clothes and opened the door. At first I couldn't see anything, because as short as Steve is, this tiny lady was half hidden behind him. Then I knew. The tiny lady said, in a surprisingly strong voice, 'Jane! Finally! Jane!' I threw my arms around her and we hugged. It was a very emotional moment."

Rivers says, "I'll say it was an emotional moment. Here we had come on a wing and a prayer, suffering from twelve hours of jet lag. They had never said, yes, you can see her. They had never given us a visa to visit her city. We had never been able to contact her. Yet, there she was—after all those years of just *reading* about her."

They all had dinner that night in the cavernous dining room of the Kishinev Hotel, with Ida's KGB "shadow" sitting glumly at the next table. The following three days were spent at Ida's little house in Benderi, about an hour's drive away. Jane brazenly requested an official Intourist car and driver to get there. Ida's shanty was two and a half rooms, with no hot water, just a gas ring for cooking in the closet-sized kitchen, and an outhouse—which Jane not so cheerfully used. It was Jane's idea to go to the Benderi post office to send a telegram to General Secretary Chernenko in Moscow, to ask once more for Ida's release. This caused total panic in the post office, where the supervisor told Rivers, "We do not handle telegrams for the Comrade Secretary General here," but after much persuasion, she got it off. By now people had recognized Jane, and they came to the post office to stare at her. She stood more than a foot taller than Ida, but they now looked at Ida with a newfound respect. The KGB man still kept glumly looking on.

The second day, Friday, was Ida's fifty-third birthday and they celebrated with a cake that Jane had bought in a local bakery. Jane gave Ida a necklace she had bought in Israel, and Ida gave Jane a coral necklace that had belonged to her mother. Rivers bought toys for the two young children of Rueck, Ida's neighbor whose phone had been disconnected. "We talked for hours and hours and hours," said Jane.

In a later interview with the magazine *Moment,* an organ of the Save Soviet Jewry organization in the United States, Jane went into great length about what she and Ida talked about. Here are some key excerpts:

> FONDA: Ida, what happened to you after you were arrested?
> NUDEL: I was sentenced. I was put in prison in Moscow. I was kept there about twenty days. After that, it was terrible. I was put on a train and we went through prison camps, and every town had a prison. We'd be kept in a prison for three days, and then they would send you out in another train, and so on, going east, east, east . . .
> FONDA: What happened when you reached Krivosheino?
> NUDEL: I had with me a little sack, where I kept my clothes, and a little food. When a prisoner is brought into a prison, they give him a blanket, and coat, clothes, and a pillow. It was too heavy for me and I was slow. A policewoman said I was too slow. I said, "I can't do anything. Beat me." Nobody had ever spoken to her like that before. She took my sack and carried it. . . . Later I was beaten by children criminals and I was poisoned with rat poison . . .

Jane then asked Ida about her living conditions in the Siberian camp. Nudel replied that she was the only woman in a barracks of men, mostly criminals, whose job it was to drain swamps. "They worked five days," she said, "and for two days they were in the barrack, getting drunk and wanting to rape. I was in a little room, where I did the clerical work. When they came in to rape, I said to them 'You are human beings, I speak to you as human beings.' " By constantly talking to the men in this vein, she somehow got them to leave her alone.

Jane, an animal lover, got most emotional when she told the story of what happened when Ida somehow acquired a dog, a collie puppy, whose name, in Russian, meant "friendly eyes":

FONDA: In Krivosheino, Ida would go for walks in the town outside the prison. You have to understand that there are no TVs, no movies there; the children in this Siberian town have little distraction. So a dog to play with is wonderful. And she would let the children play with her dog after school.

Now, understand, the people in this town had been programmed to hate her. They were told literally that this woman was the devil. . . .

But the children would play with her dog. And it became something they would look forward to every afternoon, And little by little, she said, first the children would smile at her, so it was not just the dog's friendly eyes, but also the children's friendly eyes. And then she said that as the months would go by, she began to see in the eyes of the parents little signs of friendship.

INTERVIEWER: And why did Ida go through all this?

FONDA: To be free, to practice her religion, to live where she wanted to live. She wanted the same for her fellow dissidents.

INTERVIEWER: And you, why did you go through all this?

FONDA: I cannot turn a blind eye to the abuse of human rights in the Soviet Union.

Fonda, Rivers, and Grossman left for Moscow on April 27. By now, the whole country was abuzz with the news that the film star Jane Fonda had been in Benderi and that Miss Fonda even had telegraphed Chief of State Chernenko for an audience about Ida Nudel.

Steve Rivers says, "They tried to hold us up at the airport by insisting Jane speak at a luncheon of the Moscow Film Society that day. They knew I had phoned an American reporter to set up an interview with Jane at Moscow's other airport. Then they tried to hold us up by telling us our luggage was lost. When I said I'd go down and find it myself, the luggage showed up on the carousel in less than thirty seconds.

"Anyway, we did the interview and got off to Paris and then to New York. From that point on, some amazing things happened. Jane and Ida were able to correspond directly. And Ida told Jane that all harassment of her in Benderi, and even in Moscow, had completely stopped."

Rivers concludes: "On October 3, 1987—by coincidence, perhaps, it was Yom Kippur Eve—Ida suddenly got a phone call from Rudolf Kuznetzov. That was the same Kuznetzov, the head of the Soviet Emigration Agency, into whose office we had bulled our way on our first day in Moscow. Kuznetzov told Ida—who was in Moscow for the holiday—'You're getting your exit visa. Go back to Benderi as soon as you can to fill out the papers.' Jane, when she heard the news on her movie location in Mexico, burst into tears."

On October 16, Ida Nudel arrived in Israel on industrialist Armand Hammer's private jet. Climbing on board the plane to greet her were the prime minister, the foreign minister of Israel, a host of other officials, and her sister, Elana, and her family.

At the foot of the landing ramp stood Jane Fonda and

Tom Hayden, there by special invitation. Ida nearly fell down the stairs in her rush to greet them.

Jane hugged her, picked up the tiny woman and swung her around. And Ida kept saying the same thing she had said when they first met in Kishinev: "Jane! Finally! Jane!"

4

The most astounding contradiction for this lady of contradictions is that Jane Fonda has always appeared strong, self-assured, and totally in control of her own destiny. From her image on the screen and in public, you would never dream that she could be an addict. And yet she was—for twenty-three years, including the most controversial periods of her life. She was not addicted to alcohol or drugs. In a remarkable interview with writer Leo Janos in *Cosmopolitan* in 1985, she admitted for the first time that she had been a victim of bulimia, which, in her own words, "is as serious an addiction as drugs and alcohol, and it nearly destroyed my life."

What was this then little-known disorder called bulimia? The medical journal *Developmental Disorders* defines it this way:

Often known as the binge-purge syndrome, it consists of episodes of gross overeating, followed by induced vomiting to rid the body of the enormous amount of food just ingested. . . . The bulimic has a morbid fear of becoming fat. . . . The foods bulimics choose have a texture that allows them to be eaten rapidly. They gobble them down with little chewing, in a short span of time, and then may go in search of more food. A typical binge might consist of two packages of cookies and a loaf of bread, a gallon of milk and a half gallon of ice cream, and fistfuls of candy and pastries. Bulimics are painfully aware that their uncontrollable eating pattern is abnormal, but they can't stop. They often feel disgust, helplessness and panic. . . . Bingeing-purging cycles may occur as often as thirty times a week.

Bulimics frequently suffer periods of depression and anxiety as well as guilt over their inability to control (their addiction). Their costly binge-purges can take up so many of their hours that social activities are restricted, financial resources squandered. Many bulimics are suicidal as well. . . . One estimate is that in the United States, more than five million people, mostly women, are bulimic, bingeing-purging at least once a week, and sometimes spending upwards of a hundred dollars a day on food. The prevalence of bulimia is difficult to estimate because the eating and purging is done in private, in great secrecy. The guilt-ridden victims are so careful to hide their disorder that those who live with them may not know of it. . . . It must be concluded that very little is known about the effective treatment of bulimia, reflecting our inadequate understanding of the disorder.

When she was a child, Jane showed many of the symptoms of becoming a bulimic, but this serious disorder was even less understood *then*. Her godfather, the great director Joshua Logan, told me: "When Jane was a kid, I could never understand why she thought she was fat, when she had the exact same dimensions of other young girls her age. Even when I signed her for her first film, *Tall Story,* and we set her up for publicity photos, she said, 'Don't. My face looks like a chipmunk's with a nut in each cheek.' I told her she was crazy, that her face was thinner than Lauren Bacall's, and we took the photos anyway."

In coming out of the closet with that *Cosmopolitan* interview some twenty-five years later, it took much courage and many tears before she voluntarily brought up "the nightmare that almost destroyed my life." She told writer Leo Janos, "Twenty-three years of agony. This is something I never talk about, never. And the only reason I'm doing so now is that the disease has reached epic proportions. Twenty to thirty percent of American women are suffering from it right now. Bulimia will destroy their lives. I know."

She said, "It began when I was twelve and in boarding school. It started as a lark. I loved to eat, but I wanted to be wonderfully thin. It didn't take long for me to become a serious bulimic—bingeing and purging fifteen to twenty times a day. You eat, have a tremendous euphoria, then suffer a big drop in blood sugar that makes you crave more food, so you're always bingeing and purging in a never-ending cycle. I would literally empty a refrigerator. I spent most of every day either thinking about food, shopping for it, or bingeing and purging. It's not only an addiction, but it's tremendously debilitating. You're constantly upsetting your chemical and electrolyte balance."

In this interview with Janos, Jane was a bit glib about the beginnings of her bulimia, when she described it as a "lark." Psychiatrists say this is a common form of denial among patients with eating disorders. They do not like to look back on the deep emotional disturbances that actually precipitated the onset of bingeing and purging. For example, Susan Wooley, co-founder of the Eating Disorders Clinic at the University of

Cincinnati College of Medicine, reports that 57 percent of her patients had been sexually abused through incest or child molestation.

Such was not the case with Jane, but there certainly were plenty of other causes of underlying conflict in herself and in her family life. She had a father who frequently was absent and paid little attention to her when he was home. She had a mother who was flighty and distant, and openly favored Jane's younger brother, Peter. She had few personal friends among the girls in her peer group. Because of her father's acting career, she was uprooted from California to Connecticut at a very delicate stage of her prepuberty years. She was aware that her father wanted a divorce, with impending remarriage to another woman. And then came the most devastating blow of all—the suicide of her mother under particularly horrible circumstances.

Dr. Mark Strickland of the Cleveland Clinic says, "The bulimic child is like a lightning rod for family conflict. She is a fight waiting to happen." For Jane it was a series of fights with *herself* that went on for more than twenty-four years.

As a child, how did Jane hide her bulimia from her family and friends? The Fonda household was a loosely run affair, with the servants casually refilling the depradations on the refrigerator by two supposedly healthy children—Jane and her brother, Peter, three years younger. A school chum, Carole Peterson, now a psychoanalyst, took no notice either. She says, "Jane would eat a lot, like we all did. Then she'd go to the bathroom and come back and eat some more. We didn't pay much attention to what people were *doing* in the bathroom in those days."

Jane says that trying to stop bulimia is harder than giving up drugs or booze, "because you can't get food out of your life." She says that she never lost a lot of weight, but instead looked haggard and usually was depressed, fatigued, irritable, listless, and hostile. She labels bulimia an antisocial disease: "You don't want to go out, you can't get things done, because it takes an enormous amount of time out of the day. You buy the food, bring it back, consume it, and throw up. And you have to sleep. You're too tired to do anything, so everything else falls by the wayside. Some women are intermittent bulimics. I was hard-core."

Dr. Strickland says, "Severe body chemistry disturbances, due to repeated vomiting, can cause profound heart irregularities and even cardiac arrest." Some three million bulimics in the United States (ninety percent of them women) face this grim prospect, but Dr. Strickland is equally concerned with the psychological devastation. He says, "While the world of change and conflict rages about her, the bulimic actually takes *refuge* in her eating disorder. It's easier to cope with food, calories, and dress sizes. This is a very dangerous form of coping because it is increasingly addictive."

And there is another footnote, which is especially applicable in Jane Fonda's case. The bulimic is trying to model her life after her father, rather than her mother. There is an actual cultural rejection of the female body, curves and all, according to the University of Cincinnati's Susan Wooley. In effect, it is a denial of womanhood.

Psychotherapy helps some bulimics, some grow out of it as they advance further into adulthood, and some hit bottom and ask themselves the same question that recovering alcoholics do: "Do I want to live or do I want to die?" Many opt for life and have cured themselves successfully.

With Jane Fonda, it seems to have been a combination of all three. After bulimia had continued through the most tumultuous years of her life—bad relationships with men, bad business decisions, her hyperkinetic career as a political activist—she indeed began to grow out of it, but she knew she needed help. First she tried psychiatry, but that didn't work for her. She says, "Looking back, it was the wrong psychiatrist. I think women should go to a female therapist and would probably benefit most from group therapy with other bulimics, sharing with women who are going through the same agony." Indeed, there is evidence that Jane *did* benefit from this type of group therapy.

But the key decision for Jane was finally asking herself a variation of that do-I-want-to-live-or-die question. It was 1973. She had married Tom Hayden and was pregnant with his son, Troy, her second child. She says, "What finally made me stop was the realization that life was important to me and the choice was between being a good mother and wife, and being a bulimic. I wasn't as good a mother to my daughter, Vanessa, as I wanted to be. How could I be? I was preoccupied with food."

So having made the choice, she abruptly stopped her bingeing and purging. It was a tough go, analogous to an alcoholic going "cold turkey" and "white-knuckling it." She had to learn how to eat all over again, like a child. She says, "I had to take it one step at a time, because I had lost all sense of what normal eating was." She completely forbade herself the rich carbohydrates so dear to the bulimic. She began a regimen of three small meals a day, mostly vegetables stir-fried in a wok without animal fat—the most common meal for her even today. She had to fight off the constant urges to vomit, which, in a strange way, produces a high in a bulimic. To allay her fears of getting fat, without the vomiting, she concentrated more and more on physical exercise to shed pounds—which eventually led to her workout businesses. Day by day, week by week, the old bulimic urges began to recede. Her husband, Tom, was unaware of this titanic struggle within Jane. He just wondered why her appetite seemed to be less, but was gratified that her old moodiness was disappearing.

In a little more than a year, Jane had won the struggle. "One day in 1974," she says, "I told myself, 'Boy, I think I've got this thing licked. Thank God! How different this day is because I'm not a bulimic. I actually sat down on this day and enjoyed a normal meal. How much quality has been restored to my life! I'll never let it happen again.' "

Perhaps Jane still has the old urges from time to time, but now she seems to know how to handle them, she says, "Thanks to the advances in our knowledge of this previously unpublicized disease."

Looking back at her bulimic period, with its debilitating physical toll and emotional stress, one must wonder again about this lady of contradictions. She did some of her worst film work during this time, but occasionally some of her best—*They Shoot Horses, Don't They* (her first Academy Award nomination) and *Klute* (her first Oscar).

How ironic that such accomplishments may have been an unexpected by-product of the trauma of a mother's suicide and a daughter's struggle against a deadly addiction.

5

I do not ordinarily indulge in pop psychology, but I continue to be struck by the connections between Jane's bulimia addiction, the extremely contradictory behavior of the first thirty-six years of her life, and what she herself admits was "a rather mixed-up childhood, devoid of much love." You don't have to be a Ph.D. to follow the probable straight-line progression from early-life heartache to the confused young adult who emerged. For those who do not know about the bulimia, she usually is portrayed as the typical poor little rich girl, Hollywood style. It was far more than that.

Actually, she wasn't even born in Hollywood or its environs. She came into the world at Doctors Hospital in New York City on December 21, 1937. She was born there because her father had come east to rehearse a new Broadway play, *Blow Ye Winds,* by Valentine Davies, which had opened and closed abruptly in October, just a couple of months before Jane was born. Her mother was Frances Seymour, Henry's second wife. His first wife had been Margaret Sullavan, who then married the famous agent, Leland Hayward, and became the mother of Brooke Hayward, later one of Jane's best friends. Such an intermarital mélange can be totally confusing to a child. Jane remembers asking Brooke such questions as, "What did your mommy do when my daddy came home from work and wouldn't talk to her?"

Fonda, known to his friends as Hank, had been doing well as an actor in Hollywood, but was not yet a full-fledged superstar. The glory days of *The Grapes of Wrath* and *Mister Roberts* were still ahead of him. He had done *The Farmer Takes a Wife* at Fox, and *The Trail of the Lonesome Pine* at Paramount, but also such nondescript films as *Spendthrift* and the disastrously timid *Blockade,* about the Spanish Civil War, in which it was difficult to tell who was fighting whom, and in what country. Around the time of Jane's birth, Hank was working for Warner Brothers and unhappy about it. Thus he occasionally returned to the Broadway stage.

Whereas the Fondas trace their heritage to a famous rebel Italian nobleman, the Marchese de Fonda in the 1300s, whose descendants had to flee to Holland in 1642, Jane's mother's heritage was equally illustrious, claiming descent from Lady Jane Seymour, one of the unbeheaded wives of England's Henry VIII. Jane was christened Jane Seymour Fonda and, as a child, was known as Lady Jane by her mother and everyone else. Hank Fonda's movie earnings were making him rich; Frances Seymour *already* was rich, having previously been married at age twenty-four (widowed at twenty-eight) to an elderly but extremely wealthy industrialist/ex-Congressman named George Brokaw, who earlier had been married to Clare Boothe, who later married publishing czar Henry Luce of Time, Inc. Such were the mating practices of the Hollywood–New York elite in those days. Another practice was boozing. George Brokaw died of a heart attack in a nursing home to which he had been sent for alcoholic detoxification (then known as "drying out").

Infant Jane went back to Los Angeles with her parents just a few weeks after she was born. Frances and Hank then lived in a little rented house on Chadbourne Drive in Brentwood, an upper-class suburb west of Hollywood and not too far from the Pacific Ocean. Many film industry notables lived there—and many still do. Strangely enough, just two blocks away were Fonda's ex-wife, Margaret Sullavan, and her husband, Leland Hayward, who was Fonda's agent. The Fondas' rented house was too small by Frances's standards, and she upgraded it with an infusion of antiques from her former dwelling with George Brokaw. She and Fonda almost immediately began to look for a larger lot in Brentwood, on which they could build their own dream house. Infant Jane was unconcerned by these grandiose plans. She was a chubby and apparently happy baby, in the almost constant care of the nanny of Pan, Frances's daughter from her previous marriage. Pan was five years older than Jane and quite an efficient little mother's helper, and, later, a good friend to Jane.

Jane acquired her own nurse, the faithful old Mary, not long after the family's return to Brentwood. This was mostly because Hank's fortunes really changed. Though he hated Darryl Zanuck, he switched to Zanuck's Twentieth Century–Fox company because of the quality of the properties that that studio was buying. One of them was *Young Mr. Lincoln* in which, on some serious urging by Leland Hayward, Fonda finally was cast. The film was directed by John Ford and was an enormous success. All future Lincolns were to be thenceforth judged in comparison with Fonda's performance. Hank finally had made the big time. He was up there with Paul Muni and Edward G. Robinson—and also with his pal Jimmy Stewart, with whom he had come west at about the same time.

To one-year-old Jane, all this meant nothing, of course. But in her infant mind—as she commented later—she learned a bitter lesson: "Mom and Dad would go away a lot to celebrate his successes. After *Young Mr. Lincoln,* for example, they told me later they had gone for several weeks' vacation in

South America. They went to Ecuador and a lot of other places. They showed me photos of the trip when I was older, and I remember Mom complaining a lot about the food. I loved Mary and Pan, but I think that even at the age of one, I missed Mom and Dad and wished they would be with me more."

The following year there was another huge success for Hank—*The Grapes of Wrath,* the film version of John Steinbeck's Pulitzer Prize–winning novel—and more loneliness for Jane. Her father was away or distracted throughout the production, and so was Frances. More time with Mary and Pan. At age three, Jane was still too young to realize that her father now had become one of the great acting idols of the international film world. All her child's mind knew was that they moved into a bigger house.

The house was at 900 North Tigertail Road in Brentwood. Hank and Frances had it custom-built for them on the nine-acre plot they had coveted for some time. The house was a replica of a clapboard New England farmhouse and it had stables, a vegetable garden (which Hank ploughed, with horse-drawn equipment), and also an art studio in which Hank segregated himself to paint Andrew Wyeth–type landscapes (he later became a fine gallery-level artist). It left less time to spend with little Lady Jane, however.

Jane's brother, Peter, was born on January 25, 1940. Three months later, Frances decided to have a double christening for Peter and Jane (albeit a couple of years belated). Two godfathers were named—one was a friend of Frances's; the other was Josh Logan.

Over the years, I had many conversations about the Fondas with Logan, the troubled genius of both stage and film. I first met Logan when he was directing Marilyn Monroe in the movie *Bus Stop,* but his mind was filled with memories of his earlier associations with Hank Fonda, Jimmy Stewart, and others. "You've got to remember," he said, "that Hank is one of my best friends from a long time back. When I left Princeton in my senior year, a lot of us guys who had been in college dramatics formed our own theater, the University Players on Cape Cod. Hank was one of the guys—along with Jimmy Stewart, Myron McCormick, and that terrific actress Maggie Sullavan, whom Hank married for a while. Later, Hank, Jimmy Stewart, and I shared a ratty apartment in New York. Then, things got better for all of us, and we remained friends. When Hank married Jane's mother, Frances, I was the best man at the wedding.

"I first knew Jane and Peter as babies. Jane was a sturdy little tot, with enormous inquisitive eyes. She always seemed to be in motion. Peter was a more sickly child; he kept coming down with things and took longer than Jane to get over them. From the very beginning, Frances seemed to favor Peter. She kept calling him 'my adorable child' and spoiled him in a way that she never spoiled Jane."

Logan continued: "Under the circumstances, the little girl turned to Hank for affection, but Hank wasn't capable of it. So much of his world was centered on his work as an actor and his hobby as a painter. He'd go to the studio at five in the morning and maybe not get home until eight at night. Being a perfectionist at his craft, he'd study his lines after dinner and then try to relax a bit in his art studio. That didn't leave much time for a little girl crying out for affection. Oh, Hank tried; I remember him teaching Jane how to swim in the family pool when she couldn't have been more than three years old, but he couldn't sustain his interest very long and gave up.

"Also, Jane doesn't realize to this day that Hank had a lot on his mind. He was constantly fighting with studio heads over dreadful pictures he didn't want to make. His relationship with Darryl Zanuck, for example, was almost constant war. The only reason he signed with Zanuck was because Zanuck and Fox owned the film rights to *The Grapes of Wrath,* and that was the only way Hank could get to play it. He considered the property one of the great liberal-social documents of our time. Considering her later political activity, Jane made her father look like a conservative at times. He wasn't. He fought to do pictures with progressive ideas, and fought against doing pictures with reactionary themes. For example, he defied Zanuck to make *The Ox-Bow Incident* with William Wellman. The film was about a lynching, and it died at the box office. Hank always was a Democrat, supporting Roosevelt, Truman and, later on, the Kennedys."

Logan looked thoughtful. He said, "Still, I guess he could have been a more affectionate father to a lonely little girl. For a child, it must have been difficult to understand his strange habit of going into prolonged silences. You'd ask him a question and he'd just look past you, as if you weren't there. I got to know those silences of his very well when I worked with him. He could do that for maybe an hour. I knew he was very fond of me, so I'd just let it go until he was ready to speak again."

Logan concluded, "I knew he loved little Jane, but he didn't know how to express love in a verbal way."

Hank Fonda brought up the subject himself in a soul-searching interview with my late wife, Muriel Davidson, in August 1972. This was at the height of all the political controversy swirling around Jane, and Hank was protective, like a bear defending its cub. "Yet," he said ruefully, "maybe, in a way, I was partly to blame. I didn't give her enough of my time when she was a little girl. She didn't relate well to Frances, who was the frilly type, and besides, Frances was all wrapped up with Peter, who was openly her favorite. Little Lady Jane was begging for my affection, but I didn't realize it. She wanted to be like *me*. She was riding one of my horses at five and she even helped me when I ploughed the vegetable garden. In truth, she was a tomboy."

Fonda went on: "Jane hated little girls' parties, and there seemed to be one every week for kids of people in the industry. There was always an excuse, a birthday or some such, and every mother tried to outdo everyone else, with clowns, carousels, jugglers. That also went for the way they dressed their little girls for these parties—in silks, satins, and ruffled taffetas. Jane couldn't stand that. Frances would make her go to a party at Candace Bergen's—Edgar Bergen's kid—or at

Christina Crawford's—Joan's daughter—and she'd come home crying. She'd say that everyone was prettier than she was, and that she was fat and ugly. I'd try to tell her, 'You're not, sweetheart, you're the most beautiful girl in the world,' but I guess I wasn't very good at expressing such tender thoughts. Anyway, Jane would soon seem to get over it. She'd rather be out rolling in the dust and the mud with her little brother, Peter. She was a tomboy, all right.

"But I figured she'd grow out of it when she started going to school and got interested in boys. Instead, she got more interested in horses. I once told her, 'I think you'll end up marrying a horse.' "

.

6

Jane (and later, Peter, too) began their education at the Brentwood Town and Country School, owned and run by Cathryn Dye, just a few blocks from the Fonda home. Mrs. Dye was a tough, no-nonsense educator, with formal routines, like pledging allegiance to the flag every morning, forced communal poetic readings to nature, and compulsory nap time on cots every afternoon. The children of many film celebrities and executives attended the school for their primary education. Among Jane's classmates were Gary Cooper's daughter, Maria; Fred MacMurray's daughter, Susan; agent Paul Kohner's daughter, Susan Kohner; and director Mervyn LeRoy's daughter, Linda LeRoy.

Jane didn't mix well with these celebrity tots, even in the first grade. Instead, she clung almost immediately to a tall, big-boned, blonde child named Sue-Sally Jones, who became her best (some say only) friend throughout her seven years at the school. What brought them together originally—according to classmate Carole Peterson, now a psychologist—was their mutual love of horses. Jane had full access to her father's steeds, and Sue-Sally had two horses of her own. Much of Brentwood was still undeveloped land, with large sections of brush and trees, and the two girls rode incessantly through this semiwilderness after school. They also dominated the use of the school's own horse, Traveller, which was supposed to be available to all the children.

Carole Peterson remembers that Sue-Sally, who later was to become a veterinarian, was the Queen of the May and played the lead in all the school pageants. "Jane was in her shadow, her pal," says Carole, "and she sparkled when she was with Sue-Sally. The rest of the time she was rather a moody child. But it seems right to me that she should have gone through the evolution of becoming a movie star and then a political activist. She was tough and independent. She didn't want to be done in by anybody and she didn't want to be outdone by anybody. Except Sue-Sally."

Jane also had a streak of meanness in her. One day, she invited Carole over to her house to play. Jane then had two burros that were trained to be ridden by children. Jane said to Carole, "This burro is the mean one; the other is the nice one. I'll let you ride the nice one." Carole clambered onto the alleged nice one, and immediately got thrown, banging her elbow as she fell. Jane had deliberately put her on the mean burro. Jane and Sue-Sally laughed; Carole cried. "It's an incident I'll never forget," says Carole, some forty years later.

Yet again, we have the contradictory views of Jane, even at that early age. In London, I spoke with Jill Schary, another classmate, who as Jill Robinson had become famous as an author *(Bed Time Story),* and was the daughter of M-G-M production chief Dore Schary. Jill said, "I was Carole Peterson's best friend at Brentwood Town and Country, but I don't remember Jane Fonda as being tough and independent. I thought she was extremely shy. In those days, we all were interested in horses, and in drawing horses—Jane was the best at that in art class—and we talked a lot about what we would be when we grew up. We were sure, for instance, that Linda LeRoy would marry the Aga Khan. And at that time, I would have guessed that Jane would become a senator or a scientist or a landscape painter.

"Jane was tall and had long skinny legs, which was what we all wanted to have at the time, but she thought she was fat. I could never understand that, because her best friend, Sue-Sally, was bigger and heavier, and Jane never thought Sue-Sally was fat. I also can't understand how some people thought Jane was mean. To me, she was a very kind little girl."

Jill paused and thought for a moment. "But then again," she continued, "maybe my point of view is colored by what happened later on—more than twenty years later on. Jane had a house on the beach at Malibu then. It was when she was married to Roger Vadim. Brooke Hayward called and said Jane had a very exciting party coming up and would like me to be there. I was bedazzled and I went. But I couldn't keep my head. My drinking problem caught up with me and I went out onto the beach where I passed out.

"The rest was a nightmare. A group of guys picked me up—I think they were surfers—and to make a long story short, they took me to a hotel and gang-raped me. When I came to, I staggered back to Jane's house. I *had* to go back there because I needed my car keys to get home. The party was still going on, but when Jane saw me, she rushed right over. She mothered me, she cuddled me, she shielded me. She rushed me up to her bedroom and took care of me like I was her little child. She called a doctor. She didn't let me call the police because of the ordeal I'd have to go through in my condition, in which I might be accused of having brought on the rape myself by being zonked out on the beach. So now you know why I think of Jane as being one of the kindest, most compassionate people I've ever known."

The headmistress of the Brentwood Town and Country

School, Cathryn Dye, did not think of Jane with any such superlatives—in fact, with no superlatives at all. Mrs. Dye said, "Jane was an average student and an average mischief-maker who was always smart enough to avoid getting caught and punished for her mischievousness and occasional rebellion against our tough rules."

At home things were changing for Jane. It was World War II and, in 1943, when Jane was six, Hank enlisted in the Navy. He was commissioned a lieutenant and sent to the Pacific as an intelligence officer. Jane saw very little of her father for the next two years, except for the times he came home on short leaves.

Frances became a much more attentive mother to Jane during Hank's long absences. She spent much more time with both her children, braiding Jane's long pigtails, getting the children off to school, making sure they had nourishing dinners together, helping with their homework after dinner, running the household, cutting down on her own social activities—and dispensing equally all the affection of which she was capable. Her mother, Grandma Sophie Seymour, whom Jane liked, moved nearby and did all she could to help out. Hank's sister, Harriet, also came frequently from Omaha, where she lived. Jane often wondered about the differences between Hank and Harriet, brother and sister: "It was so easy to talk with Harriet; with Dad it was a struggle, with occasional moments of genuine tenderness."

The war ended in 1945 and Hank came home. Jane said, "He had changed. He seemed sadder. He seemed to be drawing away from Mom. Mom being Mom, she did everything to please him, but so much of the time, it didn't work. She still liked parties and her society friends. Dad, who never liked parties, now wouldn't go to them at all. He just seemed to want to throw himself into his work—even more than he did before."

There was plenty of work. He quickly did two films, one of which was *My Darling Clementine,* one of his finest. It ended his contentious relationship with Darryl Zanuck. It was the last picture he was required to do under the contract he had signed long ago in order to play Tom Joad in *The Grapes of Wrath.* While he was pondering what to do with his career, Hank got an exciting phone call from Josh Logan, who said, "I've just finished the best novel I've ever read in my life. It's called *Mister Roberts.* It'll make an incredible play for Broadway. When I finish writing the play with Tom Heggen, the book's author, I want you to come east to do it with me."

Jane didn't know it, but her days at the Brentwood Town and Country School, with Sue-Sally and the horses, were soon about to come to an end—as were some other key components of her young life.

1

Actually, it was another two years before Jane would find her life turned upside down—the first of many times it would happen to her—but she began to pick up intimations of it in 1947. Hank kept going east to confer with Logan and Heggen "and he was away so much that it almost was like he was in the Navy again." Finally, Jane heard Hank tell her mother, "I'm going to do Josh's play." She remembers her mother saying, "If the play's a hit, do we keep living here, or do we live there?" Hank said, with finality, "We live there, of course." Jane said later, "As usual, Mom always gave in to Dad, even though she protested that all her friends now were in California and even Grandma Sophie was in Los Angeles. She knew no one in Connecticut, where Dad already had decided he wanted to live throughout the run of the play. Dad said, 'You'll only be an hour from

New York, and you've got friends in New York.' As usual with Dad, it was settled."

That summer, Hank sent Jane and Peter to a summer camp in New Hampshire, to acclimate them to living in the East. He was in Connecticut with Logan and Heggen, preparing to go into rehearsals for the play, and Frances remained in Brentwood.

After tryouts in New Haven, Philadelphia, and Baltimore, *Mister Roberts* opened with rave reviews at the Alvin Theatre in New York. The date was February 19, 1948. The critics predicted a run of two or three years for Broadway's new hit play and agreed that Henry Fonda's performance was so magnificent that the only danger was the possibility that he might be seduced back to Hollywood. He wasn't. He told Frances to sell their Brentwood home and to rent something similar in Greenwich, Connecticut. The family moved, in 1949. Jane went into the seventh grade at Greenwich Academy.

Such a drastic change can be traumatic for a twelve-year-old, but for Jane, it was eased somewhat by being reunited with her old childhood chum, Brooke Hayward, who already was living in Greenwich with her mother, Margaret Sullavan (soon to be divorced from Leland Hayward). This was the period so hauntingly described by Brooke in her later fine book *Haywire.* She wrote that she was as delighted to be with Jane again as Jane was to see her.

Brooke and Jane were the same age and in the same class at Greenwich Academy. Brooke noted that Jane had become more rebellious and was prone to such mischief-making as throwing spitballs at her classmates and letting the air out of neighbors' tires. What she did *not* note in her book was that the agonizing family problems Brooke was undergoing at home were being duplicated, to some extent, in the Fonda household.

Things were not going well between Hank and Frances Fonda. Already distressed by the move to Connecticut, Frances almost immediately developed physical problems as well. She had to undergo kidney surgery, which, in those days, required a long hospital stay and left ugly scars. During her recuperation, she brooded incessantly about whether or not she would still be attractive to Hank. She was only forty-one and still a beautiful woman, but she always had been extremely vain about her appearance. She became preoccupied with her scarred body, to the point where little Jane would avoid her "so as not to hear about the scar, which wasn't that noticeable anyway, no more than the Caesarean scar she already had from when I was born."

For his part, Hank was becoming more remote and more authoritarian. Because of his acting schedule in the play, he spent many of his nights in New York, causing Jane to feel more alone than ever—especially with her mother's growing depressions and her father's mostly Sunday-only appearances at home. When he was home, Hank preoccupied himself with his painting. Brooke Hayward says, "He tried to be friendly with his children, but he usually managed to turn them off by doing some horrible thing."

One of the horrible things Brooke remembered she described in gory detail in a 1988 television interview by saying, "Jane always loved animals and she stocked their Greenwich place with all kinds of beasts—dogs, cats, even chickens. At that point, I think she felt closer, and safer, with animals than with people. Well, one day one of their dogs—I think it was a Dalmatian—killed one of the chickens. Hank grabbed the dog and fastened the dead chicken around the dog's neck with a chain. The poor dog had to run around with the chicken carcass tied to its neck until it finally rotted and fell off."

It was not evident to anyone at the time, but there was a reason for Hank's absences and for his crankiness at home. A young woman, Susan Blanchard, had come backstage to meet him after one of his performances at the Alvin. He was seeing Susan more and more during that second year of the *Mister Roberts* run. Susan was the daughter (by a previous marriage) of Dorothy Hammerstein, Oscar Hammerstein's wife. Like the last three of Hank's wives, Susan was considerably younger than he was. She was only twenty.

Suspicious but unsure, Frances took a trip to Paris in the summer of 1949 with her daughter, Pan, who had just married a young man named Bun Abry. She was invited to go along on the young couple's honeymoon. Frances apparently was trying the absence-makes-the-heart-grow-fonder ploy, hoping that being away in gay Paree would rekindle Hank's interest in her.

The ploy didn't work. Soon after her return, Hank confronted Frances with the news. He told her all about Susan, that he wanted to get a divorce and marry her. According to what Frances relayed to friends, Hank also said that he had been unhappy during the entire thirteen years of their marriage.

"Not true," Josh Logan told me in 1964. "That was very cruel of Hank. I know for a fact that he and Frances were *very* happy together until he came back from the war in that increasingly sullen mood of his. The problem with Hank is that he gets bored with the status quo. When he gets bored, he thinks that a change in his life will cure everything. I used to keep talking to him about his rigid mid-American, Protestant-ethic upbringing. Several times, I had to kid him, saying, 'You don't have to marry everybody you fuck, you know.'"

In any event, when Hank broke the news about his divorce and marriage plans to Frances, she went into deep shock. Jane says she herself didn't know what was going on, "except that Dad now was living in an apartment in New York and Mom's depression was getting worse. I thought the depression was still the result of her kidney operation."

Shortly after what was a very grim Christmas for Jane and Peter, the children *knew* what was going on. Frances filed for divorce and the news broke in all the newspapers, even the *Greenwich Time,* which was read at school. It didn't cause too much of a stir at school, especially among the girls, who were accustomed to reading the fan magazines of the day, and there were so *many* show-business divorces. Besides, the Fondas were fairly new in town. Jane, distraught, would not discuss it with anybody—even Brooke Hayward.

Jane tried to discuss it with her mother, but soon gave up. Frances's depression was deepening, especially during the ensuing prolonged divorce negotiations between her lawyers and Hank's about property settlements, alimony, and such.

The negotiations came to an abrupt halt when Frances's mother, Jane's Grandma Sophie, came east to help out. Sophie spent just a couple of hours with her daughter, noted her condition, called Frances's psychiatrist, and had her sent to the Craig House Sanitorium (it would be called a psychiatric hospital today) in Beacon, New York, about twenty-five miles away. There was a postponement of the divorce negotiations until Frances's condition improved.

And she *did* improve. In about six weeks, she was allowed to go home for brief visits with her children, but always accompanied by a nurse. The visits were cheerful and Frances even concerned herself with what she thought the servants were doing wrong in the running of the house. Jane took that as a good sign, "the return to the old Mom."

On the third of the visits, Frances and the nurse were chatting with the children and Grandma Sophie, when Frances suddenly dashed upstairs to go to the bathroom. Realizing there was a *downstairs* bathroom, the nurse ran after her and found her in the master bedroom, taking something out of one of the dresser drawers. She held the item up for the nurse to see. It was a small expensive hand-painted porcelain box from England. Frances said, "This little box is an important keepsake for me. I want to take it back to the hospital." The nurse neglected to look inside the box. Hank, the utilitarian, had used the antique box as a container for his razor blades.

On the afternoon of April 25, 1950, a nurse at Craig House named Amy Grey left Frances alone in her room for a few minutes. She came back to find a note on the bedstand: "Amy dear, *don't* go in the bathroom."

Miss Grey, of course, did open the bathroom door and

couldn't suppress a scream at what she saw. Frances was lying on the floor in a pool of blood, which was still pulsing weakly from a gash in her throat. Nearby was a bloody razor blade and the little porcelain box she had taken from home on her last visit. Other nurses and a doctor rushed in and did what they could, but it was too late for Frances. She had severed her jugular vein and was dead in twenty minutes. She had left a suicide note that made it clear to the later medical inquiry that her grisly use of the smuggled razor blade "was the best way out."

The first to be summoned was Frances's mother, Sophie, who phoned Hank backstage at *Mister Roberts*. Josh Logan told me, "Hank fell apart. I don't know how he did it, but he insisted on doing that night's performance and somehow got through it. He told me, 'The children are never to know. I told Sophie to say that their mother had died of a heart attack.' "

The ruse worked for a while, although Jane confessed later that she didn't quite believe it. She was unprepared, however, for the details of her mother's suicide, which she found out about some months later in the most unfortuitous way possible. A friend had seen a fan magazine in a beauty shop. Fan magazines in those days printed gory details in the manner of today's scandal tabloids. All the gory details of Frances's suicide were there for Jane to see.

She was only thirteen, but the images tormented her for years to come. Later, at boarding school, she was reported by her dormitory mates to have suffered recurring screaming nightmares. She never could bring herself to talk about it— even to psychiatrists. Susan Strasberg, who knew Jane later at the Actors Studio, told me, "Nearly all of us went into psychoanalysis. It was part of our system at that time. Jane went for only two weeks. She said, 'The doctor wanted me to talk about my mother's death, but I just couldn't do it.' "

This is interesting because it falls into the denial patterns of bulimics—who not only do not want to own up to their embarrassing disease, but most especially do not want to face the *real* cause of what started it in the past. One can theorize that the thirteen-year-old Jane, finding out in a particularly cruel way that her mother was a suicide and not a heart-attack victim, found solace in the bingeing-and-purging addiction, with which she admittedly had begun experimenting when she was twelve. It was a controlled world she could enter, where her mind could focus almost solely on the intake of food, how to get rid of it, and how many pounds she was losing. It was all-encompassing. She didn't have to think of Mom's body lying bleeding on the bathroom floor, or of the icy coldness that Dad had exhibited, even going onstage that night. It's a form of coping—but one of the worst possible kinds.

In 1950, in the period after Frances's death, Hank spent more time at home with the children. Grandma Sophie was there, too. She said, "To his credit, Hank was warmer and more responsive to the children. He maintained the fiction of Frances's heart attack, but he seemed to be trying to make it up to them for her absence. He even fought against those periods of silence of his."

In the meantime, though, Fonda kept working in *Mister Roberts,* now driving back to Greenwich after most performances. He also kept up his relationship with Susan Blanchard. She became the third Mrs. Fonda in December 1950—eight months after Frances's death.

The effect of her father's new marriage was imperceptible on Jane. Her bingeing and purging was well underway, but, as with most bulimics, no one was aware of it.

Her brother Peter's reaction was more specific. Jane used bulimia; Peter used a gun. While Hank and Susan were on their honeymoon in the Virgin Islands, Peter, not yet ten, was spending a weekend with a friend in Peekskill, New York, which is not far from Greenwich. Peter was playing with a loaded shotgun. It still is not clear what happened next. At various times Peter has said it was an accident; at other times he has intimated that it was a suicide attempt. But the shotgun went off, the blast ripping through the right side of Peter's abdomen.

Bleeding profusely, Peter was taken to Ossining Hospital. The buckshot had torn through his liver and he was rushed into immediate emergency surgery. The liver was repaired and other torn blood vessels were sutured, but the boy was on the operating table for hours. He required several blood transfusions, and he says that a couple of times his heart stopped and had to be restarted.

In a 1988 television interview with Barbara Howar, Peter described the ordeal in detail. He said, "I was very close to dying, and I knew it. I was lying there in my bed after the operation, when Dad and Susan walked in. They had been called back from the Virgin Islands."

What Peter said next is curious because it did not jibe with the fact that Peter had long since made peace with his father and was quite friendly with Hank before his death in 1982. Perhaps it was a throwback to earlier repressed emotions, but Peter said, "Dad walked into the hospital room and the first words out of his mouth were, 'You spoiled my honeymoon.' "

Then Peter muttered three letters, "B.F.D.," the meaning of which was lost on most viewers.

"B.F.D." means "big fuckin' deal."

8

Jane, in an interview with *The New York Times,* once said, "I was lonely until I was thirty years old," a statement which is not exactly true. She had rare periods of good relations with her father, and she did have some good close friends—Sue-Sally Jones, for example, and certainly Brooke Hayward.

The most unlikely close friend of all, after the shock of her mother's death, was her new stepmother, Susan Blanchard. Susan was a warm, friendly young woman who went out of her way to become close with both Jane and Peter. She seemed to sense that someone had to fill the gap between them and their cool disciplinarian father, and she did a pretty good job of it—especially with Jane.

Only eight years older than Jane, there was little generational gap between them. Having been an adolescent so recently herself, Susan knew all the problems of a child just beginning puberty who was so confused and unsure of herself. With almost constant girl-to-girl talks, Susan tried desperately to convince Jane that she was not ungainly and ugly but a beautifully blossoming young woman with all the striking facial characteristics of her famous father.

Susan couldn't make the uncertainties disappear completely (ten years later, with her bulimic tendencies gnawing at her, Jane, at 128 pounds, *still* thought she was fat) but there were miracles in the improvement of Jane's appearance. Susan went shopping with her, induced her to buy new chic clothes, even restyled Jane's thick light brown hair away from the pigtailed little-girl look. Jane and Susan were to remain close friends for years to come, even when the stepmother connection was severed by yet another Hank Fonda divorce.

Susan also brought another quotient into Jane's life, a little sister named Amy, whom Hank and Susan adopted. Jane was very maternal to the newcomer, playing with Amy in an almost obsessive way.

Susan was not so successful with Peter, who kept getting kicked out of schools for fighting, for wearing weird clothing and oddly painted hair-styles, and for dosing himself with phenobarbital. Peter eventually was sent to live with Hank's sister, Harriet, in Omaha.

Jane had now finished the eighth grade at Greenwich Academy and decided to go away to boarding school for her high school years. She chose Emma Willard, a prep school for Vassar, in Troy, New York, several hundred miles upstate. Hank and Susan had sold the Greenwich home and were moving into a town house on New York's East Seventy-fourth Street. No one knows why Jane chose a school such a distance away, but Josh Logan theorizes that despite her genuine liking for Susan, she wanted to exorcise the horrors of her mother's death that she associated with both Greenwich and New York. "Besides," said Logan, "she could have gone to any school she wanted to. Hank had plenty of money and so did Jane herself. She had inherited a bundle from Frances."

Exorcising the horrors did not come easily. It was at Emma Willard that schoolmate Kevin Bellows reports the screaming nightmares in the dormitory. There also were distressing side-effect symptoms of advancing bulimia—sleeping many hours in the daytime, irritability. listlessness, erratic behavior. Despite all this, Jane was quite popular with the girls at Emma Willard. Her new chic persona (devised by Susan) did not hurt, and neither did the fact that she was Henry Fonda's daughter.

During her four years at Emma Willard, Jane was not a good student. She was prone to skipping classes and climbing over the walls at night for dates with boys from nearby colleges. She had never before been much interested in the opposite sex, but now she was pursuing men with a vengeance. She still was seeing Brooke Hayward during school breaks and vacations, and Brooke is the source of much of the information about these sudden carnal extracurricular activities. (Could it have been another manifestation of erratic bulimic behavior?)

Brooke says, "When I'd see Jane, she'd fill me in on all the intimate details of her dates. I got furious when I learned she had beaten me out in the matter of our losing our virginity. She said it was an older man, not a college kid, that he was so experienced, knew what he was doing, not fumbling around like some boy. I think she said he was an Italian, *much* older."

On her breaks, Jane would stay with Hank and Susan in their Manhattan town house. She seemed to enjoy these visits. Probably under the influence of Susan, Hank was much kinder to her. But in the matter of going out with boys, she was, more or less, grounded. Hank was still the tough disciplinarian with his children and he didn't think Jane, at sixteen or seventeen, was old enough for dating.

On her last trip home from Emma Willard in 1955, Jane was distressed. She noticed the same grumpiness and lack of attention to Susan that she had remembered in the period preceding Hank's breakup with her mother. Jane went back to school with a sense of foreboding. She graduated that year

60

with grades that were hardly spectacular but good enough to get her into Vassar.

Jane's sense of foreboding proved to be prophetic. She returned home to find a weepy Susan. Hank had finished the film version of *Mister Roberts,* and was in Italy doing a huge Dino De Laurentiis–Carlo Ponti version of Tolstoy's *War and Peace,* co-starring with Audrey Hepburn. At a party for the cast, he had met an Italian aristocrat, fiery twenty-three-year-old Afdera Franchetti, sister of a baroness. A tempestuous romance had begun and for Fonda, then fifty, history seemed to be repeating itself. Still, there was no talk of divorce yet, and Jane prepared to leave for her freshman year at Vassar.

But first came an interesting—and significant—interlude. This is the way Henry Fonda told it to my wife, Muriel, for her *Family Circle* article in 1972:

> Nothing, I mean absolutely *nothing* in her early childhood gave me a clue that Jane would one day become an actress. Peter was something else. By the time he was fourteen, he'd produced, directed and played five parts in a play he wrote at his prep school.
>
> I think it was in the late summer of 1955 when I got a phone call from my sister Harriet in Omaha. Harriet was very active in the Omaha Community Playhouse, which Marlon Brando's mother had founded. Harriet told me the playhouse was running out of space and wanted to do a fund-raising play in order to buy a bigger building. She asked me if I'd come out from New York and do a couple of weeks of *Country Girl.*
>
> I groaned a lot because I'd soon have to go back to Europe for the *War and Peace* movie, but I said yes. Then Harriet threw me a real clinker. She said she wanted Jane to play the ingenue role. "Ridiculous!" I told Harriet. "Jane won't do it. She doesn't know *how* to do it." So, of course, true to the experience of wise fathers everywhere, my daughter not

only agreed to do the play, but said she thought it might be fun. I tried to tell Jane that most acting isn't "fun." It's just hard work with possibly little or no rewards. Well, I tell you, she knocked me out with her performance.

On opening night, I was standing in the wings sweating out my first entrance, when Jane came over. "Daddy," she said, "I've got this crying scene to do and I don't think I'll be able to cry." I remember thinking to myself, "Lord, haven't I got enough on my mind, and now I've got to worry whether or not Jane can cry on cue." I told her, "You don't actually have to cry, baby. Just make the audience *think* you're crying." Well, as I came off, she went on. And if anything, I was sweating her entrance more than my own. Then I looked at her. And there she stood on stage. Crying. I knew then what she still didn't know. There was going to be another acting Fonda.

Hank Fonda, being Hank Fonda, didn't tell this to Jane. In fact, he continued to discourage her from thinking of an acting career—although he later allowed her to play some tiny roles with him in summer stock—repeating that "acting is a brutal profession, with rejection always around the corner."

In another interview with Muriel a year or so later, Hank expressed sorrow over Jane's record in school and college. "She has a fine mind," he said, "and there are any number of good careers she could have gone into, but she's not a well-educated person. By just playing around, her four years in high school and her two years at Vassar were mostly a waste."

That was true. When Jane got to Vassar for her freshman year, all thoughts of her performance on the Omaha stage were forgotten, and, too, all thoughts of seriously taking up acting as a profession. She herself admits that Vassar was an extension of her playgirl activities at Emma Willard. Dating was her first priority, and she hardly had time to cram for exams to get barely passing grades. Sometimes she was out all night and completely missed classes the next day. She expressed a dislike for segregated female education, which she had experienced at Emma Willard and now was experiencing at Vassar. She said, "Women should not be second-class citizens to be locked up together, away from the real world." Time proved her right. Most schools and colleges are now co-ed.

When asked about acting by the school paper, she said, "Never. I watch my father and look at my own limitations, and I realize I'll never be good enough. I don't want to go into anything where I can't be the very best."

At the end of that first year at Vassar, other things were troubling Jane. She came home to the family's East Seventy-fourth Street house to find only Susan, Amy, and the servants there. She cried when Susan told her Hank was now constantly with Afdera Franchetti in Europe. Hank and Susan's divorce was already in the hands of their respective lawyers. Susan was calm and resolute, totally different from the way Jane's own mother, Frances, had handled the same situation.

After spending some time with Susan, vowing continuing friendship, Jane went off to meet her new stepmother-to-be on Cape Cod, where Hank had rented a house for the summer with his sister, Harriet. Afdera liked Jane on sight, called her "a typical sweet, beautiful American girl, with her father's eyes, but still with baby fat on her bones." Jane, at first, didn't know what to make of Afdera, only five years her senior. The daughter of an extremely wealthy Venetian family, Afdera was typical of the European jet-setter of the day. Bejeweled and wrapped in furs, her whole life seemed to concentrate on going to parties for international society at such places as Cap D'Antibes on the French Riviera. She consorted with people like the Duke and Duchess of Windsor. Jane was stunned that her father, always noted for his frugal nature previously in Jane's life, would go along with Afdera's uncontrolled profligacy. But he did. Thus, Jane returned to Vassar for her second year, totally puzzled and increasingly resentful. She stopped wearing jewelry and designer clothes, possibly in an attempt to make herself as different as possible from Afdera.

Jane's second year at Vassar was no different from the first—lots of dating, minimum attention to her studies. She decided not to go back for her junior year and became a college dropout.

Afdera and Hank Fonda were married on March 10, 1957, at the East Seventy-fourth Street town house. Jane and Peter were both present for the nuptials. The honeymoon was delayed because Hank had to finish the movie *12 Angry Men,* and was in preparation for Paramount's *The Tin Star* and for the play *Two for the Seesaw.* But in July, the newlyweds finally took off for a summer of jet-set revelry in Venice, Pamplona, and Cap Ferrat. Jane was invited along. The scene was like something out of an early Hemingway novel. There were endless parties, dancing until dawn, and a profusion of swains circling around Jane like bees in the bougainvillea. She had a fairly serious relationship with James Franciscus for a while, and then (through Afdera) with Count Giovanni Volpi, whose father had founded the Venice Film Festival.

For Hank Fonda, at fifty-one, the pace got to be too brisk and he finally slowed it down by organizing word games, at which he was very good. The change of pace delighted Afdera and her European compatriots, who revised the games to include several languages, and Hank had plenty of companions for his evening contests—sometimes even including Jane. For Jane, as well, the pace was slowing down, with more naps in the afternoon, as bulimia took its toll on her.

Hank told my wife: "I may not have been the best father outwardly, but I loved my children and worried about them. Jane was eating a lot, but seemed to be getting thinner, not so much in the body but in the face. Even with the way she ran around at night, I couldn't understand why she had to sleep so much. She'd be very good at the word games, but then she'd drift off into total indifference."

Hank also noted that Jane didn't like his new wife very much. "It was nothing like the warm relationship Jane had had with Susan, but I had my own life to lead, and I knew there was nothing I could do about it. It hurt me when people told me Jane had a collection of 'Afdera jokes,' about Afdera's buying sprees, which she told to her American friends like Jim Franciscus."

Hank said that he had no further discussions with Jane at that time about her going into acting. "I was just as happy about that," he said, "because even though I was tempted with the idea of a Fonda acting dynasty, I would have preferred that my children lead normal lives."

For Henry Fonda, a normal life would have been a career in the art world, such as painting, in which, as an avocation, he had derived so much satisfaction for himself. He was over-joyed, therefore, when Jane came to him at the end of that crazy summer and said she didn't want to go back to Vassar, but instead, would like to go to Paris to study Renoir, Cézanne, Monet, and the other Impressionists her father so admired.

So off Jane went to Paris and what she thought would be a whole new non-Hank, non-Afdera–type life. As she later said, "I was desperately trying to find myself, to do something special with my life, something in which I could express my own personality. I still wanted to be like my father, but not *exactly* like him. It's tough growing up in the shadow of a national monument."

9

An aimless rich kid, a little on the wild side—that's the only way one could describe Jane Fonda in 1957. A lot of her flitting about had to do with the mood swings and irrational behavior suffered by all bulimics. She was like a hummingbird, seeking nectar wherever she could find it. The nectar she was seeking was male affection.

She obviously wasn't getting it at home. Even when he tried, Hank Fonda continued to be unable to express love and warmth to his daughter—and to his son as well. At this particular point, he was more remote than ever, being totally preoccupied with keeping up with the unaccustomed fast pace of his new young bride. Yet, strangely, he *did* have a father's love for his daughter—but only in his own restrictive, undemonstrative way.

Unfortunately Jane, an already-messed-up twenty-year-old, didn't understand that. She wanted out-and-out affection in the standard style. So she looked for it wherever she could. This is speculation, of course, but for a young woman engaged in this sort of emotional tug-of-war with her father, just the very fact of attention from another man could be construed by her as a form of affection—even if their motives were less than sincere. If their interest was purely sexual, *that* was a form of affection. And if they manipulated her for their own gains—as many later did—that was the *ultimate* form of affection to a love-starved little girl. At least, unlike her father, they were giving her *attention.*

And so, hummingbird style, she flitted about in search of the nectar. In 1957, after conning her father into sending her to Paris to study the French Impressionists and to paint, there is no evidence that she did much of either.

Jane said, "I moved in with Countess Somebody or the other. It was a dark, elegant apartment where young ladies weren't supposed to talk at the table. And while I attended classes at l'Ecole de la Chauvierre, I really played hooky most of the time."

One of Jane's problems was that she didn't do well with the French language and was too lazy to take French lessons; so communication with her art instructors was hopeless. (Later, of course, she became fluent enough in French to make French movies, albeit with a heavy American accent.)

In lieu of learning French in the orthodox way, Jane got it into her head that she could do just as well at picking up the language by hanging around student cafés and listening to the people talk. Instead, she fell in mostly with American youths and didn't have to exercise her linguistic muscles with them. She soon was up to the old indiscriminate dating practices she had learned at Emma Willard and Vassar.

Among her plethora of new friends were several who worked on the staff of the little literary magazine *Paris Review,* then edited by another American rich kid, George Plimpton, who grew up to become a well-known author and sports satirist. Jane did menial jobs for Plimpton and others on the *Paris*

Review, running errands, getting coffee, and serving as an unofficial copy girl. She was unpaid but had plenty of money from Hank and from her own funds, so she was able to hang out in the Left Bank cafés after hours.

A New York gossip writer came through Paris and reported in his column that "Henry Fonda's daughter is having a high old time, hopping from bed to bed." There was an implication that the beds contained women as well as men, possibly a mudslinger's hyperbole. Hank Fonda's reaction on reading this dispatch was to hit the ceiling and to order his daughter home immediately.

"When I got back to New York," said Jane, "Dad first chewed my ass really good. Then, when he calmed down, he said, 'What the hell are you going to *do* with your life?' I thought I'd calm him down further, so I said I'd register at the Art Students' League in New York, where I wouldn't have any language problems."

Concerning this bizarre year in Jane's life, her brother, Peter, said, "She was demanding our father's attention in any way she could get it—running away from Vassar and doing far-out, freaky numbers in Paris—where she was supposed to be going to art school but was running around with the top playboys of the jet-set world. When Dad ordered her home, she was still trying to make him believe she was a serious art student, but she was still just dabbling and partying."

In truth, Jane spent a bare minimum of time in life classes (painting nudes) at the Art Students' League. She spent much more time at the New York office of the *Paris Review,* taking mail-order subscriptions on the telephone and dating members of the staff. She also began dabbling in modeling. She had met the famous photographer Richard Avedon ("I don't remember whether it was in Paris or New York"), and Avedon tentatively began to use her in some of his fashion layouts. Although she disliked her long-legged figure (now, at twenty, she was five-eight and weighed only 120 bulimia-induced pounds), Avedon found her attractive. He particularly liked her wide-eyed, expressive face with its hint of sexuality and vulnerability. She later appeared in an Avedon cover for *Vogue,* but Jane was hardly a top model in the amount of work she got. As with everything else, she was still dabbling.

How, then, did this perennial dilettante suddenly focus on the single career of acting, which she had previously derogated for herself all her life? Again, it is part of her contradictory nature. She was expressing her rebellion again, along with self-interest. She wanted to be like her father, but not *exactly* like her father, as Josh Logan had frequently said. The answer was to plunge herself into a type of acting that was totally different from that of her father, who was a traditionalist in his craft. The exact opposite of Hank's style was "the Method," taught at the Actors Studio by Lee Strasberg. It emphasized inner stimulation from concentrating on one's past experiences, rather than from listening to others acting and reacting, as Hank did. Hank had just done *Two for the Seesaw* with Anne Bancroft, a Strasberg disciple, and he had hated the technique (especially since most critics felt that Bancroft had stolen the play from him).

Josh Logan also hated the Method, which was supposed to have been derived from Stanislavski's techniques in Russia. Logan always sneered at such assertions, saying, "I'm the only American who ever studied with Stanislavski, and this so-called Method is not what I studied. Lee Strasberg got his ideas second-hand from some Russian actors who maybe studied with Stanislavski and emigrated to the United States, and a lot was lost in the voyage across the Atlantic." Notwithstanding, the Method and Strasberg produced some very fine actors, among them Marlon Brando, Paul Newman, Joanne Woodward, James Dean, Geraldine Page—and later, Dustin Hoffman and Al Pacino.

How Jane got involved with Strasberg and the Actors Studio is a matter of some dispute. Some published sources have reported that Jane met Susan Strasberg, the guru's actress daughter, when Susan was making the film *Stage Struck* with Hank in New York. According to this version, the two girls, about the same age and both of them daughters of brilliant but unaffectionate, difficult fathers, immediately hit it off and Susan convinced Jane that she should reconsider going into acting as a career, but with Actors Studio training.

"Not so," Susan told me. "I didn't even meet Jane until the summer after she got back from Paris, and it wasn't in New York; it was on the beach in Santa Monica. My mother, Paula, was on the Coast, coaching Marilyn Monroe for a film—I think it was *Some Like It Hot*—and Dad had rented a house on the beach for the summer. My brother, John, and I drove out to be with them. It was a tough time for me. I was getting over an affair I had had with Richard Burton, and we had just broken up.

"Anyway, we were all sitting on the beach with people who lived around there—the Peter Lawfords, Lauren Bacall, Marilyn, and Arthur Miller—when this pretty girl wandered over. It was Jane Fonda. She was not pretty in the breathtaking sense, like Vivien Leigh and Ava Gardner, but she had a soft lushness about her. She reminded me of a ripe peach, some-one just blooming. My brother, who knew *her* brother, Peter, brought her over to talk with Dad. In the following order, my father loved geniuses, psychotics, and beautiful women. He obviously thought that Jane fell in the last category. I heard him say to her, 'Yes, you can be an actress,' and he spent a lot of time telling her about the Method, as only Lee Strasberg could."

What was Jane doing on Santa Monica beach? She had come west to spend the summer with Hank and Afdera in a house rented from the ex-Mrs. Tyrone Power, Linda Chris-tian. But when Hank had objected rather strenuously to her late-hour dating practices with a young man named Sandy Whitelaw, Jane had petulantly moved out and rented her own Santa Monica apartment. And so, she first met Marty Fried, one of Lee Strasberg's students (whom she dated), and then the guru of Method acting himself.

At summer's end, Jane made her peace with Hank and Afdera and went back to New York with them. She immedi-ately registered for classes at the Actors Studio. In one of her first exercises in class, Lee Strasberg stopped by and complimented her—and she was allocated to an elite group of select Strasberg students. She said at the time, "Lee Strasberg told me I had talent. *Real* talent. It was the first time anyone told me I was good. At *anything.* It was a turning point in my life. I went to bed thinking about acting. I woke up thinking about acting. It was like the roof had come off my life."

And so, for the first time since her childhood obsession with horses, Jane had a genuine passion about something. She attended her Actors Studio classes religiously. Gone were her hooky-playing days. She loved the instruction; she loved being with her classmates, nearly all of whom were in psychoanalysis and spoke incessantly about their "inner conflicts," of which she herself had plenty. Susan Strasberg remembers Jane as being "fiery and impulsive, a confronter, which was a veneer covering her basic insecurity." Kevin McCarthy, one of the founding members of the Actors Studio, remembers her as "almost immediately showing the signs of becoming a very good actress."

Soon, as was her custom at that time, Jane was romantically involved with a young man named Timmy Everett. He was a fellow student who already had played a small part on Broadway in *Dark at the Top of the Stairs.* Jane and Timmy teamed up in their class and did scenes together. One such scene, from a dramatic work by Dylan Thomas, drew the plaudits of the instructors and also of the other members of the class. Thereafter, love blossomed, and Jane and Timmy were an acknowledged duo, both in and out of the Actors Studio. They lived in Jane's half of a luxury apartment she shared with another California rich kid, Susan Stein, daughter of MCA's Jules Stein (again Jane had moved out of the Hank-Afdera household to be on her own).

From time to time, however, she did bring Timmy over to the Fondas' East Seventy-fourth Street town house. Hank liked Timmy; Afdera, remembering Jane's European liaisons with counts and barons, sneered at the quiet, unspectacular young man. He and Jane made a strange-looking couple. As they walked along, he was at least three inches shorter than Jane and comparatively puny-looking. Yet they seem to have had a satisfactory relationship. With her admission into the Actors Studio circle, Jane's tastes in men certainly had changed. Susan Strasberg recalls Timmy as being bright and caring, "but like so many people at the Studio, he did some incomprehensible things. He came to a New Year's Eve party with Jane that year, rolled up his sleeves, and showed us the scars where he had slashed both wrists."

Susan, already a big star by that time after *The Diary of Anne Frank,* adds, "Jane was a little crazy, too. She kept getting facial massages. Her face wasn't thin enough, she thought. I also have memory of going to her house for dinner one night. She ate like a horse and then went to the bathroom. I could hear her vomiting, quite loudly. She came out and openly said she had been throwing up." Susan, who is very astute about psychological things, soon became aware that Jane was bulimic—one of the few people to do so.

While her relationship with Timmy Everett was still on-going, Jane attracted another swain at the Actors Studio. His name was Andreas Voutsinas, and he was studying with Lee Strasberg to be a director, not an actor. He was to become very important in the next phase of Jane's tumultuous life. Voutsinas was a Greek whose father had made a fortune by going to Ethiopia and siding with the Italians in the war against Emperor Haile Selassie. When the emperor returned, the Voutsinas family was expelled and wiped out financially. Young Andreas had then gone to England and to the United States to study acting and directing. He ended up at the Actors Studio on the recommendation of his fellow Greek, the great director Elia Kazan. When he first met Jane, Voutsinas was twenty-five and Jane was twenty.

Like most of the others at the Actors Studio, Voutsinas was in psychoanalysis. He told several people that he and his therapist had agreed he was bisexual. "I assumed he was gay," says Susan Strasberg, "but that didn't matter to me. He was a wonderful young director. When I had to do a scene at the studio, I wanted Andreas to direct me more than anyone else, because I knew he'd take care of me. The props would always be right, the cues would always be right. But Andreas was kind of a weird guy. He always dressed completely in black, and with his black cape, black hair, black moustache, and pointed black beard, he looked like Mephistopheles—an impression I'm sure he wanted to give."

Susan continues: "How did he get involved with Jane? I'm sure that after all the years of inattention from her father, Jane needed an authority figure she could count on. Andreas certainly was that. He loved to be involved in molding talent. He wanted to do everything he could to show you at your best. He wanted you to feel 'I'm getting all this attention from someone who cares how I look, what I wear, how I behave.' He coached Jane at the Studio and directed her in some small outside productions. He was very tough and demanding with her. He got angry and yelled a lot. But that, apparently, is what Jane needed. Even anger is a manifestation of caring."

So Jane, who already had had some strange relationships with men, now was involved in one of the strangest of all. There was Timmy Everett, with whom she lived, who was sensitive and loving. She bought many gifts for him. Then, as another part of the trio, there was Voutsinas, the authoritarian father-figure she apparently needed. Lee Strasberg, after his initial interest in Jane, never thought of her as another Marilyn Monroe, and Voutsinas, with his concentrated attention on Jane's development as an actress, seems to have filled the void.

This is not to say that the Jane-Timmy-Andreas trio was a ménage à trois. Voutsinas patiently waited until the Timmy Everett relationship cooled off, which it eventually did; and only then did he move in. In the meantime, she raised eyebrows by bestowing her affections on both men at the Tuesday and Friday sessions of the group. Perhaps it was later, but writer Maurice Zolotow (Marilyn Monroe's biographer) was invited by Lee Strasberg to sit in on all the classes for a while. "The one thing I remember about Jane Fonda," Zolotow told me, "was that she always was sitting off to one side with

Voutsinas, holding his hand and staring up at him with puppy eyes."

Hank Fonda made no secret of his loathing of Andreas Voutsinas. To more than one interviewer he said, "That guy's a goddam Svengali."

If so, Voutsinas was to be the first of several Svengalis in Jane's life. And Hank, with his straightforward, midwestern style of thinking, never considered that he was at least partially responsible for it. *He* could have become Jane's Svengali (in a positive way), but in their peculiar father-daughter relationship, they could not even communicate.

Jane apparently *wanted* a Svengali comparable to her father, the national monument, as she called him. So she kept looking for an equivalent elsewhere: Lee Strasberg, now Andreas Voutsinas, later Roger Vadim, later the various gurus who molded her political convictions.

It's all a painful evocation of how Hank and Jane deeply affected one another—through failure to communicate—in a relationship that was seriously troubled, but with underlying love.

10

There is no way of proving it (the events, however, are too clear-cut to be coincidental), but in 1959, when Jane was not yet twenty-two, Hank Fonda hatched an ingenious plot to get Jane away from both Voutsinas and the Actors Studio. It didn't completely work, but it was typical of Hank's cunning when frustrated.

Suddenly, Jane was called in by Josh Logan. Logan was then at the peak of his career. Among his other memorable work he had previously extracted an extraordinary performance from Marilyn Monroe when he directed her in the film *Bus Stop* (although her drama coach, Lee Strasberg's wife, Paula, of the Actors Studio, deserves some of the credit). Without sharing credit with anyone, Logan had also performed somewhat of a miracle with the near-neophyte Kim Novak in the movie *Picnic.*

When Jane arrived at his office, Logan (who steadfastly denied any collusion with Hank) told her of these successes and said, "Jane, I want to sign you to a long-term contract to do both films and plays for me." Since she had not yet acted professionally in *anything,* Jane was rightfully stunned. Logan went on: "I own the film rights to the Howard Lindsay and Russel Crouse play *Tall Story.* That's the first thing I would want you to do. It's about a smart coed who chases and catches a basketball star in college."

Jane, accustomed to Ibsen and Eugene O'Neill at the Actors Studio, said "Ugh."

Logan said, "Don't worry, honey. It isn't Shakespeare, but it'll be a good start for you. I need two unknown young people for this picture. I already have the boy. I've put a boy named Warren Beatty under contract, the same contract I'm giving to you."

Although Logan's offer was not much monetarily ($250 a week, plus expenses, the standard terms for an unknown young actress in those days), it was too good an opportunity to turn down, and Jane finally accepted it—but with misgivings about how it would affect her work at the Actors Studio. Hank was ecstatic about the deal; so was Timmy Everett. Voutsinas was morosely negative, saying Jane was "selling out."

Negotiations went on for a while between Logan and Warner Brothers, which was financing the picture. Jack Warner turned down Warren Beatty, on the grounds that he had no name value (which, in his eyes, Jane did because she was a Fonda), and Anthony Perkins was signed for the role of the basketball player. When Jane finally got out to Hollywood to begin production, Warner, seeing her tests, apparently began to have misgivings about Jane, too. In a now-legendary stupid remark, Warner said, "She's got a good future if you dye her hair blonde, break her jaw and reshape it, and shoot some silicone into her tits or get her falsies."

Despite Logan's soothing guidance, Jane had a miserable time during the filming. Having been brought up in the business, she knew all about the marketing side of movie-making—the constant pull and tug of publicists and photographers. She longed to be back in the comparative quiet of the Actors Studio "where you're only judged by your peers, some of them better than you are." She later told *The New York Times* about her total lack of confidence during the filming. She said, "One night, I was so afraid of blowing a big love scene, that I had a sleepwalking nightmare and woke up naked in the street at three o'clock in the morning."

The picture completed, Jane rushed back to New York—and the bosom of the Actors Studio. She had made up her mind about her tangled love life. Timmy Everett was out; Voutsinas was in. She rented an apartment of her own on East Fifty-fifth Street, and Voutsinas settled in with her. Jane paid a brief visit to her father and spoke only desultorily about *Tall Story*. Henry Fonda later said, "I don't understand that kid of mine. Here, she gets a one-in-a-million opportunity for a young actress, and she just kisses it off in talking to me about it."

As Maurice Zolotow noted, Andreas Voutsinas now was with Jane everywhere, every day. They made no secret of their relationship, embarrassing many Actors Studio members—who were used to everything—by kissing and fondling in public almost constantly. It also was evident that he had taken complete charge of her career. He was her drama coach now in everything she did at the Studio, and he directed her scenes as frequently as he was allowed to by the Studio powers. He announced that he was looking for a Broadway play that he could direct and in which Jane could star.

It was now 1960. *Tall Story* had not yet been released, so there were no reviews to tell how Jane had fared in her first film. Members of the Actors Studio were indifferent to the possible results, having seen the rather shallow play on which the movie was based, and having deemed it "not quite Actors Studio material."

The irrepressible Josh Logan didn't care about what the critics thought of *Tall Story*. He acquired a play, written by

Dan Taradash, called *There Was a Little Girl,* and told Jane it was a perfect vehicle for her. She was flattered and excited because it would be her first appearance in a starring role on Broadway. First, however, she consulted with Voutsinas, who listened gravely to the plot, as outlined by Jane, and then told her to go ahead with it. He said he would be at her side throughout the rehearsals and the production—as her drama coach—whether director Logan liked it or not.

There Was a Little Girl had an interesting premise. As Logan related it to me, "It was about a middle-class girl who goes out for her first night of dalliance with her young boyfriend in a motel, but because of his puritanical doubts about premarital sex, they get sidetracked into a bar. They get drunk, and the girl is taken out of the bar and gang-raped by a group of punks who hang out in the bar. She tracks down her attackers and confronts them. They assure her that she had resisted their advances and had not 'been asking for it,' which had plagued her conscience. This changes her whole attitude about sex because she now feels she owns herself."

The play had a rather improbable ending—the girl picks up a stranger and goes to bed with him—but Voutsinas did not raise any objections to it, vocally at least. So Jane went into rehearsals for the play, with Voutsinas at her side. Logan was outraged. He had heard about him from Hank Fonda, of course, but, he told me, "I had no idea of the influence the guy had over Jane. I'd tell her to do something, and she'd go back to her dressing room, where this Voutsinas was waiting, and then she'd come back and give me an argument. It wasn't a pleasant experience for me."

The play opened in New York on February 29, 1960, and was creamed by the critics. *The New York Times*'s Brooks Atkinson called it a "highly unsavory melodrama." However, Atkinson went out of his way to praise Jane in her role as "the wretched heroine." He wrote, "She gives an alert, many-sided performance that is professionally mature and suggests that she has found a career that suits her."

Although *There Was a Little Girl* closed in less than two

weeks, Jane finally had become somewhat of a celebrity, and on her own—not as Hank Fonda's little girl. She was interviewed by *Life,* which reported that "she never had received any help or even encouragement from her father." The magazine quoted a stunned Henry Fonda as saying, "Jane has made more progress in one year than I have in thirty." Andreas Voutsinas was neither interviewed nor quoted.

Later that year, however, Voutsinas crept into some of the news reports, described as "Miss Fonda's coach," when she was voted the most promising actress of the season by the New York Drama Critics Circle.

Shortly after *There Was a Little Girl* came and went, the movie *Tall Story* opened in the film houses and also came and went. The reviews had hardly been worth waiting for—bad enough for Voutsinas to say, "I told you so."

Time said, "Nothing could save the picture, not even the painfully personable Anthony Perkins, doing his famous awkward act, not even a second-generation Fonda, with a smile like her father's and legs like a chorus girl." And in *The New York Times,* Howard Thompson wrote, "A frantic attempt at sophistication and a steady barrage of jazzy wisecracks, most of them pretty stale, about campus sex and the business of education. . . . On the basketball court, the gangly Mr. Perkins jounces around convincingly enough. Near Miss Fonda, he generally gapes and freezes, and who can blame him? If Miss Fonda appears to be looking askance now and then, who can blame her?"

Disasterville. Yet, in her first two starts as an actress, and while still doing beginner's exercises at the Actors Studio, Jane had starred in a major movie and a major Broadway play, albeit both bad. Most young women of her age were still struggling through regional stock companies on the stage, or, if they were lucky, were working their way up through small supporting roles in movies. In the Actors Studio, only Susan Strasberg had progressed faster than Jane, thanks to *The Diary of Anne Frank.* At Jane's age, twenty-two at the time, Marilyn Monroe was doing something called *Ladies of the Chorus* at

Columbia Pictures. Nevertheless, egged on by Andreas Voutsinas, Jane already was expressing dissatisfaction with Josh Logan, openly claiming that Logan was "exploiting" her.

It also was one of those periods of deep estrangement from her father. She said, "I'd go over to see him from time to time, but Afdera, with her social agenda, always had a cocktail party or a dinner party going at the town house, and I didn't feel comfortable." Her father never had seen *her* East Fifty-fifth Street apartment because of his dislike of Voutsinas, who also was living there. So one night Jane invited Hank over for a visit and an attempt at a father-daughter chat. She made sure that Voutsinas would not be there during Hank's visit.

Many people at the Actors Studio are aware of what happened that night, having heard the story from both Jane and Voutsinas. Jane's said: "I told Andreas to go to a movie and to be sure not to come home until eleven o'clock. Dad came over at about eight. He was stiff and formal at first. He looked around the apartment and admired it. He didn't look in the closets. I don't think he wanted to see Andreas's clothes. Then we sat down and began to talk and he loosened up a bit. He told me he was hearing good things about my work and how pleased Josh was. He talked about his own projects, how he was probably going to do the play *Critic's Choice* and the big movie *Advise and Consent.* We talked about Peter, who was in college at the University of Nebraska and was beginning to talk seriously about a career in acting. I asked why Afdera hadn't come with him and he suddenly became quiet and wistful. I got a hint that things weren't going too well in this marriage, too. Poor Dad. Was it happening to him again? I wanted to reach out and hug him, but you didn't do that with Dad."

Apparently, Jane looked at her watch at 10:45 and told her father he'd have to go, that Andreas was coming home at any moment. Jane said, "Dad looked distraught, clapped his hat on his head and stalked out."

Andreas later said, "I got home at eleven o'clock and Jane

was very upset and crying. She said she had looked out the window after her father had left and saw him sitting on the curb with his head in his hands."

It's hard to imagine: the great Henry Fonda, sitting on a curbstone in New York, sunk in despair.

11

The strange thing about the Henry Fonda–Jane Fonda relationship was that they had this capacity to hurt one another. There was love there, but it always was tempered by external forces, for which one always blamed the other.

Years later, she was to tell *Ms.* magazine:

My only major influence was my father. He had power. Everything was done around his presence, even when he wasn't there . . . I became my father's "son," a tomboy. I was going to be brave, to make him love me, to be tough and strong. . . . He's so honest. He's just full of good intentions and honesty. I've even learned to love the things that are strange about him, like how he can say things that are extremely warm and intimate to the press about me, but he won't say them to me directly. . . . I really love him but it's just that he won't tell me; he tells the world. On the other hand, when I was twenty-three and flexing my own muscles and trying to become independent of him, my anger came through the press rather than dealing with him directly.

At twenty-three, the last person she wanted to deal with was her father as she faced the problems of finding her own identity. Instead, she turned to Voutsinas. There were to be a lot of Voutsinases in her life. It was to change later, but at that stage of insecurity, it seems that she needed men to help shape her. Had she relied on Josh Logan, who had her under contract, her life might have been much different. But Logan was a lot like her father—immersed in his own projects, diffident, not available to help her cope with her lack of self-esteem twenty-four hours a day—as was Voutsinas.

Such was her lack of self-esteem at the time that she said in an Associated Press interview: "Just to get up in the Actors Studio and do a scene is hard, mainly because I know that there are people there who have far more talent than I do. I do know that I have something else: I have star quality; I have a personality. I have presence on the stage, which may make me more important than they are. What I have is obvious—it's like a commodity and it's in demand. But in terms of acting ability, they have more. That's why it's so hard."

Under Josh Logan's direction, this star quality had already come to light, but, urged on by Voutsinas, she began to resent, more and more, Logan's capitalizing on her as a commodity. In his contract with Jane, Logan had the right to "loan her out" to other producers and to pocket her acting fees while still paying her the agreed-upon weekly salary plus expenses. Logan didn't have any immediate projects for Jane after *Tall Story* and *There Was a Little Girl,* but there were many seekers of "loan-outs" for Jane.

The first was a Broadway play, *Invitation to a March,* written by Arthur Laurents, who previously had done the hit *Home of the Brave.* Co-starring with Jane was Celeste Holm, and there were two other fine actresses in the cast, Eileen Heckart and Madeleine Sherwood. The play was about a young woman who is so bored with life that she becomes sort of a Sleeping Beauty, and involves the efforts of her mother and the others to mold her into something different, in order to cope with her condition. It was the kind of moralistic fable so popular on Broadway in those days.

Invitation to a March was not much fun for Jane. Laurents, also the director, was an outspoken opponent of Lee Strasberg's Method, and he insisted on Jane's hewing to his more traditional techniques of acting. Madeleine Sherwood, also an Actors Studio disciple, was equally unhappy. In the end, however, a fairly good play was put together and it lasted on Broadway for nearly four months. The reviews were from fair to good, with Jane, once again getting some extraordinary kudos.

Newsday wrote, "Miss Fonda has a glow which almost dims the moonlight. Here is surely the loveliest and most gifted of all our new young actresses." And in *The New Yorker* the tough Kenneth Tynan said, "Jane Fonda can quiver like a tuning fork and her neurotic outbursts are as shocking as the wanton, piecemeal destruction of a priceless harpsichord. What is more, she has extraordinary physical resources."

Nonetheless, displaying the ruthlessness she was to exhibit from time to time, Jane decided she had to get rid of her discoverer, Josh Logan. She commenced legal action to buy herself out of her contract with Logan. Because of his longtime relationship with Jane and Hank Fonda, and because the buy-out would cost Jane upward of a hundred thousand dollars, Logan didn't take these negotiations too seriously. He just continued, as usual, to loan her out to other movie producers who coveted her services. There were three terrible pictures in a row, all of them beset with problems, and all hardly worth mentioning in Jane's otherwise fairly distinguished list of movie credits.

The first was Columbia's *Walk on the Wild Side,* in which Jane evolves into a hooker in a whorehouse presided over by a lesbian madam, played by an old Fonda family friend, Barbara Stanwyck. Stanwyck's relationship with the Fonda family went so far back that throughout the film Ms. Stanwyck still called Jane by her childhood name, Lady Jane. Halfway through the movie, the distinguished director, Edward Dmytryk, was fired. There were all sorts of contending forces at work off-camera, with Laurence Harvey being involved with Joan Cohn, the wife of Columbia mogul Harry Cohn; and Capucine being involved with the film's producer, Charles K. Feldman. The result was tripe, a bastardization of a good Nelson Algren novel.

The second of these bombs for Jane was *The Chapman Report* for Warner Brothers. This was a story about the kinky love life of a group of Kinsey-type sex researchers, which had to be written and rewritten and rewritten to make it palatable for the movie standards of the day. In the rewriting, most of the flavor and meaning of the work was lost. Andreas Voutsinas now had developed the theory that Jane's future lay in roles exuding heavy sexuality, but he ran into conflict with director George Cukor, who cast Jane as a tight-lipped upper-class frigid young woman instead of in the nymphomaniac role Voutsinas wanted her to play. The result of all this was a resounding flop.

Even worse in this terrible trio was M-G-M's *In the Cool of the Day.* Angela Lansbury was in it, and when I asked Angela for her recollections of Jane Fonda, she replied that the film was too horrible to remember, to the point where she had blotted it completely out of her mind. The film was shot in Greece and was produced by the otherwise brilliant John Houseman. For Jane, the entire experience started off on the wrong foot. Andreas Voutsinas couldn't go with her because, as a Greek citizen, he would have been subject to being drafted into the Greek army (a requirement he had previously neglected). The story basically was a soap opera in which Jane played a tubercular in love with Peter Finch, who later admitted he took the role "solely to have a paid vacation in Greece." Not even the talents of Houseman and Angela Lansbury could save this one, as Finch, concentrating on his sightseeing, and Jane, bereft without Voutsinas, wallowed their way through the trashy script. "And it's not even *good* trash," wrote *The New York Times* in its subsequent review.

Miracle of miracles, this trio of trash pictures, while they did nothing to enhance the reputations of the other participants in them, actually benefited Jane's. She was making fans out of tough critics. Consider the following out-and-out encomium from one of the toughest, Stanley Kauffman of *The New Republic*:

> A new talent is rising—Jane Fonda. Her light is hardly under a bushel, but as far as adequate appreciation is concerned, she might as well be another Sandra Dee. I have now seen Miss Fonda in three films. In all of them, she gives performances that are not only fundamentally different from one another but are conceived without acting cliché, and executed with skill. Through them all can be heard, figuratively, the hum of that magnetism without which acting intelligence and technique are admirable but uncompelling. . . . It would be unfair to Miss Fonda and the reader to skimp her sex appeal. Not conventionally pretty, she has the kind of blunt startling features and generous mouth that can be charged with passion, or the cartoon of passion, as she chooses. Her slim, tall figure has thoroughbred gawky grace. Her voice is attractive and versatile. Her ear for inflections is secure. What lies ahead of this gifted and appealing young actress? With good parts in good plays and films, she could develop into a first-rate artist. Meanwhile, it would be a pity if her gifts were not fully appreciated in these lesser, though large roles.

For a review written more than twenty-five years ago, Kauffman's comments explain, better than I could, the roots of Jane Fonda's enormous appeal as an actress over the last quarter century—sexiness tempered with intelligence, an innate skill at her craft. Kauffman did not mention another quality emerging in Jane that was to shape her reputation later in life. Even in her early twenties, she was making points for herself among journalists for her contentiousness and tendency to make outrageous statements—all of which got her frequently into the newspaper columns and fan magazines. She did not hesitate to call *In the Cool of the Day* a film "I'd just as soon forget"; and she went into a long harangue with an interviewer, in which, explaining her relationship with Voutsinas, she flatly stated that marriage was obsolete, an artificial social necessity not particularly beneficial to women. She said, "Why should a woman *have* to marry? I couldn't get married now, if my life depended on it."

A harbinger of the future controversial Jane Fonda?

Yet, lady of contradictions as she was even then, there was an underlying, not-so-hard-nosed sentimentality there.

She grieved for her father when Afdera left him for another man and Hank, divorced again, was alone and melancholy in the Manhattan town house.

She grieved for her brother, Peter, when he fell in love with Brooke Hayward's sister, Bridget, and later was shattered when Bridget committed suicide.

She grieved when Marilyn Monroe died of an overdose in 1962.

She even grieved when her childhood home at 900 Tigertail Road was burned to the ground in the big Bel Air fire of 1961.

Although she was diverted by all these misadventures, Jane always got back on the course she now firmly believed was right for herself. She drifted away from the Actors Studio, even having passed the rigid test for full-scale membership, and her coach-director-companion-roommate, Andreas Voutsinas, was in total control. He was now spending much of his

87

time looking for that one Broadway play in which Jane would star, and in which he would emerge as one of the Great White Way's top directors.

Only one thing stood in the way: Jane's long-term contract with Josh Logan.

Jane's negotiations to get herself out of the contract had limped along for some months. Considering the four movies and the two plays he had generated for her—plus his godfatherhood and their long-standing relationship—Logan never thought Jane seriously meant to ditch him. Besides, M-G-M wanted her on loan-out for *Period of Adjustment,* based on the Tennessee Williams play, and Logan thought this would satisfy Jane's cravings to do what she called "a more meaningful movie."

He underestimated Jane's slyness. Through her agent, she went directly to M-G-M and persuaded them to advance her the money to buy her out of the Logan contract—after which she would do *Period of Adjustment* for them. The amount necessary for the buyout never has been made public.

The stunned Logan, confronted with this fait accompli, put up no resistance and gave Jane her release. They parted with some residual bitterness and Jane never saw Logan again.

12

My very last interview with Josh Logan helped explain some of these strange manipulations. It was a sad visit. The date was October 22, 1987, and Logan was only a shadow of the bearlike, vigorous, eloquent man I had known for many years. He was suffering from a rare, paralytic disease, and was, in fact, near death. We saw one another in the famous drawing room of his apartment overlooking the East River in New York. The walls were still hung with all the memorabilia of his illustrious career, including several original Henry Fonda oil paintings.

Logan's shrunken form was huddled in one corner of an enormous sofa. Attending him was a nurse with a wheelchair—the only way he could be moved. Also in the room was Nedda, his lovely wife of many years; and a young man, a secretary named Chris, who basically was Logan's translator.

Though Logan's mind was as sharp as ever, no one could understand him—not even Nedda—because his paralysis had seriously affected his vocal cords. His voice was a feeble mixture of incomprehensible groans and whispers. As in the case of the renowned scientist Dr. Stephen Hawking, only one man could decipher what he was saying and convert it into recognizable English. Here, that man was Chris.

Speaking through Chris, Logan began with reminiscences of Jane as a child, repeating much of what he had told me before. He added something new and touching: "I really felt terrible for Jane when her mother, Frances, committed suicide and everyone told her it had been a heart attack, and she didn't learn until later that her mother had slit her throat. Exactly the same thing happened to me. My father committed suicide in a mental institution. I was fifty-three years old before I finally found out that he didn't die a natural death. An uncle told me."

Nedda Logan interjected: "Let's talk about Jane's contract with Josh. It came about, basically, when she came to visit us one Sunday afternoon in our country house in Connecticut. We hadn't seen her for some time because she had been away at Emma Willard, and then at Vassar. When she walked in I said, 'Oh, my God, look at this beautiful girl. You should be on the stage.' Jane said, 'I wouldn't be an actress for all the money in the world.' She was quite adamant about it. But a few months later, when Josh called her in to sign her for *Tall Story,* she apparently had changed her mind."

Josh Logan said, "I remember the exact date when I put her under contract. She signed it on January 15, 1959."

Intermittently and haltingly, Josh explained the contract. He said, through his interpreter, Chris, "After *Tall Story,* she was supposed to do seven more pictures for me. The entire contract was worth one hundred thousand dollars to her. Her monthly pay of a thousand dollars—plus makeup, wardrobe, and other expenses—might seen low by today's standards, but at that time it was generous. Studios were then signing unknown young actresses for as little as one hundred and fifty dollars a week."

Josh went on: "Anyway, she did *Tall Story,* and though the picture wasn't so hot, she got some good reviews and attracted a lot of attention. The next film I wanted to do was *Fanny,* with Jane in the lead role. *Fanny* was an institution in France—part of a trilogy: *Marius, Fanny,* and *Cesar,* which had been best-selling books, and even inspired sets of porcelain figurines—one of which I have—which sold like hotcakes all over France."

A flash of the old Logan humor suddenly came through, as Josh said, "Well, the producer, David Merrick, rushed over to France and bought the rights from one of his many illegitimate children—of which he had plenty—and we did the musical *Fanny* on Broadway. Now it was time for the nonmusical *Fanny,* as a film. I talked to Jane about it. She loved the idea at first, but then she talked to her pal, Andreas Voutsinas, and decided that the French people would be outraged if one of their classics was played by an American actress, rather than a French one. I thought maybe she was right, and I ended up casting Leslie Caron in the part. But I still think that if Jane had done it, she would have become a huge star overnight, in only her second picture."

Instead, there was Logan's play, *There Was a Little Girl.* Nedda said, "That was a strange experience. There was this boy, Timmy Everett, who showed up with Jane every day and went home with her every night; and in her dressing room, there was this Andreas Voutsinas." Josh said, "Yeah. He'd be back there, playing records to get Jane in the mood for her scenes. I'd tell Jane, 'Hogwash. Just go out there and do it, like we rehearsed it.'"

According to Logan, the contract problems with Jane began immediately after *There Was a Little Girl.* Logan recalled, "Jane came to me and said she wanted to get out of her contract. She also said she wanted the one hundred thousand dollars I owed her. I said, 'Jane, that's ridiculous. You've still got four years to go on this five-year contract, and you haven't yet come close to *earning* the one hundred thousand dollars.' "

Logan continued, "Then I got hit from another angle. Ray Stark was becoming a big-time producer at Columbia Pictures, and his people came to me and said, literally, that Stark wanted me to sell Jane to him. He offered a whale of a lot of money, but my attorney, Bill Feitelson, said it wasn't enough to compensate his law office for the time they had spent in negotiating the original contract between Jane and me."

The story now got muddy, in Logan's telling, but he said, "I didn't feel badly about Jane wanting to leave me because, after all, she was my best friend's daughter, so I eventually told Bill Feitelson to set the minimum price in order to compensate him, and only to sell the contract to Jane herself, not to anyone else. Bill set the price at one hundred thousand dollars, and Jane later came up with the money. I hugged her and wished her Godspeed. I wasn't aware that the money came from M-G-M, who wanted to be sure she'd do *Period of Adjustment* for them.

"To this day, I feel that as far as Jane was concerned, I was her Abraham Lincoln, freeing her from slavery. By selling her contract to Jane, and not to another producer or studio, I kept her out of the hands of people who would have tied her up for years. Instead, she became her own woman, making her own decisions, as she has been able to do to this day. Since that couple of years with me, she has never been owned by anybody."

A cloud of sorrow passed over Logan's wasted face. He said, "And yet, she wiped me off her slate and I never saw her or spoke to her again. Since I became sick, she never called to see how I was doing. I've gotten anonymous phone calls asking, 'Why did you gouge Jane?' and her brother, Peter, asked me the same question when we appeared together once on 'The Merv Griffin Show.' During a commercial, I explained to him, as I'm explaining to you, how, rather than exploiting her, I actually was her Abraham Lincoln, and willingly let her go for a minimal sum, rather than selling her as a slave to someone else. I think Peter understood."

That sad meeting with Logan ended with Josh plaintively asking me, "Can *you* explain why Jane turned against me with such vindictiveness?"

I had to answer, with total honesty, "I'm sorry, Josh, but I just don't know."

Logan died a few months later—on July 12, 1988.

13

For Jane, it was onward but not yet upward, after her final split with Josh Logan in 1962. *Period of Adjustment* turned out to be far less than she had expected. The 1959 Broadway play, from which the film was adapted, was second-rate Tennessee Williams, nowhere in the same class with some of his previous triumphs, such as *The Rose Tattoo,* and his Pulitzer Prize–winning *Cat on a Hot Tin Roof.* Unlike much of his other work, this was Williams's attempt at light bittersweet comedy—about the tribulations of a young couple, newly married, set against the squabbling of an older married couple at the point of separation and divorce.

In the M-G-M film, Jane and Jim Hutton were cast as the newlyweds; Tony Franciosa and Lois Nettleton were the other twosome. Jane and Andreas (neither of whom had seen the Broadway play) set out for Hollywood with high hopes. Jane rented a house for the duration of the M-G-M production, but soon discovered that M-G-M's hypocritical sense of morality, enunciated by Louis B. Mayer (who was long gone from the studio), was still in effect. Mayer used to say, "Our stars are America's royalty and cannot be allowed to sully themselves in the eyes of the American people." That's why the William Randolph Hearst–Marion Davies and the Spencer Tracy–Katharine Hepburn liaisons were so effectively hushed up by M-G-M's publicity mogul, Howard Strickling. Strickling told me, "Jane Fonda was called in and told that Mr. Voutsinas—or whatever his name was—could not live in her house. He'd have to move to a hotel."

Which is what Voutsinas did, though he was with Jane every moment on the set. He continued to coach her off-camera, which did not bother the director, George Roy Hill, who had directed the play on Broadway and was a newcomer to films. Unlike Josh Logan's rough treatment of Voutsinas, Hill said, "Andreas had good instincts in preparing Jane for her scenes. I appreciated his help."

For the first time, Jane's hair was dyed pure blonde. She showed a lot of cleavage and wore tight dresses—all the sexist things she had abhorred and was to abhor much more vigorously later. Under the watchful eye of Voutsinas, her early-1960s sex-kitten image was taking shape.

But not without some protest from Jane. During the filming, she told an interviewer on the *Hollywood Citizen-News*: "As a bride who cries most of the time throughout this picture, I don't know how pretty I'll look, even with the makeup and the wardrobe. The whole story covers a period of twenty-four hours following the wedding, and everything goes wrong. It's a story of the lack of communication between male and female—the old idea that a man must show off his masculinity and a girl must be dainty and weak. They're both so busy living in this framework that they go right past each other."

Interesting, because that framework—with some modifications—was the framework of her relationship with Voutsinas. He was the strong planner; she was the weak doer. Or so it was at that time. So mercurial was Jane that who knew when Andreas's days, like Logan's, would be numbered.

Bolstered by the Tennessee Williams and Jane Fonda names, *Period of Adjustment* did fairly well at the box office when it was released. The reviews were kind (Bosley Crowther of *The New York Times* termed it "better than the play") and Jane's consistent fan, Stanley Kauffman of *The New Republic,* wrote, "Her comic touch is as sure as her serious one. . . . Her performance is full of delights."

Back in New York again, Jane was far from happy. The film, though it had enhanced her image as a minor star, had not, as expected, made her a major one. At twenty-five, she was becoming impatient. She longed to return to the stage, remembering, in particular, the excitement she had felt doing Josh Logan's *There Was a Little Girl,* with Voutsinas backstage guiding her. Although the play was short-lived, it had brought her some of her best reviews; *Life* had devoted an entire article to her. And even though she was estranged from Josh Logan, she liked the creative push-and-pull between actress and director on the stage, as opposed to the less immediate push and pull between actress and director in a film.

Voutsinas couldn't have been more delighted. While he never had abandoned his search for a Broadway play in which he could emerge in his own right as Jane's director, he now redoubled his efforts. A few weeks after he and Jane got back from Hollywood in 1962, he suddenly came up with a play that he thought would be perfect for both him and Jane.

The play was called *The Fun Couple.* It didn't matter that the play had been written by a dentist (with a collaborator). The dentist had backers with enough money to produce the play on Broadway. And most important of all, the backers had no objection to signing Voutsinas on as the director, even though he had no previous major credits at staging a play. Jane was ecstatic. She told a reporter from the New York *Daily News,* "This play will make Andreas Voutsinas a name to be reckoned with in the American theater."

The Fun Couple basically was about a boy and girl, both

96

extremely puritanical and fresh from religiously oriented colleges, who meet in wicked Tijuana, fall in love, and get married—all in the space of one day. Playing Jane's swain was Bradford Dillman, and a very young Dyan Cannon also was in the cast.

Rehearsals began that summer. Things were complicated by the fact that Time-Life films chose to do a television documentary on Jane and the making of the play. Cameras were everywhere—onstage, backstage, in Jane's apartment, even following her from her apartment to the theater. Dyan Cannon said, "It was crazy. Not enough that we had a first-time director who seemed to be a little crazy, too. He flapped around the stage, his long hair flying, yelling most of the time. He kept yelling, 'No, that's not the way I want it.' 'Stop, do it again.' 'You're getting me angry.' Andreas was toughest on Jane. He did most of his yelling at her."

But Jane took it, unwhimperingly. She kept kissing and hugging Andreas between hollerings. When the dentist's play began its first tryout in Wilmington, everybody knew the production was in trouble. It was supposed to be a comedy, but nobody laughed. The entire first act was rewritten, and the actors were told to prune their own lines to make them shorter and snappier.

When the play opened in Philadelphia, the audience reacted just as tepidly, the changes in the script notwithstanding. Lee Strasberg came down to see how two of his prize pupils were doing. His daughter, Susan, was with him, and she reports, "Dad just threw up his hands, telling Voutsinas, 'There are too many mistakes being made here. I don't know how you can fix it at this stage.' "

The play opened at the Lyceum Theatre in New York on October 26, 1962. Before the performance, Jane received flowers from Peter but nothing, not even a telegram, from her father. The Time-Life cameras were still everywhere in pursuit of their documentary. The documentarians faded away during the performance when their cameras picked up the reactions of the audience. There were yawns, then a lot of people getting up and walking out of the theater. It was one of the worst disasters in the history of Broadway.

After the show, the cast went to Sardi's for the time-honored custom of taking the applause of the diners and waiting for the reviews in the midnight editions of the newspapers. Voutsinas was still very much the Broadway director, cheerfully greeting other theater people at other tables, and obviously hoping for a miracle. The miracle never happened. The first review came in and it was typical of the rest. Walter Kerr, in the *New York Herald Tribune,* wrote: "I find it impossible to believe that *The Fun Couple* ever went out of town for tryouts. It did, and they should have closed it then."

The next day, the Shubert Organization counted up less than two hundred dollars in advance reservations at the box office. They closed down the play on the spot.

It had lasted for exactly one night on Broadway.

It took a little longer for Voutsinas and Jane's relationship to reach its termination point, but this was the beginning of the end.

14

After the fiasco of *The Fun Couple,* Jane and Andreas went into seclusion for a while in their East Fifty-fifth Street apartment. Voutsinas apparently was hoping that someone would see *some* merit in his direction of the play and would offer him another directing job. No one did.

The fiasco, on the other hand, did not affect Jane's continuing promise as an actress—in films, anyway. Producers and studios kept calling her agent, Dick Clayton, who told me: "Jane was not exactly a household word as yet, but she had proved herself in a lot of lousy films, doing both comedy and melodrama. People figured she had been better than her material. She also was reaching the full bloom of her beauty—that oval face, the full sexy mouth, the clear alabaster skin. Also, the baby fat was disappearing. So, there was a lot of interest in her, and we were trying to work out deals."

However, this did not abet the growing strain in the Jane-Andreas relationship. After all, the main objective of *The Fun Couple* project had been to make Voutsinas "a name to be reckoned with" on Broadway, and it failed. Voutsinas couldn't forget that, and neither could Jane. They continued to live together, though, and Andreas's main function now was to continue as her drama coach in whatever work she got.

The next work Jane got turned out to be her last appearance in the theater. It was early in 1963, and she had just turned twenty-six, when the Actors Studio decided to stage a Broadway revival of Eugene O'Neill's 1928 marathon play *Strange Interlude.* The director, José Quintero, cast Jane in the role of Madeline Arnold, which gave her a lift after her last catastrophic stage production. She was also exhilarated at the prospect of being reunited with some of the Actors Studio's greatest superstars.

It didn't turn out the way she thought, however. Madeline Arnold appears only in the last two of eight acts, and Jane's performance, while more than adequate, was pretty much overshadowed by the superstars in the cast, which included Geraldine Page, Ben Gazzara, Betty Field, Pat Hingle, William Prince, and Franchot Tone. Andreas Voutsinas, as usual, prepared Jane for her role, but she was disconsolate when the play's limited run ended. Friends say she decided then to forego the theater in her future plans, and to concentrate solely on "selling myself as a commodity" in films.

That still was to prove to be a rather slippery objective. The industry continued to look at her as a girl-next-door type, who could be believable with either good or bad morals. Jane's next picture continued the trend. In M-G-M's *Sunday in New York,* an old-fashioned comedy in the early Doris Day tradition, she was a virgin whose brother kept rushing into her New York apartment to save her from the carnal intentions of a man she had casually met. The movie, written by Norman Krasna, was pure titillation—up to and including the wedlock ending required of such sex comedies in those days. The film did nothing to enhance Jane's reputation—except in the eyes of Stanley Kauffman, the critic who continued to love *everything* Jane did.

Jane now was in one of her periods of great discontent. She had turned her back on the stage and felt that she was not progressing in her movie career; it was stable but not moving forward. Voutsinas was brooding and more or less just hanging around. Her father, disconsolate over his divorce from Afdera, was losing himself in his own films and was even less available to Jane for advice and encouragement, if she had wanted it from him, which she didn't. Jane's brother, Peter, had now married and had launched his own acting career, and, at the time, was busily at work in Robert Rossen's film *Lilith,* in which he had the second male lead. The picture starred Jean Seberg.

Jane met Peter briefly in New York and they talked about Miss Seberg's unusual career. Seberg had begun fairly inauspiciously in the United States in Otto Preminger's *Saint Joan,* in which she had been selected for the part from among eighteen thousand unknown actresses. She had then gone to France and had become a huge international star overnight in Jean-Luc Godard's gangster epic, *Breathless.* She was one of the heroines of the *Nouvelle Vague* (New Wave) of young French filmmakers whose work at the time was the most talked about in the film industry, and the envy of Hollywood directors who tried the same techniques and failed.

Jane Fonda, already becoming a self-educated student of film, got to know all she could learn about the giants of the New Wave: Godard, Chabrol, Truffaut, Resnais. She was utterly fascinated with the ferment going on in the French film industry. She decided that perhaps that was where the future of her career lay, as it had for Jean Seberg. Seberg now was married to the famous French novelist Romain Gary.

And suddenly, out of the blue, came Jane's chance. Or so she thought. Her agent got a call from M-G-M, which was trying to capitalize on the popularity of the New Wave in the United States. The studio had signed a deal to partially finance a film to be made in France by director René Clément. In the United States, the picture would be titled *Joy House.*

M-G-M, as it did rather frequently in those post–Louis B. Mayer days, had made a mistake. Clément was not one of the young New Wave directors, but rather an older, more traditional director, trying to alter his style to take advantage of the New Wave boom. Why someone at M-G-M didn't know that is a mystery. Or why Jane Fonda, with her newfound wisdom, didn't know either.

But Jane gleefully signed and flew off to Paris with Andreas Voutsinas. Since M-G-M was involved, an entire publicity staff was there to greet them. I was in France at the time, and I recall that both the French press and radio were surfeited with Jane Fonda interviews. She answered hundreds of questions about her famous father; she talked about her previous art-student days in Paris (with some exaggeration, indicating, for example, that she was a full-time scholar at the Sorbonne); she discussed such serious subjects as female sexuality.

How did Jane get through such interviews, considering that seven years earlier she had foundered in her art studies because of her inability to master the French language? The answer is that, thanks to M-G-M's munificence, she was provided with a full-time language professor, who, on her insistence, was a woman. All this was before production on *Joy House* even got under way. Jane bubbled: "My personal linguist did not allow me to speak one word of English for two months. And all that publicity, with reporters constantly crowding in—they adore my father in Europe. All this, mind you, in *my* French. I never felt so good."

One cynical French journalist pointed out, however, that Jane's French was not so hot yet. The reporter wrote, "Miss Fonda's accent is atrocious. Also, she constantly uses the *tu* form in addressing anyone with whom she is speaking. She should be reminded that the *tu* form, the familiar, should only be addressed to husbands, lovers, personal friends, children, and pet animals."

Jane's persistence eventually overcame the *tu* form problem, but not the strong American accent, which, in fact, enchanted most reporters. They constantly called her "the American BB," thus comparing her with the ruling French movie queen, Brigitte Bardot, whom Jane slightly resembled. Jane's photo even made the cover of *Cahiers du Cinema,* the serious, high-class French movie magazine. Their columnist, Georges Belmont, wrote, "On the outside, Mademoiselle Fonda is true to her image: tall, blonde, the perfect American, with long flexible movements. Inside, she is sultry and dangerous, like a caged animal."

Living as she did at the plush Hotel Relais Bisson, Jane was hardly caged. But, as she renewed her old friendships in Paris, Andreas Voutsinas acted more and more as if *he* were caged. They shared the same suite, and he accompanied Jane to the set every day, but his almost perpetual gloom deepened. In one of her giggling interviews with a reporter, Jane had discussed her unusually handsome co-star, Alain Delon. Said Jane, "I will undoubtedly fall in love with Alain. I can only play love scenes well when I'm in love with my partner." That was standard Hollywood pap to evoke interest in an upcoming film.

But it happened. Jane got involved with Delon in a genuine romance, so intense, in fact, that it caused Delon's long-time lover, Romy Schneider, to break up with him in a much-publicized spat. Soon thereafter, Andreas Voutsinas announced to Jane that he was ill, that he no longer could continue as her coach, and that he was immediately flying back to New York—which he did.

And as Josh Logan had predicted, that was the end of Andreas in Jane's life. At last report, Voutsinas had returned to Paris and was conducting Lee Strasberg–like drama classes there.

If this makes Jane sound as if she had the habit of squeezing people dry and then throwing them away, it may have been true only of her early bulimia-addled years. Her later history does not indicate the same tendencies.

Actually, with Voutsinas gone, *she* felt abandoned; but

she soon got caught up in the new intricacies of her life in Paris. Her romance with Alain Delon was a brief one; she said she found him "handsome, but dull." Even more serious to her was the fact that she sensed she was in another bad movie. She said, "It was all very haphazard in production. There was no script and very little organization. It sort of threw me, because I'm used to working within a structured framework. There was too much playing it by ear for my taste."

As director Clément went along, trying to imitate the New Wave directors, the story became increasingly more ridiculous. Titled initially in French *Ni Saints, Ni Saufs (Neither Saints nor Saviors),* the evolving plot bore little relationship to the title. It was about a small-time criminal (played by Delon) who is fleeing mob retribution and ends up in a flophouse on the Riviera, where he is served soup by two rich women volunteers (Jane and Lola Albright). The ladies take him home to their mansion. Jane sleeps with him. Albright sleeps with him. Albright keeps a shrunken human head in a case. Someone is trying to poison the Delon character. An insane former lover wanders the premises. Jane has some sort of mysterious hold over Albright, which never is explained. Jane keeps ending up in Delon's bed, even as the mob is closing in on him. What a mish-mash!

Critic Judith Crist, reporting that Jane played her role as if she were doing a combination of *The Madwoman of Chaillot* and *Baby Doll,* listed the film among the Ten Worst of 1965. Even Jane's biggest booster, Stanley Kauffman, had to lament, "Jane Fonda's development as an actress is beclouded by her poor choice of vehicles. Her latest film is an absurd suspense picture called *Joy House.* . . . No summary of the silly plot is needed."

It was another terrible film, but was it the end of Jane's experimental incursion into the world of the French New Wave? Most certainly not.

Because, during the production of Clément's *Joy House* at the Epinay Studio outside Paris, she became involved with a *real* New Wave director, Roger Vadim. Vadim wrote, in *Bar-*

dot, Deneuve, Fonda, that he was visiting Epinay and having a drink at the studio bar when Jane burst in dripping wet, having heard that he was there.

"And at that instant," Vadim wrote, "I knew I was in love."

15

Roger Vadim, the son of a Russian immigrant (real name: Plemiannikov), had burst onto the New Wave scene in 1956 with his bold and innovative film *And God Created Woman*. Vadim was not rated in the same class with Godard and Truffaut, but he had earned considerable respect for some of his other pictures, such as *Les Liaisons Dangereuses*.

In France, and throughout the world, Vadim was best known for his libertine ways—both in his films and in his personal life. His pictures shamelessly exploited women for their sexuality, and scenes of female nudity had become his hallmark. Vadim, himself, caused shock waves with his lifestyle, if not so much in France, certainly in the more puritanical United States. He was noted for his wild parties, nude-bathing beach gatherings, and, by his own admission, casual use of drugs.

He had discovered Brigitte Bardot when she was fifteen, built her up in his films as the universal "sex-kitten," and married her when she was eighteen. To Vadim, Bardot was the symbol of female sexual liberation; to others, he was just perpetuating the age-old concept of woman as a man's possession, a plaything. The controversy—along with the nudity—made smash box-office hits of most of the Vadim-Bardot films.

After Bardot, Vadim had married Annette Stroyberg, with whom he did *Les Liaisons Dangereuses,* and with whom he had a child. Then came his long-running affair with Catherine Deneuve (he sired another child with her, out of wedlock). Because they never married, their tempestuous romance became one of the favorite continuing subjects for the scandal presses everywhere.

Jane had had previous contacts with Vadim before their fateful meeting at the bar at the Epinay movie studio—none of them earth-shaking. During her art-student days in Paris, when she was eighteen, Vadim saw her dancing at Maxim's restaurant with a friend of his, and he asked to be introduced to "Henry Fonda's daughter." Jane was noticeably cool at that brief meeting, and Vadim observed only that "Jane's ankles seemed to have been swollen that day."

Their next contact came when Vadim was staying at the Beverly Hills Hotel in California, and he asked Jane to join him in the hotel's coffee shop to discuss a film she might be interested in doing. She said no to the film. She issued an even more emphatic no when she received a telegram, sometime later, from French producer Francis Cosne, regarding another film Vadim was slated to direct. Her answer was in a telegram from her agent, which Cosne showed to Vadim: "JANE FONDA IS NOT INTERESTED IN A COSTUME DRAMA. SHE ALSO ASKS ME TO TELL YOU SHE WILL NEVER MAKE A FILM WITH ROGER VADIM."

Concerning these early parryings with Vadim, Jane said,

"I met him that first time in Paris when I went to study painting. I heard things about him then that would curl your hair. That he was sadistic, vicious, perverted, that he was a manipulator of women. . . . Then I saw him again in Beverly Hills a couple of years later, and he asked me to meet him for a drink to talk about doing a picture. I went, but I was terrified. Like I thought he was going to rape me there in the Polo Lounge. But he was terribly quiet and polite. I thought, 'Boy, what a clever act.' When I met him again in Paris while I was making *Joy House,* it was all totally different."

Why the difference? For one thing, Voutsinas had gone out of Jane's life, the attraction to Alain Delon had passed, and Jane felt extremely lonely. For another thing, Vadim had continued to be unexpectedly gentlemanly when Jane's French agent, Olga Horstig, invited him to a birthday party for Jane at her home. Thus, the stage had been set for that rainy afternoon at the Epinay studio, when Jane heard that Vadim was on the lot and rushed over to meet him in the studio bar.

They chatted comfortably in the bar for two hours, and Jane's remaining anxieties about Vadim apparently disappeared. They left the bar and went to Jane's hotel. As Vadim himself later wrote in his autobiography about the incident, they ascended to Jane's suite, stripped, and fell passionately into bed. But by Vadim's own written admission, an inconceivable thing—for him—happened. He became suddenly impotent and couldn't perform. He kept seeing Jane, and kept trying, but he admits that he continued to be impotent for three weeks, until one night "when the curse finally was broken," and he was able to make love. He opined that "There was one positive result of this experience, so wounding to my pride: Jane no longer had any reason to be frightened of my reputation."

She wasn't. She told Vadim that she was in love with him, and they lived together in her hotel suite for the duration of the filming of *Joy House.* Vadim was different from most men with whom she had been involved. He was not handsome, like Timmy Everett and Alain Delon, or weirdly striking-looking, like Andreas Voutsinas. Vadim's face, in fact, was slightly craggy and more like that of a factory worker or miner than a movie director. But he was charmingly intellectual. Not being very intellectual herself at that point in her life, she allowed herself to be taught by Vadim, and eagerly read the books he selected for her: works by Malraux, Gorky, and Machiavelli.

Vadim, by now, had signed Jane to star in his next picture, *La Ronde,* so she was not too upset when *Joy House* finished and she, like everyone else in the production, knew that René Clément's experiment was doomed to be devastated by the critics and the public. With M-G-M no longer paying Jane's hotel bill, she and Vadim moved into an apartment at 12 Rue de Seguier, near the Seine. She remembers the apartment as having a huge fireplace, craggy beams, and vast living spaces. It was very expensive. She paid the rent.

The filming of *La Ronde* began in Paris in early 1964. It was the second French film remake of Arthur Schnitzler's erotic work about various couples making love, the last making a complete circle with the first—hence the American title, *Circle of Love.* The first version, produced fourteen years earlier, had starred Danielle Darrieux and had been an enormous hit. Jane was to play the Darrieux role of the wife, in the first episode of the circle, in bed with her husband and then her lover. Why make the film again? Its American producer, Joseph E. Levine, may have wanted to capitalize on Vadim's scandalous reputation in America.

Jane and Vadim got along extremely well during the production. "She was eager to learn," says Vadim, "and I only had to convince her she was a beautiful woman, which, for some reason, she doubted. I also had to get her to shed some bad acting practices she had learned somewhere along the way. But basically she already was a very good actress, professional, punctual—unlike many of my French leading ladies. I like to describe her as a fine diamond, which only had to be shaped by the diamond-cutter—me."

Vadim adds that in certain matters, she was as immovable

"as the Great Wall of China." She refused to strip to the buff for her romps in bed in the film, and Vadim didn't press the issue too hard. He allowed her to be only semi-nude in her scenes, "showing just her back and shoulders—mostly shoulders."

These precautions came to naught later on, however, when the picture opened in the United States. New Yorkers were astounded one day to see an enormous signboard overlooking Times Square, advertising the film, and consisting totally of a representation of Jane with her totally nude buttocks facing the public. Vadim denied any complicity in this matter and blamed it on producer Levine. The irate Jane sued, and her derriere on the sign was covered with a black patch of paint. That made it worse. It provoked even more giggles, and the sign itself was taken down, under the threat of more legal action by Jane.

This contretemps did not hurt the box office, of course, and *La Ronde* a.k.a. *Circle of Love* went on to become a hit. Although most reviews compared Jane unfavorably with Danielle Darrieux, the picture made a lot of money, much more than any of her previous seven films. The world press trumpeted the fact that Jane had succeeded Brigitte Bardot as Vadim's newest sex-kitten—an appellation which Jane didn't seem to mind, in *those* days.

Earlier, back in Paris, Vadim had no other film projects after they finished production on *La Ronde,* nor did Jane, so she devoted herself to fitting into Vadim's rather hectic social life. There were parties at their apartment on the Rue de Seguier; there were parties on the beach at St. Tropez, which Vadim previously had helped found as the recreational hangout for the French movie-making set. There were a lot of drugs, up to and including hard ones like heroin, but according to Christian Marquand, Vadim's best friend, Jane never indulged in anything more than an occasional nervous puff on a marijuana joint.

As Jane and Vadim settled in as a couple, there were more tranquil pursuits, as well. They visited art museums; they made a quick sightseeing trip to Vadim's ancestral roots in Soviet Russia. As opposed to the St. Tropez madness, Vadim took Jane to quiet, solitary inns in rural France, where nobody knew them. Vadim was a good father and he arranged for his two children, Nathalie (Annette Stroyberg's daughter) and little Christian (Catherine Deneuve's son), to spend days and weeks with him and Jane. Jane became quite motherly with the two youngsters.

This involvement with Vadim's children seems to have evoked latent instincts in Jane. She suddenly bought a farm at Saint Ouen-Marchefroid, about thirty-seven miles outside of Paris. In a strange transition, she reverted back to the way her mother had been in Brentwood, California. She made lists, she planted trees, she bought antiques, she ruled their two servants with an iron hand. Vadim complained that she was trying to make the farm a replica of her childhood home, and that frequently she would chase him back to their Paris apartment, while she remained on the farm alone.

If it was homesickness, the antidote for it came unexpectedly to Jane in the summer of 1964. A property named *Cat Ballou* had been kicking around Hollywood for years. No one wanted to do the movie because it was a satirical Western, and in the parlance of the Broadway stage, satire—especially of the revered Western movie—"is what closes on Saturday night." Now, however, producer Harold Hecht had acquired the film rights at Columbia Pictures, and it was he who contacted Jane in France. He wanted her to play the lead role of Cat, Catherine Ballou, opposite Lee Marvin.

Jane read the script and liked it. "I just kept laughing out loud," she said, "which I had never done before while reading a script." She gave the script to Vadim to read. He didn't laugh, not getting the American nuances, but he told Jane, "I think this could be a success. I think you should do it." So off they went to Hollywood. They rented a house on the beach at Malibu, which, with its many film industry residents, reminded Vadim of St. Tropez. Part of the picture was to be shot in the Los Angeles area, at the Columbia Ranch, where many serious Westerns had been done. The rest of the filming was to be in Colorado.

While Vadim lolled about on the beach and read current and past issues of *Mad* magazine, which he found fascinating, Jane went to work every day. Although she often has been accused of having no sense of humor, Jane was delighted by the wild and crazy goings-on in the Cat Ballou story. Cat is a prim and proper young lady who sees her father killed in cold blood by a heinous villain, Jim Strawn (played by Lee Marvin), who has a silver nose because his own nose was bitten off in a fight. To get revenge and her ranch back, she joins forces with Kid Shelleen (also played by Lee Marvin), a drunken sot who used to be a famous gunfighter, but who now can't shoot straight. Cat and Shelleen form a gang of miscreants, who clumsily rob a train and perform other unlikely alcohol-induced acts. Cat ends up being accused of a murder, and narrowly escapes the gallows—to the tune of Nat King Cole singing *The Ballad of Cat Ballou.*

Presiding over this delightful nonsense was director Elliot Silverstein, who says: "When Jane arrived, I was immediately impressed with her dedication to work, her innate sense of filmmaking. I worried, at first, about her Actors Studio training, because this film was such a spoof and could have been loused up by a lot of introspective analysis. I didn't have to worry because Jane acknowledged that and took to my direction very well. We used a technique that worked perfectly: Jane played her part absolutely straight, as if this was a real Western. That made everyone else's crazy antics seem even crazier, especially Lee Marvin's. So I believe that Jane, playing it straight and taking everything seriously, and being a Little Mary Sunshine, was the key to the success of the entire picture."

Silverstein, a scholarly Yale graduate, had some personal comments as well: "I liked Jane so much that I wanted to ask her out. Then I discovered that the Frenchman with her was Roger Vadim and that they were pretty much a couple. So I gave up the idea of dating. Funny, but I got to like Vadim a lot, too. He had this reputation as a sex-nut, but he turned out to be a nice, quiet, intellectual guy, who played chess and read the classics. Seeing them together, it was obvious to me that he and Jane were very much in love—a tender, caring couple."

When *Cat Ballou* was released it became an almost instantaneous hit. It won the 1965 Best Actor Oscar for Lee Marvin, and the Directors Guild Award for Silverstein. Despite Silverstein's praise of Jane as being the key factor in holding the picture together, Jane didn't even get a nomination. She was consoled, however, by the fact that *Cat Ballou* became one of the top-ten box-office hits of the year. Also, Hollywood insiders recognized her worth in the film, and her per-picture acting fee rose to $400,000, a high figure for those days. *Cat Ballou,* following the money-making *La Ronde,* had made her a genuine international film star.

As such things happen, however, Jane's newfound status—after six years of financially floundering film involvements—led her into a couple of high-paying movie roles that were so bad that they are hardly worth mentioning. Her later perspicacity in choosing the right screen vehicles had not yet developed. Vadim seemed to be content to let Jane do what she wanted.

The first of these flops was *The Chase,* directed surprisingly by the able Arthur Penn, and co-starring, just as surprisingly, Marlon Brando and Robert Redford. The film was an example of the old show-business adage: "If it ain't on the page, it ain't on the stage." In this case, what was on the page was written, believe it or not, by the great playwright Lillian Hellman. Suffice it to say, it was "a picture to leave you cold. . . . It's phoney and tasteless," as Bosley Crowther of *The New York Times* summed it up. It was one of Columbia Pictures' biggest bombs of the 1960s.

Jane's second bomb of that year was Warner Brothers' *Any Wednesday,* in which she was chosen over Audrey Hepburn for the role of Jason Robards's mistress. Rex Reed said: "Simply everything is wrong with this loud-mouthed movie based on Muriel Resnick's warm and funny Broadway play." That's about it.

By now, Jane was commuting back and forth from France to Hollywood with Vadim. Her lengthy stays in the United States brought about some good things, as counterweight to the bad pictures. After three years of practically no contact with her father, Jane affected a rapprochement of sorts. Maybe she still needed Papa's approbation, but she brought Vadim to see Hank both on the West Coast and in New York. Vadim says, "My relations with Henry Fonda were superficial but pleasant. He didn't exactly think of me as the ideal prospective son-in-law, but I must have stood up well in comparison with Jane's previous fiancés. He thought I was responsible for getting Jane away from Andreas Voutsinas, which wasn't true, of course, but I didn't disabuse him of the idea. He came to visit us from time to time in Malibu, and once we stayed in his town house on East Seventy-fourth Street in New York."

Although he was not the epitome of warmness to his children, Hank Fonda had mellowed considerably. Much of this was due to his relationship with Shirlee Adams, a young charming former airline stewardess who was destined to become Hank's fifth and last wife. Jane got along famously with Shirlee. Like Jane's first stepmother, Susan Blanchard, Shirlee was close to Jane's age, and they were able to chat and to confide in one another, like girl friends. They still do.

Perhaps buoyed by this newfound familial feeling (Vadim's mother also was visiting them in Malibu), Jane and Vadim suddenly decided to get married in the summer of 1965. Some previous reports have said that Vadim suggested it and Jane merely acceded—a theory which Vadim vehemently denies. He says, "Jane has never let anyone make the important decisions in her life for her"—a statement not yet borne out by her past history with Strasberg, Voutsinas, and others.

The wedding was almost a secret one. There were no hordes of international press to cover the legal uniting of a big movie star and her equally celebrated husband-to-be. They flew to Las Vegas from Los Angeles in a private plane, and the ceremony was performed by a judge in their room at the Dunes Hotel on August 14, 1965. Present were only eight witnesses: Peter Fonda and his wife, Susan; Dennis Hopper; Brooke Hayward; three of Vadim's friends from France; and Vadim's mother. Henry Fonda did not attend. He was rehearsing his new play for Broadway, *Generation*.

16

Mr. and Mrs. Roger Vladimir Plemiannikov, better known as Roger Vadim and Jane Fonda, flew back to France a few days after their Las Vegas wedding. Why did Jane marry after all her nonbinding relationships with men? Vadim theorizes: "She was twenty-eight years old, she was still subject to the traditional American values of her Nebraska father, she felt it was the time in her life to become a legal wife and mother."

They settled in at the Saint Ouen farm. Jane had no film commitments for the rest of 1965, and she attacked her newfound "housewife period," as she later termed it, with enormous vigor. By now, she had torn parts of the old farmhouse apart, and a small army of carpenters and stonemasons was replacing walls and partitions. She brought in new truckloads of trees—pine, birch, cedars, and beech—surrounding the house with them and causing Vadim to ask, "If you wanted a house with trees, why didn't you buy a house with trees already there?" Just as when she was a little girl she had to have her own horse on the property, so she brought over the pony she had ridden in *Cat Ballou,* a gift from Columbia Pictures. The pony delighted little Nathalie, whose mother, Annette Stroyberg, was away almost constantly now on her own adventures, leaving Nathalie with Vadim for long periods of time. Nathalie rode the pony nearly everywhere, and as Jane watched this reincarnation of herself as a child, her maternalism bloomed.

Vadim being Vadim, there were frequent dinner parties and weekend guests at the farmhouse. Jane remained the perfect hostess, but her gusto for these social activities was diminishing. She says she would rather have spent her time with the stonemasons. She was busy scouting nearby castle ruins for medieval paving stones for her courtyard.

By January 1966, Vadim, with two collaborators, had finished the screenplay of his next film with Jane, *La Curée,* taken from a short story by Émile Zola. Vadim, who customarily took two years to prepare a film property, had been working on the script while he was with Jane in the United States on her pictures. As was customary with Vadim, the principal theme was sex. It was about a woman who marries a wealthy older man, but who then falls in love with her husband's handsome, sensual son. Vadim had transposed the classic Zola story to modern-day France and intended it as an exploration of the foibles and morals of the 1960s upper classes in his country. It became somewhat of a horror story as the husband takes revenge on his faithless wife, driving her into total madness. Hence, the change of title to *The Game Is Over* for English-speaking audiences.

La Curée was one of Vadim's better pictures, still considered somewhat of a classic in France. It was exquisitely photographed. The settings were opulent baronial estates, which he had scouted in southern France. As a director, he had complete control of his wife, the star, for the first time (in his *La*

Ronde, she had only been in a segment). They got along well as star and director, though Vadim complained that "she was still trying to analyze every scene, constantly looking for motivation." In his autobiography, Vadim also wondered why this extremely talented, extremely beautiful woman was so unsure of herself, and was still trying to find her own identity "as if she didn't know who she was."

As part of her search for identity, Jane apparently had decided it was okay to appear nude in her husband's films. This was an interesting flip-flop from her strenuous objections to doing so in *La Ronde.* In *La Curée,* as she cavorted with her young lover, played by Peter McEnery, she displayed practically *all* of her anatomy. Unfortunately, some paparazzi were lurking about at the locations, and a choice collection of Fonda-in-the-nude photos showed up in *Playboy* magazine in the United States. Again, Vadim pleaded innocence, probably rightly so, and the litigious Jane sued *Playboy.* The case dragged on for months, and she finally lost it.

No matter. Although *La Curée* didn't do anywhere as well in the United States as it did in France, the picture got mostly good reviews from the American critics, though some, like Rex Reed, had reservations about the excessive sensuality. Reed wrote in the *Daily News:* "I counted seven full-face bare-breast shots of Fonda, whose father must be purple-faced with embarrassment."

After *La Curée,* it was back to the United States again for Jane. With her still undeveloped sense of film quality, she had chosen two pictures to work in. One was terrible; the other was good. First, the terrible one: *Hurry Sundown.* This was produced and directed by Otto Preminger with a good cast, including Michael Caine, Diahann Carroll, Burgess Meredith, and Faye Dunaway. It was about black-white racial conflict in the South; pro–civil rights, but filmed like a tasteless soap opera. Preminger obviously wanted to cash in on Jane's sex-goddess image and he used her in some allegedly erotic scenes, such as her using a saxophone to arouse her husband (Michael Caine) out of his impotency.

Jane, who had never before exercised temperament with a director, could not abide the Teutonically tyrannical Preminger. Diahann Carroll said, "There was a lot of screaming and yelling between Jane and Otto. I guess she couldn't believe the story we were trying to tell, but then again, none of us could." The picture bombed. It alienated both black and white audiences, and once again, a Jane Fonda film was nominated by Judith Crist as "one of the worst movies of any number of years."

The next American film in which Jane worked in 1966 was a happier experience. This was *Barefoot in the Park,* which had a good script (adapted by Neil Simon from his hit play) and a pliable, thoughtful director, Gene Saks. The producer, Hal Wallis, picked Jane as the female lead over Elizabeth Ashley, who had played the role on Broadway with Robert Redford. Wallis told me, "Jane was developing into a big box-office name, and I needed her to carry Redford, whom I also wanted, but who was not that well-known at the time." Such are the ironies of movie casting, considering Redford's status as a box-office giant, starting with *Butch Cassidy and the Sundance Kid* only a couple of years later.

Jane recalls that she really enjoyed doing this picture, which was about a newlywed couple—a stuffy young man and a free-spirit wife who inhabit a fifth-floor walkup apartment in a kooky Greenwich Village building in New York. The story basically is about the wife, Corrie (Jane), curing the husband, Paul (Redford), of his stuffiness mainly through some bizarre machinations.

Jane, who previously had worked with Redford in *The Chase,* had barely gotten to know him during the production of that film debacle. In fact, her reputation was—and still is—that she is so intent on her acting that she rarely finds time to become friendly with any of her co-actors. Redford seems to be one of the exceptions. Jane says, "That's because we have mutually liberal ideas, which we discovered when we worked together again in *Barefoot in the Park.*" Redford later recalled, "At that time, I think, most of Jane's liberal ideas had come from her father." Redford, in 1967, had not yet become involved in the environmental issues that preoccupy him now, and Jane, by her own admission, was not yet aware of the social issues about which she became obsessive later. With incredible candor, she told an interviewer, "I didn't even know where Vietnam was."

On *Barefoot in the Park* she also broke her own rule by hobnobbing with Charles Boyer, who delightfully played an aging, eccentric hippie, who gets involved romantically with her mother in the picture (Mildred Natwick). Jane said that she and Boyer talked a lot about the work of his countryman, Vadim, whose films he found interesting but did not particularly admire. Boyer remembered Jane as a charming young woman "who impressed me because she was more interested in her performance than her makeup and her hair."

The film itself was a hit, and it reinforced Jane's image as an expert at doing sexy comedy (though, this time, there was no actual nudity). In the United States, at least, what she longed for most—recognition of her ability to play meaningful dramatic roles—was yet to come.

Nor did it come when she returned to France, where she spent most of 1967 in the Saint Ouen farmhouse, occasionally in her Paris apartment, while her husband, Vadim, prepared to make *Barbarella,* probably Jane's most notorious sex comedy of all. Vadim had gotten the idea from a well-known French adult comic strip of the same name. He was intrigued with doing with *Barbarella* what others had done with the *Superman* comic strips. Here, he not only had a lot of science-fiction action, but in addition, a lot of science-fiction sex.

While Vadim worked on the *Barbarella* movie script with the incredible number of *seven* writer-collaborators (including American Terry Southern), Jane receded into the period of her greatest domesticity. She was the ultimate housewife. In Vadim's strange household, his former wife, Brigitte Bardot, came to visit quite frequently, and she and Jane became fairly good friends. Brigitte had now become an animal activist and was devoting her time to the rescue and shelter of stray cats, dogs, and horses. This was one of the mutual bonds she shared with Jane. Also, Jane was continuing her relationship with Vadim's children, Nathalie (now seven) and Christian (three), who came to stay with her and Vadim more and more often.

As for Vadim himself, he sensed (as he wrote) that Jane was growing away from him. He responded in some peculiar ways. In *Bardot, Deneuve, Fonda,* he writes: "After three years of living with Jane, I had convinced myself that the solution was to be found in sexual freedom based on reciprocal honesty. . . . When I made love to another woman, I talked to Jane about it. With time, I went further. I brought home some of my conquests—sometimes even into our bed. I did not demand that Jane share in my frolics. . . . Jane seemed to understand. . . . As for Jane, she did not allow herself extramarital escapades. This should have opened my eyes. I was heading down a one-way street."

How understanding *was* Jane about this one-way street? She has never commented on it. Was she playing the part of the ideal French wife, inured to a husband's infidelities? Or was it growing indifference? Probably not. Because at the end of that year, 1967, she was to become pregnant with Vadim's child.

17

It was with mixed feelings that Jane began production on Vadim's *Barbarella* late in 1967. She was nearing the end of her sex-kitten phase, and she seemed to sense it. She was stung when, on a whim, she called her father about his playing a cameo role as a galactic statesman in the film, and Hank snorted, "Will I have to take my clothes off?" and then he declined. In reporting this conversation to an Associated Press columnist, Bob Thomas, Hank added, "Jane has survived more bad movies than any actress should be able to do in a lifetime."

The film began production in Rome and then moved to Paris. There was a huge budget, for those days. Paramount was financing *Barbarella,* and Dino De Laurentiis was its producer. Much of the money went into special effects, crude by today's *Star Wars* standards, but effective for the 1960s.

In the very first scene, Jane had a flap with Vadim, again over the *extent* of the nudity. While the film's credits roll on the screen in graphic form, behind them we see Jane, apparently weightless, in her one-woman spaceship, doing a complete striptease as she sensuously removes segments of her space suit. The striptease remained in the film, but after Jane's protests, Vadim cut out the most intimate exposures of portions of Jane's body—but not enough to avoid the X rating the film later received.

There was more nudity in the picture, but not so drastic. But there were other problems with the censors. Jane has a sex scene with a blind angel, played by John Philip Law, and unmistakable intimations of lesbianism in scenes between Jane and the female heavy (Anita Pallenberg). Most controversial of all (and probably the funniest sequence in the picture), for punishment, Jane is placed in a orgasm-producing machine that is supposed to "pleasure her to death." Instead, Jane, while being pleasured, blows out all the fuses in the machine and wrecks it.

To Jane's credit, she played the role much as she had played Cat Ballou (no one has ever said she isn't a quick learner), with deadpan seriousness, extreme naïveté about the bizarre goings-on around her, in effect a fortieth-century Alice-in-Wonderland.

Although she later would denounce the film as the nadir of her career, in terms of expounding the sexual exploitation of women, she was quite defensive about it while the picture was in production. For example: Earl Wilson quoted her in the *New York Post* as saying: "I don't think of it as an erotic film. It's just funny and free and nice. You know, Vadim only has me completely nude behind the opening titles. He said, 'Everybody will be waiting for that, so why don't we get it over with right away, and get on with the picture.' That's how he thinks about it all. . . . If I have anything as an actress, I have variety. Why *not* go out on a limb and do something like *Barbarella*?"

Despite these brave words, Jane was extremely depressed

when the film was finished, according to her friend, Elizabeth Vailland. "She was worried about two things," said Mrs. Vailland. "Her next birthday was arriving soon on December 21, and she was going to be thirty years old. Her second worry was that *Barbarella* was going to be a failure, and that her career would be adrift again on a sea of poor films."

As it turned out, worry number two was paranoia. *Barbarella* did get some good reviews (notably one by the ultra-tough Pauline Kael of *The New Yorker*), and although it indeed was labeled "a poor film" and "a lewd smoker-room joke" by most other critics, the picture made money. This was the 1960s and *Barbarella* fit neatly into the philosophies of the Age of Permissiveness. Strangely, the film still is popular in art houses, and its videotape version still sells briskly in the home-video-rental stores.

Worry number one, Jane's anxieties about becoming thirty years old, was another matter. Her surrogate-mother role with Vadim's daughter, Nathalie (now eight), had become increasingly strong, and, as Vadim put it, "Jane wanted a child of her own, with a legitimate father, before she got much older."

So Jane, acting with the incipient resoluteness she was to display later, celebrated her thirtieth birthday with Vadim on December 21, 1967; and they went off on a skiing vacation in Megève in the French Alps. Her doctor later confirmed that Jane had become pregnant shortly after Christmas, during that vacation.

Vadim was ecstatic; Jane, he says, acted with slowly mounting exhilaration "as she felt the child growing within her." It was a fairly easy pregnancy, and in the early months Jane went to work on another Vadim film—or rather, it was the Vadim segment of a three-part trilogy called *Spirits of the Dead,* the other two segments to be directed by Federico Fellini and Louis Malle.

Vadim's participation in this tripartite venture came about mainly because of his flair for showmanship. Jane's brother, Peter, had just completed *Easy Rider,* which was on its way to becoming a worldwide smash-hit film. Vadim reasoned that putting the now-renowned Peter in a film, for the first time, with his already renowned sister, would attract vast audiences.

Although Peter and Jane had a marvelous time being together (Hank's continuing standoffishness had made them even closer), Vadim's hunch didn't work. This was because Vadim's sequence, "Metzengerstein" (loosely based on an Edgar Allan Poe short story), was another of those dreadful films Jane would prefer to forget. In a medieval setting, Jane and Peter played cousins, with an overtone of incest. There also was a mysterious horse, who might or might not have been an incarnation of the cousin played by Peter. The horse was both loved and hated by Jane. There was an orgy, some bisexuality, and preposterous medieval costumes for Jane, with see-through panels that exposed even the pregnant part of her.

None of the critics could make any sense out of this mess, and *Spirits of the Dead* is mainly remembered for the infinitely better segment directed by Fellini. So overlooked was Vadim's "Metzengerstein," that few people, even film scholars, are aware that Jane and Peter Fonda ever worked together.

With the completion of the picture, Jane went back to the farmhouse to await the birth of her child. She had had a slight case of the mumps and was terribly worried—as was Vadim— that the baby might be deformed, physically or mentally. There were frequent visits to her gynecologist-obstretrician. Amniocentesis had not yet come into general use, and the doctor was worried, too, but as far as he could tell, the fetus was developing normally.

American friends came to see Jane at the farmhouse (among them was Warren Beatty, who then was romancing Brigitte Bardot) and they reported that Jane was in a period of deep introspection, her only interest being her impending motherhood. They noticed a strain in her relations with Vadim, and that she emphasized only one attribute in him:

what a tender and loving father he was to Nathalie and Christian. There was a lot of expressed worry by Jane about the seeming purposelessness of her career after eight years in the business. Despite the money she was making, did she really *want* to continue doing light comedy and what amounted to soft-core pornography? Was she ever going to get to do an important film like her father—one that Hank would be proud of?

Jane's baby was born in a Paris hospital on September 28, 1968. She and Vadim both sagged with relief when they were told that Jane's mumps had had no effect; the child was perfectly healthy and normal in every respect. Curiously, the only Fonda present during the birth was Jane's first stepmother, Susan Blanchard, who volunteered to fly over from New York to help out. Hank and Peter Fonda both cabled their congratulations. The baby was a girl and Jane named her Vanessa. It has been reported elsewhere that "the child was named after Jane's fellow radical Vanessa Redgrave." Jane has denied this. She barely knew Redgrave at the time, and Jane herself had not yet been radicalized.

Vanessa's birth stirred up all the old Jane Fonda enthusiasms, and submerged her moodiness for a while. Vadim says she became obsessive about motherhood, constantly holding and coddling Vanessa, buying baby clothes in enormous amounts, decorating and redecorating the nursery, seeking out every book on the market about infant care. She breast-fed the baby and frequently slept with her in the nursery. Vadim had hired a baby nurse, but Jane left little for the woman to do.

But then, late in 1968, came another event that was to help change Jane's life drastically. A movie script from Hollywood arrived in the mail at the Saint Ouen farmhouse, with a notation from Jane's agent that writer-director James Poe considered that only Jane could play the heroine of the film. Jane's interest immediately was riveted on the script because, while she was pregnant, she had read and reread the Horace McCoy novel on which the film was based. The novel, written in the United States in the 1930s, was still a literary classic in France, and the French paperback edition was available everywhere. It reminded her wistfully of her father's masterpiece about the American Great Depression, *The Grapes of Wrath.* And now, here, delivered to her own doorstep, was her own chance to move—for the first time—into a possible similar masterpiece project. She could scarcely believe it.

The book—and the movie script—were titled *They Shoot Horses, Don't They?* It, too, was about the American Great Depression. The story focused on the indomitable spirit of a group of bone-weary, down-at-the-heels contestants in a 1930s dance marathon, whose last chance to make a little money was to come out on top in the twenty-four-hour-per-day grind.

Jane quickly accepted the film offer (Vadim liked the script, too), and she and Vadim and baby Vanessa flew to California, where they rented yet another house in Malibu. Not long into production, writer-director James Poe was fired for being too fanciful in his concept. His script was rewritten by Robert Thompson, and dynamic thirty-five-year-old Sydney Pollack replaced him as director. With Pollack, Jane moved into the sort of cooperative star-director relationship she had never experienced before. She said that she never knew movies could be shot that way. Pollack involved her in everything—casting, scene design, the rewriting of scenes, and, of course, there were endless discussions between Jane and Pollack about how a scene should be played. Pollack says, "We usually did it Jane's way at first, and then, only if it wasn't right, we'd refine it."

Jane's role of Gloria was the most difficult she had ever tackled. Gloria is a loser, a masochist, drowning in hopelessness when she enters the dance marathon solely as a means of survival. But she is sharp-tongued and sharp-witted as she interrelates with the other losers in the marathon, and you root for her. She sees horrors (Red Buttons's character, for example, dies of a heart attack as the result of his long exertions on the dance floor), and she suffers setbacks (she catches her boyfriend, played by Michael Sarrazin, copulating with

Susannah York's character in a storeroom off the dance floor), but she gallantly retains the one freedom left to her—to die as she pleases, at the hands of her boyfriend.

Pollack says he has rarely seen an actress so immersed in her part: "She read and reread the book, she kept living the character after we finished work for the day; after a while, she even insisted on living on the set, in a trailer with her baby and her nurse. She breast-fed her daughter on the sound-stage." Vadim, now feeling unneeded on the beach at Malibu, was acutely aware of the change in Jane. He wrote, in *Bardot, Deneuve, Fonda,* "She was living her part with an almost morbid intensity."

With Jane's intensity leading the way, the grim *They Shoot Horses, Don't They?* emerged as what critics later called "a metaphor of the human spirit." Director Pollack also extracted superb performances out of his other stars, Gig Young, Bruce Dern, Susannah York, and Bonnie Bedelia. There was a lot of camaraderie in the cast, but not with Jane. As usual, she kept to herself, except when she was onstage at work. Susannah York noted this strange predilection in Jane. Ms. York says, "We worked together for months, and I don't remember exchanging more than a half-dozen words with her."

The picture completed, Jane fled back to France with Vadim, who wrote how strongly he sensed that things would never be the same between them. They weren't. Jane obviously had attained one goal she had always longed for: even before the reviews, the word was out that this was her first *succes d'estime,* with some insiders comparing her with the early Bette Davis. But there was no outward exultation, just more quiet introspection. No one knew what her thoughts were at the time, but an entirely new Jane Fonda had emerged from her sex-kitten image, and an even more startlingly different Jane Fonda was *about* to emerge.

The reviews of *They Shoot Horses, Don't They?* confirmed the early insider speculation. The picture was hailed as "a new American film classic." John Simon wrote, in *The New York*

Times, "As Gloria, the fine little actress, Jane Fonda, graduates into a fine big actress." At Oscar time, Jane got her first Academy nomination as Best Actress, but lost out to Maggie Smith's solo bravura performance in *The Prime of Miss Jane Brodie.* She was, however, named Best Actress of the Year by the New York Film Critics.

And she received a letter from her father saying, "You've finally come into your own."

When Hank's letter arrived, Jane had just come back from seeing a French documentary about the possible massacre of hundreds of Vietnamese civilians by American forces at My Lai and elsewhere in Indochina.

18

How does a young woman, admittedly previously empty-headed about social and political matters, suddenly become rabidly socially conscious and political?

With some exaggeration, Jane said, in an interview in *The New York Times*: "I reached the age of thirty-two and discovered I'd wasted thirty-two years of my life. I reached it because of the war, because of the kinds of questions that the Vietnamese struggle is forcing us to ask ourselves about who we are, what our country means, and what we're doing."

It wasn't that clear-cut. Her father's New Deal liberalism had always stayed with her; in college, she had seen the excesses of Senator Joe McCarthy's anti-Communism. In 1973, she told writer Leroy Aarons of the *Washington Post*:

I've been trying over the last few years to figure out why it took me so long to put the pieces together. I think part of it has to do with the fact that I grew up and went through the student years in the 1950s. And what I remember about those times is very colored and conditioned by the fact that it was the McCarthy era. I remember the sort of overhanging sense that the movements for social change were fraught with danger and met with repression. I remember how certain of my teachers who expressed progressive ideas, and then they weren't around very long. . . . So I grew up feeling, "What's the use?"

The big change in Jane seems to have begun to come about in 1968, when she was pregnant with Vanessa and spending much time at home, thinking about her own problems. But because television had now come to France, she also could not escape the problems of the world. That was the year of the assassinations of both Robert Kennedy and Martin Luther King. In France, the nation was on the verge of revolution, with thousands of students rioting in the streets of Paris, mainly over educational reform, but soon abetted by leftist workers, with their own anti–de Gaulle agenda. Jane personally saw the violence and the bitterness of the riots every time she went into Paris to visit her obstetrician.

Also, French television, perhaps gloating over American failures in the war they, the French, had lost at Dien Bien Phu, flooded the airwaves with much more graphic coverage of Vietnam than the U.S. networks dared to run. Jane saw the whole of the 1968 Tet Offensive by the Vietcong and North Vietnamese, including the month-long battle for Hué. The French ran film that they had obtained from the North Vietnamese, and they did not stint on covering atrocities.

Along with the war footage, the French TV and press concentrated on unrest in the United States. Jane said then: "I didn't have any understanding of what was going on, except that people were moving. The most specific thing I can remember was watching television when there was a march of a half-million people on the Pentagon. That had a profound effect on me, because I suddenly realized to what degree the country had changed since I'd been away. I watched women leading marches. I watched women getting beaten up. I watched women walking up to the bayonets that were surrounding the Pentagon and they were not afraid. It was the soldiers who were afraid. I'll never forget that experience. It completely changed me. It began my searching for what was behind it all."

This was a landmark statement by Jane, quite startling in view of the fact that all her life she had been dominated by men. It was the first stirrings in her of feminine consciousness. Other things also began to stir in her. Through her friend Elizabeth Vailland (a French leftist acquaintance of Vadim's) she met Americans in Paris of the type she had never known before. There were soldiers who had deserted in Vietnam, soldiers who had finished their tours of duty in Vietnam and had settled in France. In both groups, there were whites who talked about poverty in Appalachia, and blacks who talked about the civil rights struggle and poverty in Harlem and Alabama.

Jane says, "I was initially defensive about America with these people, but then I began to listen more and more to things I never had known much about." This led to one of her most impulsive acts—one which was to change her life from then on. She decided to go to see poverty at first hand, in one of the worst imaginable places—India. No one knows why she chose India rather than, say, Detroit's inner city, but Vadim says, "The catalyst was a college friend of Jane's who had stopped off in Paris on her way to Bombay, and had asked Jane to accompany her." He misread Jane's purpose for going as a hippielike attempt to seek one's true identity with the gurus of Eastern spiritual religions.

Jane left for India shortly after Vanessa's first birthday in

September 1969. She did not ask for Vadim's permission to go, nor did he offer any objections. In any event, there was a minimum of communication between them at this point. Jane, her obsessive motherhood having seemingly moderated, left Vanessa in Vadim's care. As a father, she trusted him implicitly.

The India trip was devastating for Jane. Not only was the cultural shock unbearable, but she found none of the peacefulness with which her childhood friend, Mia Farrow, had returned from the subcontinent. Jane said, in a press conference in Los Angeles: "I had never seen people die from starvation, or a boy begging with the corpse of his little brother in his arms. I met a lot of American kids there, hippies from wealthy or middle-class families in search of their individualistic metaphysical trips. They accepted that poverty. They even tried to explain it away to me. But I couldn't accept the suffering and the gross injustices. It was the social system, a whole way of thinking, that was keeping so many people down."

From India, Jane went to Sikkim, the little Himalayan kingdom where Hope Cooke, an American girl her own age, was queen. Jane stayed at the palace, as a highly welcomed guest because of her film fame. The opulence of the palace, and the life-style of the royal couple, made the contrast with the common people she had seen both in India and in Sikkim itself even more appalling in Jane's mind. "For the first time," she said, "I realized how cloistered I had been all my life, how shut off I had been from the realities of ordinary people everywhere."

Jane cut short her stay in Sikkim and flew home because she was needed in Los Angeles to do publicity for *They Shoot Horses, Don't They?*, which was one of the favorites in the 1969 Oscar derby. Vadim had to go to Hollywood for one of his own film projects, so they took little Vanessa with them. They put Vanessa up at Hank Fonda's house in Bel Air (grandfatherhood had softened him somewhat) and they took a suite at the Beverly Wilshire Hotel. There was no house at Malibu this time.

Still thinking constantly about her trip to India, Jane picked up a copy of *Ramparts* magazine. It featured a story about the band of American Indians besieging and occupying the former federal penitentiary island of Alcatraz, in San Francisco Bay. It was then that Jane was reported to have made one of the most inane remarks of her life: "So *we* have Indians, too."

Whether this statement of revelation was true or not, this was the beginning of Jane's personal involvement in radical causes. She conferred with Marlon Brando, already famous for his espousal of Indian rights, and she made speeches at fundraisers for the Indians. Still bulimic and headstrong in her emotions, she soon felt that she *had* to go to Alcatraz and join forces with the beleaguered Native Americans. Her showdown with Vadim was now inevitable.

Vadim remembers the showdown well. He wrote in his autobiography: "It was in the room at the Beverly Wilshire that Jane finally said the words that I had been expecting to hear for months: 'Vadim, we must separate. I still love you very much but I need my own time, my life and my freedom. As for Vanessa, it's a problem, I know. But I can't do anything about it. We'll decide on the conditions later.' "

It soon became evident that the conditions would be that Vadim would care for Vanessa, along with his other children, and that Jane would see her daughter as often as she could, as she began a schedule of constant traveling for her causes. Technically, she and Vadim were to remain married for another three years.

Jane had contacted Peter Collier, the *Ramparts* magazine writer who had done the article about the Indians' invasion of Alcatraz, and Collier offered to escort her to the embattled island. It was, however, not so embattled. The government deliberately was holding back on assaulting Alcatraz because there was a lot of public sympathy for the Indians. They had seized the unused island as a token return of all the land that had been stolen from them in the past, and they were protesting many real injustices against them by the government's rigid Bureau of Indian Affairs. So when she arrived at the Embarcadero on San Francisco's waterfront, Jane found a carnival atmosphere: singing, dancing, wealthy yachtsmen ferrying food and supplies to the Indians on the island, the Coast Guard idly standing by, movie fans swarming around her and asking for autographs. In all, it was an easy transition for her, not unlike what she had become accustomed to in show business.

In *Ramparts* Collier reported Jane's arrival as follows: "She showed up at the San Francisco Embarcadero on the appointed morning, materializing out of a fog that seemed provided for the occasion by a Hollywood special effects crew. She was wearing tight jeans and had a helmet of hair cut in a shag. It was the proper uniform, but she didn't seem quite comfortable in it. She said she was nervous about how she would be received."

The nervousness subsided when she was ferried out to the island and sat down to talk with the Sioux leaders, who were predominant in the Indians' sit-in. The Sioux were polite but bewildered. They didn't know what to make of a famous female movie star, sitting among them and chatting about matters which, one of them complained to Collier, "she didn't seem to know very much about." She had learned a lot of it by rote, like learning a script, from what she had read in the statements of Marlon Brando and others. Yet, unlike most other celebrity visitors, Jane remained with the Indians far into the night. Eventually, they suggested to her that she visit Indian reservations, to better acquaint herself with Native American problems.

That was all the encouragement Jane needed. She took off in her station wagon, accompanied by Elizabeth Vailland, and on the next stop, Jane had her first encounter with the police. She was visiting the Washington State Indians around Puget Sound when she became entangled in a demonstration that grew violent outside Fort Lawton, a little-used army reserve base the Indians coveted. Several Indians were arrested as a result of a clash with club-swinging army military police. Arrested, too, were Jane and Mrs. Vailland, who were roughed up slightly but not hurt. After many phone calls to their superiors, the civilian police released the two ladies without clapping them in jail.

But Jane had tasted blood, as it were. She continued her tour of Indian reservations throughout the West. Everywhere she went she'd speak her piece about justice for Native Americans, and inevitably attract press coverage. The press coverage, in turn, attracted other political protesters, of which there were many in the United States at that time. Among those who enlisted her support were the Black Panthers (several of their members were in prison after armed clashes with the police, and the "Free Huey Newton" movement was in full swing). And then, of course, there was her original protest of choice: the growing outcry against President Nixon's continuation of the Vietnam War. Eager to see and hear her were antiwar activists in every town, on every college campus, and in the so-called GI Coffee Shops outside many military bases. Frantically scurrying around in a backbreaking schedule—with barely enough time to change clothes and to bathe—Jane managed to accommodate nearly all requests for her appearances.

Gone was Jane's vast wardrobe. She limited herself to jeans, one full skirt, and a couple of loose-fitting sweaters. In cold weather, she wore what seemed to be a navy pea jacket. Her only luggage was a single soft-sided bag.

It's hard to believe that just a few short months before, this was a pampered child of wealth, an efficient housewife and devoted mother, living a life of ease in a luxurious remodeled French farmhouse, most recently in a four-star hotel like the Beverly Wilshire. Why the overnight switch to crummy motels, bone-numbing auto trips, and red-eye airplane flights? Granted, her self-described political awakening was the key factor. But did the precipitous aberrant behavior of the bulimic also trigger the metamorphosis? Besides, in a couple of significant statements she made at the time, she seemed to have undergone sudden revulsion over what she had *been*.

> After India, when I first woke up in the morning at the Beverly Wilshire hotel, I still had in my eyes the crowds of Bombay, the smell of Bombay, in my ears the noise of Bombay. My first day back, and I saw those houses of Beverly Hills, those immaculate gardens, those neat silent streets, where the rich drive their big cars and send their children to the psychoanalyst, and employ exploited Mexican gardeners and black servants. I'd grown up here, but I'd never looked at it in these terms before. *(Los Angeles Mirror.)*

Later, in her peripatetic wanderings around the country:

> I was so used to being considered a sex symbol, that I began to like it. I didn't expect people to treat me as a person who thinks. But when I went to the Indians and I came in contact with the Panthers, the GI's, my new friends, I realized they were treating me as a person. This was so beautiful that I began to feel uncomfortable with people who still considered me a doll. It completed my own personal revolution, and Vadim was the first victim of it. *(The New York Times.)*

This is interesting because it translates into, "I found camaraderie with my new friends of the Left." She had not had much camaraderie before. Remember that ever since Voutsinas, she had been under the domination of one man, which had not left much time for socializing with confreres. With the intense preparation she poured into her acting chores, that left no time, either, for mixing with her fellow actors and actresses in her pictures. As previously noted, she had developed a reputation as a loner on her soundstages and movie locations, without exchanging (with very few exceptions) any bonhomie whatsoever. Now she was regarded as a thinking woman, loved by all her new confreres, admired for the fame she had brought to their various causes—"to say nothing of the money and publicity she attracted," as Dick Gregory put it.

And yet, she was honest enough with herself to recognize her limitations. She said, "When I went to talk to the Indians, I realized, of course, that when you're a movie actress, and when you go anywhere where people are in trouble, you have to be an expert. I showed up at Alcatraz and suddenly the newspapers were all over the place and they wanted to know what I thought. I didn't know what I thought. I had only just arrived. . . . Then, it was a hell of a time to drive across the country. I didn't realize there was this much motion. I'm aware, as we all are, of racism and poverty and unemployment, of protests against the war. What I had not realized is how some things are tied together. . . . I saw guys who will never be the same. You read about the post-Vietnam syndrome. I've seen hundreds of men suffering it that can't even speak. Guys who would whisper in my ear that they were incapable of doing anything else except perhaps killing. . . . You suddenly open up the floodgates and you have no words to express what you're feeling, and you grasp. I mean there were a lot of words that I was just beginning to understand what they meant, I borrowed a lot of rhetoric from a lot of people to try to give train rails to what it was that I was feeling."

How effective was Jane in the fumbling early months of her radicalization? Abbie Hoffman said, "She was too earnest, and too naïve. She thought she could lump all the world's ills into one overall cause, and that doesn't work." The Indians soon fell away because of her lack of understanding of their unique problems, and after a while, so did the Black Panthers. But she added others to her laundry list of causes. She marched with protesting welfare mothers in Nevada, and she picketed with Mexican-American vineyard workers in California. The Vietnam War protests continued as her chief commitment.

She even went to see her father in an appeal to his latent liberalism. Jane said:

> I told Dad all the things I had learned about American atrocities in Vietnam. He exploded: "You don't know what you're talking about. We don't do that. We're American. And even if the soldiers did it, they wouldn't talk about it." So I brought a couple of former Green Berets to see Dad, and they gave him first-hand accounts of what they had done and what they had seen done to the Vietnamese. Dad was moved, but he said, sadly, "I don't know what I can do besides what I'm already doing—that is, campaigning for the peace candidates." (Washington Post.)

Hank Fonda later told me, "This confrontation between me and Jane had a strange effect. Even though we got nowhere in our arguments, I began to understand her zeal. I even admired her for some, not all, of the things she said. It reminded me of the zeal I had for social causes when I was a kid. As a result, we began to get closer, as father and daughter, than we had been for years."

Elsewhere, the results of Jane's zeal were not so benign. For in June 1970—just six months after she had left Vadim at the Beverly Wilshire hotel—the FBI began its first entries in its voluminous file labeled JANE FONDA, ANARCHIST.

What exactly was Jane saying in those tumultuous times? Here are some excerpts, culled from the 763 pages elicited by me from the FBI under the Freedom of Information Act.

The speeches in her file are repetitious. She mostly said the same things to all of her audiences. Usually, an FBI informant sat in the audience and tape-recorded all of Jane's remarks. Some of the speeches were incredibly long-winded and encompassed fifty or more pages when transcribed.

Personally, I found little to justify labeling her an anarchist, a proponent of violent overthrow of the government. Others may feel differently. But read these samples and judge for yourself.

On June 19, 1970, a Special Agent of the FBI recorded a speech by Jane Fonda, internationally known film actress and supporter of militant causes, at a rally at 217 West First Street, Los Angeles, California, held in support of three inmates of Soledad Prison, Soledad, California, charged with murder. A transcript of Fonda's speech is as follows:

"Did you notice that lately whenever people get together to demand their freedom there are new symbols of repression flying overhead, the helicopter, the symbol of 20th century repression.

"We are right now, at this moment in history, locked in a struggle for survival against a monster which has been created and which we are perpetuating if we allow it to exist; and that monster is the American society. Put that on television, you'll be arrested by Spiro Agnew for freedom of speech! If you strip away the facade and the false sense of freedom and social justice and comfort that lulls the white middle class into thinking they're safe, you can see the system for what it is, racist, oppressive, totalitarian, and monstrous. And the only way that that system is going to change, particularly the courtroom system, is if we the people throw our weight entirely against it. We must denounce the unjust laws, we must denounce the unjust justice, and we must bring the system to a halt until it is again working for the people to protect the people.

"Rigged criminal trials for the purpose of wiping out anybody that the authorities don't want around, for the purpose of repressing political ideas and organizations, by exterminating the leaders and by intimidation, is nothing new in this country (will you please be quiet). If we are silent this time, we are the enemy and eventually we are the victim.

"Can any of you really believe that you are safe? Do you really think that it is sufficient to say, 'I am innocent, I have done nothing.' This is not Los Angeles in 1970. This is not Los Angeles in 1970, it is Berlin in 1936, and we are all Jews. The prisons of this country are overflowing with people who may be executed not because of what they have done but because of what they are. And this is no longer a situation reserved for the poor, the black, the starving, the unemployed, the shot at, and the afraid of. Kent State and the Chicago trial showed us all, I think, that we are all niggers to this system. White students are being shot, white lawyers are being convicted, middle-class pacifists are being sentenced and convicted for crossing state lines to incite to riot. It is all coming out, and we all better stop kidding ourselves into thinking we are safe. We must show the courts of this country that, if they try to execute the Soledad brothers, or Bobby Seale, or any other political prisoner, they will have the people to contend with. We must mobilize ourselves into massive demonstrations, we must educate ourselves and others in California as to the truth about the prisons and the courtrooms in this state, we must raise funds for research on the unconstitutionality of the Grand Jury, for investigations, for legal defense, for transcripts of court hearings, because for the lawyers of the Soledad brothers, the conventionally, the normally free transcripts have been denied. The lawyers are contributing their services but there are incredible transportation travel expenses because the witnesses in the Soledad case have been transferred to other prisons to try to prevent the truth from coming out.

"If we do nothing, if we hide our eyes and bury our head and are silent, we are as guilty as the executioners, and we will have no one to blame but ourselves when our time comes, and it will come, and the time of our children, if there are any left."

Bobby Seale is the Chairman of the Black Panther Party (see Appendix).

This document contains neither recommendations nor conclusions of the FBI. It is the property of the FBI and is loaned to your agency; it and its contents are not to be distributed outside your agency.

On December 10, 1970, Jane Fonda spoke at Texas Hall on the University of Texas at Arlington campus to an audience of approximately 2,500 persons. She spoke from 9:50 AM to 11:00 AM. . . .

The following are excerpts from Fonda's speech at the University of Texas at Arlington:

"The Administration talks a lot about terrorism and violence. I think that terrorism on the part of law enforcement officials of this country against citizens of the United States is the most dangerous kind of terrorism that exists.

"If they (law enforcement officials) isolate a political prisoner, that person is contained forever.

"I also realize that everyone that is in jail is a political prisoner.

"Truly some of the best people in the country today are behind bars.

143

"There is a law that states that if the President invades a foreign country without Congressional approval, he is to be impeached.

"The American institution is collapsing and the Administration is trying to disguise that collapse by using you as scapegoats.

"It is the antithesis of a learning institution that an officer should receive faculty status for learning how to kill. If the students don't want ROTC on campus, they shouldn't be there."

Many FBI transcripts were studded with misspelled words and frequently ended in midsentence—as if the transcriber was getting bored at the total lack of calls by Jane for violent revolution or organized mutiny by the troops in the field in Vietnam. I could find no such exhortations in any of the 763 pages in the FBI's Jane Fonda file.

True, she occasionally called for "Power to the People," and her contacts with bitter antiwar Vietnam veterans probably contributed to her exaggerating conditions in the war zone. But she never once advocated anything more drastic than *peaceful* protest against the policies of the Nixon administration—in the manner of the Reverend Martin Luther King's civil rights crusade.

And so far as her espousal of the Black Panther cause is concerned, her speeches were naïvely overemotional but entirely legal.

Despite its violent conflicts with the police, the Black Panther Party was never outlawed by either the federal or state governments.

20

ovember 2, 1970, had been a
grueling day for Jane Fonda. She was in Canada, speaking to
antiwar groups, and she traveled overland to London, Ontario, where she made a scheduled speech at Fanshawe College. Since she had another speech scheduled for the next day
at Bowling Green State University in Ohio, she took Air
Canada's "red-eye" flight number 271 late that evening from
Toronto International Airport. She was worn to a frazzle and
wearing her regular protest-rally garb of jeans and baggy
sweater.

Flight 271 touched down at Cleveland's Hopkins International Airport shortly after midnight in the early morning
of November 3. She was planning to spend the night in an
airport motel, and then move on to Bowling Green in the
morning. She never made it.

As the passengers trooped through the U.S. Customs Hall at the airport (271 having been an international flight), a single customs agent was on duty. His name was Lawrence Troiano. He rushed the other passengers through the line but told Jane to leave her luggage on the counter and to sit in a chair. He then left to make a phone call.

Jane's version of what happened next was related to my wife, writer Muriel Davidson. Jane said: "When this joker told me I'd have to sit there while he made a phone call, I asked him why I'd been singled out for special treatment. He told me to shut up, and walked away. When he came back, he opened my bag and confiscated my address book. When I got the address book back later, the pages were all out of order, and it was obvious that they had Xeroxed everything in it. The book contained such dangerous names as Norman Mailer, the novelist, and Tommy Smothers, the comic.

"The next thing Troiano did was to seize all the medicine vials in my bag. I had one bottle of Valium, for which I had a California prescription, and there were something like a hundred small vials of over-the-counter vitamin pills, which I always took to keep my strength up when I was on the road. I had marked the vitamin vials 'B,' 'L' and 'D,' for breakfast, lunch and dinner. Troiano sneered at me, 'What's this BLD? Something like LSD, I guess.' He then told me I'd have to be detained. He said he'd have to go away to phone his superior in Cleveland, and he brought in a Cleveland cop to stand guard over me."

Later court records indicate that Troiano's superior, Special Agent Richard Matuszak, arrived from Cleveland at 12:45 A.M. Jane was on the phone in the Customs Hall, talking with attorney Mark Lane, who then was handling cases for war protesters under arrest. Being far away in Boston, Lane told Jane that a Cleveland colleague, attorney Irwin Barnett, would soon be on hand to help her. Matuszak got Jane off the phone and ordered her into the airport's customs office.

In an interview in the *Cleveland Press,* Jane said: "I was about to have my period and I desperately had to go to the bathroom. Matuszak told me I couldn't go to the bathroom until two policewomen came from Cleveland to do a body search on me. Matuszak said the body search was necessary to make sure I wasn't carrying other dangerous drugs in my body cavities. I said, 'What do you mean, *other* dangerous drugs?' He just repeated that I couldn't go to the bathroom until the policewomen arrived.

"We hassled back and forth. I said, 'What do you want me to do, pee all over your floor?' I struggled to get to the bathroom, and when Matuszak grabbed me, I spun away from him. By now, two other Cleveland cops had shown up because the word had gotten around the airport that Jane Fonda was being detained. As I pulled away from Matuszak, he started yelling to these cops, 'She threw a punch at me. You're the witnesses.' Then one of the cops, Robert Pieper, got into the act. He said I had tried to kick him.

"The cops handcuffed me and Matuszak read me my rights. My Cleveland attorney, Irwin Barnett, was trying to reach me on the phone. I said, 'Don't my rights include the right to legal counsel?' Matuszak said, 'Not until the policewomen get here and search you.' He wouldn't let me talk to Barnett. Finally, the policewomen arrived and at last, I was allowed to pee, after their intimate search of me turned up absolutely nothing. It was only then that I was allowed to speak with my lawyer. I found out that there were three charges against me: assault on a federal officer, assault on a policeman, and attempting to smuggle illegal drugs into the United States."

Jane was handcuffed and driven to the Cuyahoga County Jail in Cleveland and booked at 2:45 A.M. She was put in a cell with several other women, two of whom had been charged with murdering a man and dismembering his body. Another was a genuine anarchist who had been arrested for carrying a red flag into a right-wing hard-hat rally.

Jane's Cleveland attorney, Barnett, arrived at the jail at 7:00 A.M.; Mark Lane, flying in from Boston, got there at about 11:00. The jail by now was swarming with television and newspaper reporters. After conferring with Jane, Lane held a press conference on the steps of the jail. He was roaring mad. Included among other things (police brutality against the other women in Jane's cell, for example) he said, "Miss Fonda's arrest was an act of terror, pure and simple. This is the Nixon-Agnew terror."

The law-enforcement response was weak. The federal officials said nothing. Cleveland Deputy Sheriff Albert Brockhurst made the following statement, in behalf of the local police:

> Miss Fonda deliberately and fraudulently brought drugs in from Canada, contrary to law, and there are three police witnesses to testify that she kicked the Cleveland policeman and punched the Federal officer. After she was arrested and jailed, she got hold of two Commie lawyers and they turned this thing into a circus. The lady was cursing and screaming and calling everyone "pigs," and the lawyers were holding press conferences and blaming the whole thing on President Nixon. Isn't that ridiculous?

As it turned out, it wasn't ridiculous at all.

Jane was arraigned the afternoon of her arrest, before U.S. Commissioner Clifford E. Bruce, who set bail at $5,000 and ordered her to appear for a hearing the following Monday. She faced three years in prison on the assault charge, and five years on the drug-smuggling charge. In covering the arraignment proceedings, the *Cleveland Press* came up with some interesting revelations: "The Press learned that Miss Fonda is on a Customs Department list of persons to watch as they enter and leave the country. So when she appeared at Customs, she was taken into a waiting room for a search. . . . The senior Customs officer here said orders had come from Washington, D.C. . . ."

After her federal arraignment, Jane was rearrested and taken to municipal court on the charge that she had kicked

Cleveland police officer Robert Pieper at the airport im-broglio. Again, the courtroom was jammed. Jane pleaded not guilty and Judge Edward F. Feighan set a trial date of January 6, 1971.

But that wasn't the last of her legal entanglements that day. She rushed off to catch a plane for a speaking engagement at Central Michigan University, and, at the airport, she was served with a summons. Officer Pieper had filed a civil suit against her, claiming $100,000 worth of damage to his leg during the ten-second airport scuffle.

Strangely enough, it was this simple act of greed that caused the entire case against Jane Fonda to collapse. It's a long way from a Cleveland cop to the White House, but this is how it happened:

My Freedom of Information data, plus later testimony in the Watergate hearings, proves that there *was* a so-called Ene-mies List, ordered in pique by President Nixon and compiled by his aide, Charles Colson (convicted and imprisoned there-after for Watergate improprieties). The list was not one of enemies of the nation, but enemies of the Nixon policies. Alphabetically, Jane Fonda was sixth on the list.

Orders went out to all government agencies to harass these enemies in any way they could. There were to be wire-taps, mail covers, constant income-tax audits (to their credit, then–Treasury Secretaries John Connally and George Shultz refused to go along with the audit orders). As in Jane's case, Customs and Immigration was a frequent point of contact with the enemies. With Jane, there even was a reinforcement to the mere fact of her name being on the list. Someone wanted to make *sure* the harassment would occur. The Royal Canadian Mounted Police were tipped from the United States that Jane Fonda would be flying from Toronto to Cleveland, and that she was a "notorious drug user who would be carrying contra-band drugs, which should be called to the attention of U.S. Customs in Cleveland."

As it was, the drug charges against Jane quickly fell apart. Laboratory analysis soon proved that "B," "L," and "D" indeed were harmless vitamin pills. But for U.S. Attorney Frederick Coleman, he still had the serious charge of assault on a federal officer against Jane for allegedly throwing a punch at customs agent Matuszak. This alone could possibly bring her three years in prison.

Whatever case the government had, if any, was sandbagged, however, by that silly little civil suit filed by Cleveland cop Pieper, who wanted $100,000 for damage to his leg caused by that allegedly fearsome kick by Jane when she struggled to go to the ladies' room at the airport.

Jane's Cleveland lawyer, Irwin Barnett, came up with the strategy. "In a civil suit," says Barnett, "you have the right of 'discovery,' which is not applicable in a criminal action. Before trial, you can ask all sorts of questions in depositions, which are taken under oath. By filing his civil suit, Pieper opened up a can of worms for him and for the government. I kept asking all sorts of questions about Nixon's 'enemies list,' and whether it had been used to entrap Jane at the airport."

Rather than admit that the list even *existed,* the government made a motion to dismiss all of its charges against Jane on May 28, 1971.

Pieper's case similarly was dismissed by Municipal Court Judge Feighan on June 23. In his discovery proceedings, lawyer Barnett had learned that Pieper had not even been on official duty the night of the airport imbroglio. He was moonlighting as a private guard and had no right to help Matuszak in restraining Jane from going to the bathroom. Using a legalism, Judge Feighan stated that he was dismissing the case because "Pieper's charge had been too broadly drawn."

And so, this early government assault on Jane ended embarrassingly with retreat on all fronts.

But for Jane, that was not the end of it. Two years later, she did an extraordinary thing. In October 1973—with Vice President Spiro Agnew having resigned, and with President Nixon being pushed toward resignation by the congressional

Watergate hearings—she filed a gargantuan suit in federal court against the entire government, naming Nixon, his White House staff, most of his cabinet officers, and others. She charged that the FBI and the CIA had violated her civil rights by harassing her through overt and physical surveillance, burglaries, and opening her mail. She also charged several banks with surrendering her financial records to the FBI without the court-ordered search warrants required by law. She asked for damages totaling $2.8 million.

The case dragged on for years, with some startling revelations. The CIA admitted to opening Jane's mail from overseas, including Christmas cards. The FBI admitted it had wiretapped her phone calls more than forty times, and had illegally seized her bank records without warrant or subpoena. The trial revealed the vast government files on Jane and her activities, compiled and exchanged by a half-dozen federal agencies. There was testimony about the fiasco of her arrest in Cleveland, and the confiscation and copying (without warrant) of her address book. Even J. Edgar Hoover's "Morris" letter to *Variety* came to light.

The case ebbed and flowed, mainly because of delays caused by the Justice Department seeking (and sometimes obtaining) court orders to prevent the release of FBI, CIA, and State Department material—on the grounds that public scrutiny of them in court would somehow damage national security.

Finally on May 8, 1979—nearly six years after Jane's suit was filed—a settlement was quietly reached between Jane's lawyers and the Justice Department. By agreement, the details of the settlement were kept to a minimum and released in a way that there would not be wide coverage in the media. As it was reported in the *Washington Star-News*: "The settlement includes an admission of Government wrongdoing in the FBI's surveillance of the political and private life of Miss Fonda from 1970 to 1975, and there's a promise that the Government will adhere to surveillance guidelines established after the case began. The settlement reached last month does not provide for any of the 2.8 million dollar monetary damage Fonda sought, however."

"Money," said Jane, "is not really what we were going after. We got an admission of guilt. We got a promise that they would try not to do such un-American things again.

"So it wasn't the money. We were trying to illustrate a principle."

The fabulous Fondas. Jane with her father and baby Peter. (THE BETTMANN ARCHIVE)

Above: A misleadingly happy family portrait. The new Mrs. Fonda cradles Amy, 1955. (UPI/BETT-MANN NEWSPHOTOS) *Below:* With Henry Fonda and Josh Logan while filming *Tall Story.* (KOBAL COLLECTION) *Opposite:* Relaxing in St. Tropez, 1964. (POPPERFOTO)

Above: Jane Fonda before her Hollywood career began...(KOBAL
COLLECTION) *Opposite:* ...and after. (KOBAL COLLECTION)

Marriage to Roger Vadim, 1965.
(UPI/BETTMANN NEWSPHOTOS)

With Vadim in Venice, 1966.
(UPI/BETTMANN NEWSPHOTOS)

On the set of *Cat Ballou*, 1966. (KOBAL COLLECTION)

Above: A still from *Barbarella*. (KOBAL COLLECTION) *Opposite:* In 1970 fashions were not always kind to thirty-three-year-old women. (CH. SIMONPIETRI/SYGMA)

Above: The activist. Jane in Hanoi, 1972. (SYGMA/JOHN HILLELSON) *Opposite top:* In handcuffs in 1970 following charges of assault and smuggling. (UPI/BETTMANN NEWSPHOTOS) *Opposite bottom:* Jane Fonda with Donald Sutherland in *Klute,* for which she won an Oscar. (KOBAL COLLECTION)

Above: Henry Fonda, close to death, receives his Oscar for best actor in *On Golden Pond* from a family group in 1982. He was too ill to attend the ceremony. (G. BRYSON/SYGMA) *Opposite top:* With Tom Hayden and son, Troy, in 1975. (JIM McHUGH/SYGMA) *Opposite bottom:* Jane Fonda and her workout program inspired millions of women to stay fit and beautiful. (POPPERFOTO)

Above: With husband Tom Hayden and Bishop Desmond Tutu in California, 1986. (UPI/BETTMANN NEWSPHOTOS) *Opposite:* A Vietnam veteran makes his views clear, 1988. (UPI/BETTMANN NEWSPHOTOS)

JANE UNCLE "HO" IS REAL PROUD OF YOU!!
BENIFIT NOW
THE POW's DO A
GET THEM FOR
+ MIA
THE VIET CONG
LOVE
JANE FONDA
(WE DON'T)
VETS
VETS
VETS
VETS

From *Old Gringo*, 1989, with Gregory Peck and Jimmy Smits.
(KOBAL COLLECTION)

21

One of the people closest to Jane during these troublous times was Steve Jaffe, who was her personal press agent from 1969 to 1973. A handsome young man who is now married to actress Susan Blakely and produces TV shows, Jaffe was then at the vortex of the tornadoes that swirled around Jane's forays into protest politics. Hired originally to publicize movie projects, he ended up spending most of his time fending off frequently hostile media people, writing press releases, and setting up press conferences—all in behalf of the *political* Jane.

For example, Jaffe bore the brunt of the press onslaught the morning she was arrested in Cleveland. He says, "I was in my office in Beverly Hills, preparing for a routine day, when my phone began ringing off the hook. Then someone brought in a copy of the *Los Angeles Herald Examiner.* Jane's arrest by the Feds was a big headline across the top of page one, printed in red, no less. The last time I had seen a huge red headline like that was when we were on the verge of war with Russia during the Cuban missile crisis.

"I sat there for three days, answering questions from media people from as far away as France, South Africa, and Japan. I couldn't reach either Jane or her lawyer, Mark Lane, so all I could say was that from my own many travels with Jane, I knew she carried vast quantities of vitamin pills in vials marked for breakfast, lunch, and dinner. That, at least, got out the explanation of the B, L, and D on her medicine bottles and began to raise doubts in some reporters' minds, but the story was dominated by the flood of information coming out of law-enforcement sources in Cleveland. The flap finally died down, but I was not surprised by the resolution of it, which was handled in the usual way by the press in those days. The *Herald Examiner,* which had trumpeted her arrest with the big red war-scare headline, ran a one-paragraph story on page forty-four when the charges against her were dismissed."

There were a great number of threats against Jane's life during this period, and though his job was public relations and not security, Jaffe found himself in the middle of many of these emergencies. Once, when Jane was scheduled to deliver a lecture in Bakersfield, California, Jaffe was tipped off by a friend in the media that someone had called in to a radio talk show and promised that Jane would be shot and killed on leaving the lecture hall. Says Jaffe, "I had to charter a plane to Bakersfield—Jane was en route by car—and I had to arrange for extra security with both the Bakersfield police and private guards. They actually picked up a guy backstage. He was armed with a handgun."

On another occasion, Jaffe was asked to speak for Jane on the Los Angeles radio talk show hosted by Michael Jackson (*not* the rock star of the same name). Jaffe says, "I never heard so much hate being spewed out over the airwaves, and finally Jackson had to stop it by asking his listeners to *write* their comments about Jane to the radio station, KABC-AM. Later,

I went to the station to pick up the mail. There was a huge bag of it, about six hundred letters. One letter really flipped me out. It was unsigned, but it was a very specific, chilling warning that their organization knew every move Jane made, that she could not escape them, and that she would be assassinated by sniper-rifle fire on a street in Los Angeles."

Jaffe studied this ominous letter for some time. "Then," he told me, "something about the letter rang a bell in my head. Jane previously had received occasional hate mail, which I had filed away in what I called 'my nut file.' I rushed to the nut file and, just as I had suspected, there was a letter in the same writing style and in the same handwriting as the death threat that had been mailed to KABC. Only *this* one was signed. There was the name and address of a self-ordained preacher in Arcadia, California."

Jaffe was distraught but hesitant about going to the FBI or the local police, considering their generally hostile attitudes toward Jane. "So I discussed it with her, and after thinking about it for a few minutes, she told me I had to take both letters to Ramsey Clark, the former U.S. attorney general, who would know what to do with them. So I went to see Clark. He looked at the letters and I could see he was genuinely alarmed. 'There are no two ways about this. You've *got* to go to the FBI.' "

Jaffe then phoned FBI headquarters in the Federal Building in West Los Angeles, and was told to come in with the letters. Jaffe said, "I was interviewed by two very nice young agents. They examined the death-threat letter and the preacher's letter, and they were stunned. They said they would keep the letters and send them to the FBI lab in Washington to confirm that the handwriting was the same and to analyze them for other identifying factors. They gave me photocopies of the letters. They told me the Bureau was seriously concerned about a mailed death threat to any U.S. citizen, and would keep us informed. We never heard from them again."

Asked if this lack of action was a further indication that the FBI loathed Jane Fonda to the point where it would do nothing to protect her individual rights, Jaffe was more than magnanimous. He said, "Maybe they *did* do something. We never heard from the nut preacher again. And as far as hating Jane was concerned, they were just doing their job. I think the principal hatred came from Richard Nixon and the White House—a bunch of guys who soon were to be brought down by Watergate. After all, it was *they* who put her on their enemies list, ordered surveillance, ordered the opening of her mail, the checking of her bank records, the whole bit. I later found out they even had a record of every nickel she had paid me as her press representative, so *I* was in a government file, too. I believe the Nixon bunch couldn't stand it that a mere movie actress had the audacity to keep attacking the President and his messed-up Vietnam policies every time she made a speech."

On the other hand, I got a contrary point of view from a man who was in the highest echelons of the FBI and who was an important source for me when I wrote an early complimentary magazine article on J. Edgar Hoover, and, later, in my investigative-reporter days. My own personal Deep Throat said, "The Director got some crazy ideas in his old age. He thought Martin Luther King was a Communist, and that Franklin D. Roosevelt had been a traitor to his class. I think he believed Jane Fonda was a traitor to her class, too, because Henry Fonda's daughter shouldn't do and say things like that." My source said it was Hoover who insisted on the label "Anarchist" in Jane's file, "even though we never had any evidence, beyond freedom of speech, which we could forward to the Justice Department for prosecution."

Steve Jaffe, of course, knew none of this when he went to work for Jane in 1969. After a stint as a movie publicist at Universal Pictures, he was hired by the public relations firm of Allan, Ingersoll and Weber to handle the publicity of such film-star clients as Ryan O'Neal and Gene Hackman. He didn't even know Jane Fonda, whose movie work was being publicized by another press agent in the firm, Emily Torchia.

Jaffe says: "It's funny how things happened in those crazy

days. Jane had just arrived from having lived in France and was fumbling around, trying to get her protest activities in focus. She hadn't even gone to Alcatraz yet. I was in the antiwar movement and knew Mark Lane, the antiwar attorney from Washington, D.C. One day Mark called me and said he had set up a meeting at a house in the San Fernando Valley between Jane Fonda and Donald Duncan, a decorated former Green Beret Vietnam vet who was crusading against the war—and would I come. I went. And that's where I met Jane for the first time.

"The meeting was to discuss support for the GI Coffee House movement, in which coffeehouses were being set up just outside military bases all over the country, as centers where soldiers, sailors, and airmen could vent their opposition to the war. At the end of the meeting," says Jaffe, "Mark Lane asked me if—since I already was working in Jane's public relations firm—I could handle Jane's political-protest publicity, along with her movie publicity. I said I'd ask my bosses. Not exactly knowing what they were getting into, and eager to please Jane, they said, 'Fine, if it's okay with Emily.' I went to Emily Torchia, who had been Jane's press representative for some time. She said, 'Go to it. Handle *everything* for Jane. I wouldn't have the vaguest idea what to do with political stuff, which I know absolutely nothing about.' And that's how Jane and I got to team up."

It was a very effective teaming for more than three years. Jaffe would frequently accompany Jane on her frenetic speaking tours around the country, but mostly he remained in his office and answered questions from the press. When Jaffe left Allan, Ingersoll and Weber to form his own PR firm, Jane went with him as a client—and so did Donald Sutherland, another antiwar activist. They used Jaffe's office for fund-raising and to organize Entertainment Industry for Peace and Justice, which attracted many hundreds of movie and TV people, including, strangely, Henry Fonda.

Jaffe's travels with Jane were fraught with problems. "For instance," says Jaffe, "she got heavily involved with the Winter Soldier Investigation in Detroit, where Vietnam vets testified about horrors they had seen—events similar to the My Lai massacre. It was not a meeting of wild-eyed hysterics. It included some people who later became very distinguished, such as one vet spokesman named John Kerry, who now is the junior U.S. senator from Massachusetts. The problem was that we didn't get much press coverage. Jane and I were on the phone every day to media people, but we didn't get very far. We suspected pressure by the White House to induce the media to all but ignore the event.

"Jane finally came up with an idea. *Life* magazine had been after her for some time to agree to be the subject of a cover-story profile. She called the *Life* editors and made an agreement with them: 'I'll sit still for the profile, if you include as much as possible about the Vietnam soldiers in Detroit.' The magazine lived up to its word. The ice was broken on the Winter Soldier Investigation, and others now came in and covered it. Jane didn't *want* the profile, which opened up old wounds, but she sacrificed herself. That's the way her mind worked."

Jane also sacrificed herself somewhat when she helped organize the so-called FTA Shows and participated in them as a performer. FTA stood for "fuck the Army," but was usually translated freely as "free the Army." The FTA Shows involved antiwar show-business entertainers and were designed to be antiwar musical satires of the typical Bob Hope shows that operated, with military approval, on military bases. The FTA Shows, on the other hand, operated without military approval, and took place *off* the military bases. Jane both sang and danced in them. Says co-performer Holly Near, "Jane didn't sing very well and she danced like a klutz, but her enthusiasm made up for it."

Steve Jaffe says, "We became acutely aware of the heavy hand of the Nixon administration trying to stop us when we flew to Japan to entertain the American troops stationed there. When we arrived at the airport, the Japanese Customs agents said they had been instructed not to let us into their country.

They seemed rattled because we were surrounded by what looked like hundreds of media people, with endless TV lights blinding us, but they herded us into the customs room, where we spent the whole night trying to sleep on hard benches."

In the morning, which happened to be December 7—Pearl Harbor Day—the Japanese officials said the troupe would be allowed to leave, but could only be taken to the Maranuchi Hotel, where they would have to stay, under a sort of house arrest, until their case could be decided. The hordes of press people—both Japanese and international—still swarmed around. "So we set up a press conference at the hotel," says Jaffe. "Jane and Donald Sutherland both made eloquent statements, to the effect that we were on a mission of peace on this disastrous Pearl Harbor Day. The hundreds of press people were visibly moved and the story ran in its entirety that afternoon. Later that day, the Japanese Parliament voted to let us in, against the wishes of the U.S. government, and we did our show."

Jaffe, who like many before him, was later to have an unpleasant severance from Jane, looks back on those days with warm nostalgic feelings. He says, "This is a lady who was unjustly accused of being un-American. To my way of thinking, what could be more *pro*-American than putting her money and her job at risk for her beliefs."

As close as he was to Jane, Jaffe had no idea of how much she had dug into her own pocket to finance her hundreds of speaking trips, and to help finance activities like the FTA Shows. He was astounded, therefore, when he was flying to New York with her one day, and she gave him a film script to read—after many months in which she had evinced no interest at all in going back to movie acting. Jaffe read the script and was not too impressed. He said, "Why are you interested in this?"

Jane said, simply, "Because I've run out of money, and this is the best script available to me now."

The script was *Klute,* which, sandwiched in among her continuing protest activities, was to bring her her first Oscar.

22

For Jane Fonda, lady of contradictions and mistress of the unexpected, *Klute* was one of the most contradictory and unexpected of the many turnarounds in her life. At the time she signed to do *Klute,* she hadn't made a film in two years (her last had been *They Shoot Horses, Don't They?*), and she had become so obsessively involved with her protest activities (the radical wit, Saul Alinsky, called her "a hitchhiker on the highway of causes") that many people in Hollywood thought she'd never go before the cameras again. No one knew, of course, that the money she had spent on her causes (a word she detests, preferring, as she told *Life* magazine, "involvement in specific historical events") had left her nearly broke. She not only had run through much of her own substantial movie income, but also the legacy left her by her mother.

Her personal life was a mess. Her bulimic affliction was in full flower, as evidenced by the B, L, and D vitamins seized by the U.S. Customs Service in Cleveland. Bulimics mistakenly try to compensate for vomited nutrients with huge quantities of vitamins and, according to her father, Jane was gulping seventeen to twenty-four vitamin capsules at each mealtime. Technically, she was still married to Roger Vadim, but rarely saw him. Her daughter, Vanessa, was left in Vadim's care, and, says Steve Jaffe, Jane made frenzied attempts to have Vanessa accompany her to meetings and interviews, whenever she came within range of Vadim's dwellings in the Los Angeles area.

What about men in her life during this hectic period? The protest comic Paul Krassner told me, "Every guy in the movement was in love with her," but he did not elaborate on whether, or with whom, she reciprocated these attentions. It does seem clear that she had some sort of romance with fellow actor-activist Donald Sutherland, her constant companion on the FTA soldier-entertainment/protest tours. Sutherland will not discuss Jane or the relationship, but Jane brought it up herself in an interview for *The New York Times Magazine* in 1971. She said: "I will never be a wife again. Donald and I are friends. We think the same things. When we're together, it's delightful. When we are apart, we remain friends. He is not indispensable to me. I am not indispensable to him. Our attraction involves learning and respect, and we don't intend our relationship to continue forever."

It did continue, however, through the filming of *Klute* (Sutherland was her co-star), and through two other far less memorable films, *F.T.A.* and *Steelyard Blues.* Then, as was customary with Jane, it was splitsville.

Considering all these conflicts roiling around in her head, it is totally amazing that Jane—after a two-year layoff from acting—was able to settle in and do such a professionally acute job in her filming of *Klute* in New York City. Producer-director Alan J. Pakula, who had met her previously, said: "I have to admit I was more than a little worried when Jane came to work on this picture. She had become so politicized; she had such a passion about so many things, I was genuinely concerned that her mind was not going to be on the film. But I soon discovered that she has this extraordinary capacity for concentration. She'd be engrossed in a conversation with Don Sutherland, or she'd be making endless phone calls—she'd *always* be on the phone hustling people for money for one cause or another—and I'd wonder if she knew her lines or even if she'd devoted any thought to the next scene. But I'd say, 'We're ready, Jane,' and she'd say, 'All right. Just give me three minutes.' Then she'd stop what she was doing, stand still, and concentrate. When she'd then walk into the scene, she was totally involved in the film, and nothing else existed for her. . . . When the scene was right, she'd just go back to Sutherland or to the phone calls—and that *other* world was total. It seemed to me to be an extraordinary gift—this capacity to compartmentalize her mind."

When Jane's press agent, Steve Jaffe, had first read the script of *Klute* on the plane to New York, it seemed to him to be just an unremarkable whodunit about a New York call girl, Bree Daniel, who gets involved with an out-of-town police detective who is investigating the mysterious disappearance of a friend from his community. The detective, Klute, falls in love with the prostitute, Bree, as the story proceeds to an unexpected, chilling climax. Jaffe says, "My first reaction to the script may have been negative because I didn't realize what Alan Pakula's genius could do with it; and I didn't realize how much Jane could contribute to the film, with the new-found realizations she had come up with in the protest movements." And she *did* contribute. Every time I came into her dressing room, she was tapping away on her typewriter—that is, when she wasn't on the phone. She was putting down her own ideas about the character of Bree, and how men in our society exploit women—even whores. She'd take her notes to Pakula and he accepted a lot of her suggestions. As the result of this, whole scenes were changed, and she had a lot to do with revising the ending of the film from happy-happy to bittersweet."

Indeed, this was the first time in her career that Jane incorporated her personal feelings into her work as an actress—a factor that was to become a hallmark of her own film productions later on. In an interview in *The New York Times,* she said:

> I attacked my role in *Klute* like I was doing a research project in college. I went out and watched prostitutes working on the street. Gradually, I got to know several high-priced call-girls, some of them highly intelligent, like my character, Bree, in the picture. I interviewed them, got to see the apartments where they lived. A lot of my ideas were incorporated into Bree's apartment on the set. . . . It all reinforced my previous feelings about how women, generally, are treated by our system—pitted against each other, how they are made to believe, because of the TV commercials they watch, that they only exist as a function of how they look, how they dress, of the kind of men they're with. I remembered my own exploitation as a sex object in the earlier films I had made, and I remembered what the anti-war vets told me about the lives of the vast number of prostitutes in Vietnam—many of them intelligent and trying desperately to get *out* of the system.

Alan Pakula, an exceptionally astute director (he was forty-three at the time), gave full reign to Jane's research activities and personal feelings about women. He even hired a twenty-three-year-old call girl as a technical adviser on the film. He remembers one of her conversations with Jane, almost verbatim: "The first thing you do, no matter what, is get your money. You get it before, because you're not going to get as much afterward. The second thing you do is make sure the man thinks he's different. You tell him he *is* different, and that he really turns you on. You get more money that way. I've lost all respect for men because they all believe they're different, every one that comes along."

Those attitudes were translated into a key Bree Daniel scene in a hotel room. The "different" theme even popped up in Bree's first coupling with Klute, even though she was beginning to experience genuine budding affection for him.

In all, there were a lot of creatively imaginative factors in this Jane Fonda performance. For one thing, even though the film was openly about sex for sale, there was no nudity in it. Partly at Jane's insistence, she was never seen disrobed—which was a far cry from some of her earlier films, in which she casually shed her clothing to expose a breast or a buttock for much less valid reasons.

Another unorthodox bit of creativity was the ending of the film—also partially instigated by Jane. In discussing the lady-or-the-tiger conclusion of the movie, director Pakula said: "The way it turned out, you don't know what's going to happen to the call girl. Originally it ended with her and Klute laughing and loving their way down the street. Jane said, 'There's no way I'll have anything to do with that'—and she was right. So the picture ends hopefully but enigmatically."

When production ended, Pakula was more and more convinced that he had a winner. Jane wasn't so sure. She collected her much-needed money and ran. She immediately ran back to the maelstrom of antiwar, antiracist, antichauvinist, antiestablishment politics.

Pakula was right. When the film was released later in 1971, the reviews were almost universally ecstatic. For example, *The New Yorker*'s frequently acerbic Pauline Kael gave full praise to the picture, and especially to Jane. Ms. Kael wrote:

As an actress, she has a special kind of smartness that takes the form of speed; she's always a little ahead of everybody, and this quicker beat—this quicker responsiveness—makes her more exciting to watch. This quality works to great advantage in her full-scale, definitive portrait of a call girl in *Klute.* It's a good, big role for her, and she disappears into Bree, the call girl, so totally that her performance is pure—unadorned by "acting." . . . Bree's knowledge that as a prostitute she has nowhere to go but down and her mixed-up efforts to escape make her one of the strongest feminine characters to reach the screen. . . . [Jane Fonda has] invited comparison with Bette Davis in her great days, but . . . her Bree transcends the comparison; there isn't another young dramatic actress in American films who can touch her.

Such fulsome praise immediately made Jane a favorite for that year's Best Actress Academy Award, but show-business speculations were completely overshadowed in the press by the increasing tempest of stories about her political imbroglios. This was the period when she was in the Far East with the FTA show, and the attempts of the Japanese government to sequester the troupe at the airport made front-page headlines in the United States. Also, there were a lot of accounts of internecine warfare in the touring company, with many barbs aimed at Jane and Sutherland. Country Joe McDonald quit the troupe, saying, "The movement has been duped by Fonda and Sutherland. I'm not going to be any part of their ego trip." FTA founder Fred Gardner also turned against what he called "Jane's clique," on the grounds that "they are not dedicated enough to the fight against imperialism . . . and are missionaries and fakers."

The public neither knew nor cared about these niceties of radical thought—which actually put Jane to the *right* of many more extreme activists. The nation by now had split into prowar and antiwar camps, and the perception on both sides—especially among the self-styled patriots—was that Jane was a leader of the radical Left. She wasn't, of course. As she herself admitted, "I was only two years into my awakening to the injustices of the world, and I was still learning."

All this, however, added a final dramatic note to the story of her involvement in the movie *Klute.* The drama built as the Academy Awards came closer and closer in early 1972. Would Jane—if she won the Oscar—take advantage of being on national and international television by delivering a ringing denunciation of the war and social injustice? If she did so, would the Academy cut off her microphones and hustle her off the stage, after quickly cutting to a commercial? At the very least, would she shun the gaudy feminine attire she loathed and wear peasantlike counterculture clothing as a *silent* protest?

As was frequently the case, Jane fooled everyone. She walked in, wearing a chic black pantsuit, more stylish than many of the décolleté gowns that surrounded her. She was on the arm of Donald Sutherland. They quietly took their seats, while the hall buzzed with the expectation that she soon might be making a fool of herself. She already had told an interviewer, "The Oscar is what the working class relates to when it thinks of people in the movies. It's important for those of us who speak out for social change to get that kind of acclaim." Adding to the suspense caused by this proletarian rhetoric, two months earlier, when she had won a Golden Globe from the Hollywood Foreign Press Association, she had sent a bemedaled Vietnam veteran who was against the war to accept her award for her.

As usual, on that 1972 Oscar night, the Best Actress Award came toward the end of the program. When it was announced, Jane was the winner. Some of the audience booed, some applauded. She walked calmly to the stage and stared out at the crowd for a few seconds, while everyone waited. Then she spoke: "Thank you. And thank those of you who applauded. There's a lot I could say tonight. But this isn't the time or the place. So I'll just say 'Thank you.'"

As the cameras panned over the audience, they caught

glimpses of studio moguls obviously sighing with relief over the fact that Jane had not loused up their event.

One camera focused momentarily on Henry Fonda, who had never won an Oscar. It was difficult to tell whether he was laughing or crying.

13

Hank Fonda's attitudes toward Jane had changed considerably. He bragged constantly about her Oscar and he defended her ferociously in press interviews when the subject of her antiwar activities came up. He said, "Her feelings about Vietnam are the same as mine and Senator William Fulbright and the former Secretary of Defense Clark Clifford, but she takes a different approach." He and his wife, Shirlee, continued to baby-sit Vanessa whenever Vadim was unable to watch her, and he welcomed Jane herself to his homes in Bel Air and New York on her stop-offs in her frenetic activist journeys. "Yet," said Jane, "Dad was still unable to give me the warmth of the father-daughter relationship I always had wanted so desperately. I guess it's in his makeup. He still kept telling everyone how great he thought I was, but he still couldn't bring himself to tell *me*."

In those days, Hank kept expecting two things—as he told my wife, Muriel.

The first was that, with her Oscar for *Klute,* Jane would "be swamped with movie offers that will get her career back on the success-track where it belongs."

The second was, "With a little more time and experience, Jane will moderate her political views, as we *all* do with time and experience."

Both of Hank's expectations were to be shattered within four months of the time Jane received her Oscar.

Despite the commercial success of *Klute,* the movie industry was chary of the adverse effect Jane's activism would have on the box office of any future film she might be offered. So there were no immediate offers. And then, the whole thing blew sky-high, career-wise, at least.

In July 1972, telling very few people—and especially *not* her father—she flew to North Vietnam.

In retrospect, it seems to be an extreme, foolhardy act, and, indeed, it turned out that way for Jane. But in the context of 1972, it was not that unusual an enterprise. Technically, we were not at war with North Vietnam, and there was no law forbidding anyone to go there. Steve Jaffe says, "The former attorney general, Ramsey Clark, had been to Hanoi, and so had one of my other clients, Dick Gregory. Highly respectable people like Walter Cronkite were talking about going to inform themselves about what was really happening. That's what Jane said when she told me she had used her old contacts in Paris to get a visa from the North Vietnamese government: 'I've been talking about this war, and I want to inform myself at first hand, so I know what I'm talking about. I'd go to South Vietnam, but they won't let me in.' "

You must understand our situation in Vietnam at that time. U.S. forces had been in the country for eleven years, and 50,000 had died in combat. An estimated 1.2 million Vietnamese had been killed, in both the North and the South. The war was grinding down. The Vietcong's Tet Offensive had come and gone, shattering our illusion that the war still could

be won quickly and easily. The My Lai massacre of 337 un-
armed civilians, including women and children—followed by
the conviction of Lt. William Calley—had shocked the sen-
sibilities of many Americans. The Paris Peace Talks had been
in session for years but seemed to be going nowhere. The
Nixon administration had bombed and then invaded Cam-
bodia. Nixon's so-called process of Vietnamization was under
way, leaving most of the ground fighting to the South Vietnamese Army. Our principal involvement in the war at that
time was massive bombing by the U.S. Air Force.

This is what was happening when Jane Fonda set out for
Hanoi from Los Angeles. There being no direct Pan-Am
flights, of course, she had to fly to a neutral Asian country and
transfer to a regional airline, probably in Hong Kong or
Singapore. She arrived on July 8, 1972. When she alighted in
Hanoi, she was greeted with enormous enthusiasm as "the
great progressive American actress." Unlike their carefree
friendly brothers in the South, the North Vietnamese (especially after eighteen years of Communist rule) were a rigid,
inflexible people—but highly skilled in the arts of propaganda.
They indoctrinated their more naïve Western visitors with
charm, flattery, and seemingly nondoctrinaire reasoning.

It now appears likely that Jane Fonda was among the
naïve ones. The foremost example was a seemingly innocuous
act—one of her silliest, and the one which was to cause her
the most anguish later on. A Czech journalist named Hav-
ranek was present, and this is how he described the event
when I met him in Paris in 1979: "The Government guides
took Miss Fonda on a tour of the environs of Hanoi and some
of us reporters were allowed to accompany her. We stopped
for lunch, where there were a lot of toasts in Russian wine and
Hungarian slivovitz. Then they took her to an anti-aircraft
battery. She had this fixed smile on her face as they moved her
toward one of the anti-aircraft guns. They said that this was
one of the heroic weapons that was protecting the city from
the barbaric American air bombardment. Someone put a soldier's steel helmet on her head and she joked that this was just

like a Hollywood publicity opportunity, except that her hair
didn't look right. One of the guides, a woman, then fixed her
hair so that it was arranged correctly around the edge of her
helmet. They asked her to climb up onto the gun mount,
which she did, sitting in the gunner's seat. Everybody laughed,
including Miss Fonda. I don't know whether or not she realized a camera crew was filming every moment of the incident."

The film was not seen in the West until later, when her
U.S. critics charged that this was an act of treason, in that she
was celebrating a weapon that may have shot down and killed
American air crews. Of more immediate concern back home
was what she was *saying* on Hanoi Radio. As "the great progressive American actress," she was invited to speak on Hanoi
Radio and she accepted—and thus became known to her enemies as Hanoi Jane, the latter-day equivalent of World War
II's Tokyo Rose.

At this point, the CIA, rather than the FBI, became the
principal chronicler of Jane's alleged misadventures; and the
CIA files obtained by me under the Freedom of Information
Act present detailed evidence of everything she said and did—
even down to photos of her visit to children in a Hanoi kinder-
garten class. The CIA monitored every speech she made,
every press conference at which she spoke. As she did back in
the United States, she repeated basically the same speech over
and over again, resulting in endless duplications in the 200-
odd pages of CIA files. Interestingly, some of the accounts
picked up by the CIA were from Havana Radio. Others apparently came from agents-in-place, both in North and South
Vietnam, or from electronic surveillance facilities.

Just what was it that Jane *did* say—according to these
undoubtedly accurate CIA files?

For one thing, she continued to attack Richard Nixon, as
she had done in the United States. An example:

Do you know that when Nixon says the war is wind-
ing down, he's lying. He has simply changed his

tactics. He thinks he can get away with it, because he believes we have no conscience, that if he reduces the American casualties but kills more Vietnamese, that we the American people won't care. I think he has a very low opinion of the American people. . . . He defiles our flag and all that it stands for in the eyes of the entire world.

She *did* speak directly to American military personnel in the field:

Tonight, when you're alone, ask yourselves "What are you doing?" Accept no ready answers fed to you by rote from basic training manuals, but as men, as human beings, can you justify what you are doing? Do you know why you are flying these missions, collecting extra pay on Sunday? . . . The people beneath your planes have done us no harm. They want to live in peace; they want to rebuild their country. They cannot understand what kind of people could fly over their heads and drop bombs down there. Do you know that the antipersonnel bombs that are thrown from some of your planes were outlawed by the Hague Convention of 1907? They cannot destroy bridges or factories. They cannot penetrate steel or cement. Their only target is unprotected human flesh. . . . The hospitals here are filled with babies and women and old people who will live for the rest of their lives in agony with these pellets imbedded in them. . . . Are these people so different from our own children, our mothers, or grandmothers? . . . I know that if you saw and if you knew the Vietnamese under peaceful conditions, you would hate the men who are sending you on bombing missions. I believe that in this age of remote-controlled pushbutton war, we must all try very, very hard to remain human beings.

A little naïve and one-sided, perhaps, considering the terrorist tactics of the Vietcong on the other side, but is it an incitement to. mutiny, as has been charged?

During her two weeks (that's all it was) in Hanoi and vicinity, Jane was taken on carefully guided tours of bomb-damaged hospitals, residential areas, factories, and dikes along the Red River delta. The dikes apparently upset her more than almost anything. She knew that it had taken the Vietnamese nearly four thousand years to perfect these earthen embankments that prevent the spring floods from inundating the country and destroying much of its agriculture. In a speech given on July 20, 1972, Jane said:

On July 12th, I went to Nam Sach. As you know, twelve foreign journalists were bombed there on July 11th, and yet the Pentagon denies that this bombing took place. They went to see the damage that has been done by extensive bombing to strategic points on the major dike systems of the Nam Dinh district. And I saw with my own eyes the following day, that the dike has been cut in two of the most vulnerable points, and on both sides of the dike there are many bomb craters. This is a district with a population of a hundred thousand rice growers and pig feeders. As far as the eye can see, there are rice fields. There obviously are no military targets, no gun emplacements, no trucks, no convoys. . . . The other day, Secretary of Defense Melvin Laird said that the bombing of the dikes may have taken place, but that it is accidental and it only happens if there is a military installation on top of the dike. Does he really think the Vietnamese would be foolish enough to put a military installation on top of an earth dike? And what about the new weapons the Pentagon boasts of, the smart bombs and the laser bombs that never miss their target? . . . If the floods come through the broken dikes and there is famine and disease epidemics and thousands of innocent people die, Nixon has a very clever scheme he is carrying out. He already is saying that if the floods come this year, it would be a natural disaster.

Less convincing was Jane's visit to a group of American prisoners-of-war, scrupulously selected by her North Vietnamese hosts. This was Jane at her most gullible. So conditioned was she to what she called the lies of the Nixon administration, that she seemed to believe everything the North Vietnamese told her, and nothing that emanated from the American side. For example, she accepted the North Vietnamese figure of only about three hundred POWs held by them (the actual number turned out to be far higher when they were released at the end of the war), and she believed that all U.S. POWs were being treated humanely. She heard nothing about the brutal treatment of POWs at the so-called Hanoi Hilton—well-documented later. If she had, she may not have believed it.

She discussed her visit with POWs in several of her Hanoi speeches. In one of them she said:

> Yesterday evening, July 19th, I had the opportunity of meeting seven U.S. pilots. Some of them were shot down as long ago as 1968 and some of them had been shot down very recently. They are all in good health. We had a very good talk, a very open and casual talk. We exchanged ideas freely. They asked me to bring back to the American people their sense of disgust of the war and their shame for what they have been asked to do. They told me that the pilots believe they are bombing military targets. They told me that the pilots are told they are bombing to free their buddies, but, of course, we all know that every bomb that falls on North Vietnam endangers the lives of American prisoners. . . . They all assured me that they are well cared for. They listen to the radio. They receive letters. They are in good health. . . .

We shared a sense of deep sadness that this war is a terrible crime and that Richard Nixon is doing nothing except escalating it while preaching peace, endangering their lives while saying he cares about the prisoners. . . . I'm sure that with the studying and the reading they've been doing here, these pilots will go home better citizens than when they left.

Alice-in-Wonderland time. But as usual, Jane got in some clever campaigning against Richard Nixon in that 1972 presidential race that was about to occur between Nixon and the Democratic peace candidate, George McGovern.

Jane flew out of Hanoi on July 22, after a final press conference in which she basically repeated everything she had said before—about the bombings, the POWs, the fact that Vietnam had been decreed one nation by the 1954 Geneva Conference but had been divided into two countries, North and South, by U.S. connivance. It's remarkable how much trouble she had stirred up for herself in a short fourteen-day period.

She returned to Los Angeles to face a firestorm. Steve Jaffe was frantic, having been trying to douse the fires ever since she had left. Mostly, he could only keep insisting that Jane was on a fact-finding mission and nothing more. But some of the problems he had to face were bizarre. A source in the government had leaked the fact that the passport on which Jane traveled to Hanoi was in the name of Jane Seymour Plemiannikov, causing one female reporter to speculate that Jane was using a Russian Communist pseudonym. Jaffe had to issue an explanation that Jane was still married to Roger Vadim and that was her *real* name. Another enterprising TV correspondent strongly hinted that Jane had had a personal audience with Ho Chi Minh. Jaffe had to point out—without making a fool of the man—that the North Vietnamese Communist leader had been dead for three years.

The firestorm escalated when it became known that Jane was back in the United States. That's when congressmen, state legislators, and newspapers—as previously noted—insisted that she be tried for treason and hanged, shot, or have her tongue cut out. The only area, in the government at least, where there was a noticeable lack of frenzy was, strangely enough, in Nixon's Justice Department. The CIA had sent its file of Jane's trip, and the Justice Department had to determine if she should be prosecuted for sedition—the answer was no.

I was doing a series of articles on organized crime at the time and I had many friends in the attorney general's office. One of them told me later: "We went through every word in the CIA record. Fonda was saying what she thought was true. She caused no desertions. As far as giving aid and comfort to the enemy was concerned, who was the enemy? We had never declared a state of war with North Vietnam. Remember that, legally, we were just involved in a pacification program in the South to help our friend, Mr. Thieu.

"We would have had a hell of a time trying to justify the twists of our foreign policy in a court of law."

24

Jane's movie career was in tatters. She threw herself unstintingly into the doomed George McGovern campaign for the presidency, but in many of her public appearances, she was reviled, spat upon, even doused with red paint. She was shunned by the moguls of the movie industry. Her recently acquired Oscar meant nothing to them now. She was entering the darkest period of her life. It was to be another five years before she would be seen again in a major Hollywood motion picture.

Still obsessed with her political activism, she had attempted three protest-type films. All of them bombed.

The first was a movie version of the FTA show, called simply *F.T.A.* It got few theater bookings and lasted no more than two or three days where it *was* shown. In Los Angeles, it was pulled overnight.

The second was an amateurish endeavor called *Steelyard Blues,* about an antiestablishment bunch of social misfits trying to fix an old plane and flying off into the wild blue yonder. Even with Jane and Donald Sutherland as co-stars, the film was a total disaster at the box office, like *F.T.A.,* opening and closing in a matter of days. This picture marked the end of Jane's relationship with Sutherland.

Her third bomb was *Tout va bien,* for which Jane went to France to work with her idol of the French New Wave days, director Jean-Luc Godard. Godard, in the meantime, had become even more radicalized than Jane. He was openly Marxist, even Maoist. *Tout va bien*—about the takeover of a sausage factory by its workers—was an undisguised political polemic, with very few entertainment values. It was too much, even for Jane, who expressed her frustration in public and called Godard "tyrannical to work with." This picture got practically no release in the United States.

So, with these failures (coupled with George McGovern's overwhelming defeat by Nixon in the November election), 1972, on the whole, was a very bad year for Jane. "Aside from the Oscar," she said, "the only good thing that happened to me in 1972 was Tom Hayden."

Hayden sort of sidled into Jane's life—at a time when she was without a permanent man for the first time in nearly fifteen years. She and Hayden had first met at a protest meeting in 1971, but nothing much had happened then. She learned more about him when, during the filming of *Steelyard Blues* in Berkeley, California, she had stayed in a left-wing commune, Red Family, and had enrolled Vanessa in the commune's day-care center, Blue Fairyland. Hayden recently had been expelled from the commune because of some amorous conflicts, the details of which fascinated Jane.

She was *already* fascinated by Hayden because of his history as one of the genuine New Left heroes in the United States. Every political activist knew all about his spectacular revolutionary résumé, and, indeed, he had become something of a living legend among the nation's radicals in the 1960s.

Born into a strict Roman Catholic family in Royal Oak, Michigan, the parish of the famous right-wing, anti–New Deal, anti-Semitic Father Charles E. Coughlan, the young Hayden became an early rebel against Coughlan's ideas and the physical beatings he claims the nuns administered to him in the parish schools. He continued his rebellion against structured authority at the University of Michigan, where he was the editor of the college newspaper and helped found the openly radical national organization, Students for a Democratic Society (SDS). After college, Hayden's résumé became almost a litany of all the protest movements in the United States. He got his head split open as an activist for civil rights in the South; he wrote the first draft of the famous Port Huron Statement, which became the bible for radical thought in this country; he organized a community project in the black sections of Newark, New Jersey, pressing for rent control, better playgrounds, etcetera, and then actually helping to cool down the disastrous Newark riots when they occurred in 1967; in 1968, he was one of the Chicago Seven, tried and convicted of fomenting the massive disorders outside the Democratic National Convention that nominated Hubert Humphrey, for which he received a five-year prison sentence that later was reversed by a Federal Court of Appeals.

Hayden was best-known, perhaps, for his anti–Vietnam war work. He probably was the number-one speaker on the college-campus circuit, packing in more and bigger crowds than even Jane Fonda. He had been to North Vietnam several times, beginning in 1965, and punctuated his talks with slides of photos he had taken while in Southeast Asia, emphasizing American injustices in that war-torn land. The Hayden slide shows frequently outdrew the combined audiences in all the movie theaters elsewhere in town. As far as the American Left was concerned, Hayden's greatest accomplishment came in 1967, when he went to Vietnam and brought out three U.S. POWs, released to him by the Vietcong.

To Jane, with only two years of experience as an activist, all this was the stuff of ancient heroic epics like *Beowulf* and *The Odyssey*. It didn't seem to concern her that Hayden was a fairly physically unattractive man with a large nose and an acne-scarred face, or that he was two years younger than she. Yet, her natural timidity took over and she made no effort to see Hayden again. In fact, it was Hayden who made the first move.

Hayden says, "It was before Jane took her own trip to Vietnam. She was making an antiwar speech at the Embassy Theater in Los Angeles, and I dropped by to hear her. I was impressed. She was nothing like the Barbarella I remembered in the movies. When the speech was over, I went backstage to see her. I offered to give her a few pointers about Vietnam from my own experience. Jane later told me that she knew then and there that we were destined to fall in love."

A few days later, Hayden went to see Jane in her Laurel Canyon house. Because of her diminished finances, it was a smallish rustic wood house on Canton Drive—a far cry from the villas and estates she had previously inhabited.

As Hayden reports it, he plunked himself down on the floor in front of the living-room fireplace and projected his slides on the opposite wall. The slides progressed through the little-known history of Vietnam, through the people's love of the land and their culture, to photos of Saigon with its refugees, brothels, and bars filled with teenage prostitutes. Hayden's slide talk then had a long section about how South Vietnamese women had to go through painful operations to change their eyes and their breasts, so that they'd look more like Americans. At that point, according to Hayden, he looked over at Jane and saw that she was shaking and crying. He says, "Suddenly I understood why she was weeping. I was talking about the image of superficial sexiness she once promoted and now was trying to shake. I looked at her in a new way. Maybe I could love someone like this. So Jane was right when she had predicted to herself that we were destined to fall in love. We did fall in love soon after."

That's how matches are made in the world of radical politics.

Hayden was by Jane's side when she returned from Hanoi to face her ordeal of vilification (but also praise from the Left, and from much of Europe and Asia, where U.S. involvement in the war was getting tiresome). He and Jane began to make joint appearances on the antiwar talk circuit. He toned down her rhetoric, making her speeches less hysterical and more believable.

He took great delight in Vanessa, then three, and still tells the story of how the child had walked in on them when he and Jane had first made love. He admits she made him feel wistful about never having been a father, "though I was tentative about committing myself to someone else's child." He had already done that with Christopher, the son of a former lover, and the relationship with the boy eventually had been shattered.

But as they lived together in Jane's house on Canton Drive, parenthood gradually came to be more and more on the minds of both Hayden *and* Jane. Hayden says: "It was on one lovely afternoon after Jane had come back from Vietnam, where she had seen women having children in the face of death. Apparently, that moved her to create life again. She came up behind me, naked, and whispered, 'I want to have a child with you.' With a tearful smile, I said yes."

And so, Jane was pregnant as she made the talk-circuit rounds with Hayden. (Says Hayden with becoming modesty, "We must have appeared like a remake of Beauty and the Beast.")

And Jane was still pregnant when a movie offer finally came in later that year. The picture was *A Doll's House,* a cinema version of the classic Ibsen play. It seemed, at first, to be a perfect blending for her art and her politics, since the producer-director was Joseph Losey, himself a political dissident who had had to flee the United States to escape blacklisting as a Leftist in the 1950s. Losey, based in England, had done excellent films during his exile, among them *The Go-*

181

Between and *The Servant.* He had found a British production company to finance his *A Doll's House,* arranged to film it in Ibsen's Norway in the town of Roeros, and eagerly went after Jane Fonda. He had long dreamed of her as the perfect Nora, Ibsen's flighty wife trapped in a marriage with an odious husband. The dream, unfortunately, became a nightmare—for both Losey and Jane.

She arrived in Norway with Hayden, but also with a screenwriter friend, Nancy Dowd, in tow. This immediately set up a conflict with Losey, who was perfectly happy with British writer David Mercer's revision of Ibsen's classic. Jane and Ms. Dowd wanted to make the character of Nora more noble, and more in keeping with that period's feminist thinking. Soon, the production was split into openly warring male and female camps, with co-star Delphine Seyrig siding with Jane; and the male stars, David Warner and Trevor Howard, backing Losey's point of view. The crew was mostly with Losey. Hayden, of course, supported Jane.

The hostility escalated. It was the first and only time that the usually disciplined Jane was accused of screaming and yelling on the set. She was quite bitter in an interview with *The Village Voice*:

> All the men had decided that what Ibsen had said about women didn't apply any more. I discovered that the male characters, who are somewhat shadowy, had been built up and the women were shaved down. . . . Delphine Seyrig and I were being called dykes, a gaggle of bitches. Every day there would be some nasty inscription on the camera about women's lib. . . . Most of the men were drunk all the time. They interpreted everything we did as simply wanting more lines to say. They painted it as a conspiracy of dykes ganging up on "us poor men." . . . Losey never had the guts to confront me, but he attacked women in lower positions. He tried to set us against

each other. Then he gave those interviews in which he attacked me, called me cruel, and said I was disrespectful to the crew. Actually, I got along fine with the crew. It's just that I didn't want to socialize with all of them because Tom was there and I wanted to be with him. . . . Loscy would have preferred an Elizabeth Taylor with tantrums and scenes. I was a perfectly normal, well-disciplined actress who had some ideas about the play that he couldn't handle. And this from a man who calls himself a progressive, a Marxist.

In rebuttal, Losey complained that Jane had absolutely no regard for his views as a highly respected maker of quality films. He referred to his work with her "as a bloody awful experience."

And so the Old Left and the New Left came together, and never the twain did meet.

The result was another in Jane's growing string of failures following *Klute.* The film never was picked up for movie release in the United States, and, instead, appeared on the ABC television network. It received dismal ratings. Jane's performance, however, got surprisingly good reviews.

While she was still in Norway, another series of dramas— both large and small—began to play themselves out in her personal life.

Back in Los Angeles, Steve Jaffe was still her press representative and was still parrying hostile thrusts from the press about her political activism—and now, in addition, about the rumored chauvinist-feminist struggle under way in her film in Scandinavia. Suddenly, in the middle of the night, Jaffe got a transatlantic phone call from Jane in Norway. "She told me," he says, "that she and Tom Hayden were going to get married soon after they got back, and would I handle the announcement discreetly so they wouldn't be swamped by the media. So I gave the item exclusively to Army Archerd in *Daily*

Variety, and that took the edge off it for the rest of the press."

Jaffe did not know that this was going to be the beginning of the end of his long association with Jane.

She and Hayden got back to the United States and made plans for their wedding on January 21, 1973. There was one small detail, however, that had to be taken care of first: she was still married to Roger Vadim. She met with Vadim, who was living with another woman, Catherine Schneider, at that time. Vadim says: "Jane said she was pregnant and wanted to get married again. I looked at her swelling belly and said, 'That's a good idea. Who's the father?' I already knew because I had seen Joe Losey who complimented me, bitterly, on my being in such good shape despite being married to Jane for six years, after which he told me about her being constantly with Hayden on the *A Doll's House* location. Jane confirmed that Hayden indeed was the man, and we agreed that she would get a quickie divorce in the Dominican Republic. We had no financial entanglements anymore. She had sold the farmhouse in France. . . . Vanessa would live with the future Mrs. Hayden, but I could see our daughter as often as I wanted."

So the divorce was obtained, and the Hayden-Fonda wedding took place on January 21, as scheduled. It was at Jane's house on Canton Drive in Laurel Canyon, and somewhere between fifty and a hundred people, mostly activists, were there to celebrate the nuptials. Henry Fonda and his wife, Shirlee, were there, and so were Peter and his new bride, Rebecca. The rites were performed by an activist Episcopal priest from San Francisco, Richard York, who, two days later, received a "Letter of Godly Admonition" and was suspended from further religious duties for marrying a divorced woman without permission from the bishop.

The proceedings were fairly typical of counterculture weddings of that day. According to Steve Jaffe, the guests sang Vietnamese songs and danced Irish jigs. Neighbors noticed a strong smell of pot wafting down from the house, which sat atop a little hillock. The official photographer was Steve Jaffe, who was skilled with the camera as the result of much photo-taking with Jane in four years of her tours. That was his undoing. He says: "I was fairly broke at the time, so I offered to take pictures, as my wedding gift to the couple. Jane and Tom said, 'Fine,' and I had a wonderful time, making maybe five hundred exposures of everything that went on. I stood next to Henry Fonda at the ceremony and I was moved by the great amount of emotion he showed. I left late and went home to bed in my West Los Angeles apartment.

"At about 6:00 A.M., my phone began to ring and jolted me out of bed. It was the media, calling me from all over the world, asking, 'Is it true that they got married last night?' The calls went on all day. They put a lot of pressure on me to give them details of the wedding. I held back. Then they demanded photos. They threatened that if I didn't come up with pictures they'd run one of Jane in Hanoi, wearing a coolie hat. I was desperate and didn't know what to do. I kept calling Jane at her house but she wouldn't take my calls. She and Tom were spending the whole day in bed and didn't want to be disturbed.

"Finally I took just one of my wedding photos to a guy I knew who owned a photo lab. I knew I could trust him. It was Sunday and he came in, just to help me. I carefully cropped prints of that single photo and distributed them to all those people who were threatening to use the derogatory photos of Jane in Vietnam. The processing costs came out of my own pocket.

"The next thing I knew, Jane and Tom were on the phone, haranguing me about exploiting them and selling the photos for money. I said that that was ridiculous, that I only had done it to protect Jane, and I hadn't made a nickel out of it. I told them how desperately I had tried to get them on the phone to find out what I should do. It all ended up on a pretty sour note.

"For months, Jane didn't speak to me. Then, she and Tom met me for dinner in a little Vietnamese restaurant. They said they were sorry for accusing me of personal gain. And at that time, we pretty much parted company."

Like so many others before him who had been discarded by Jane, beginning with Josh Logan, Jaffe said, wistfully, "I kind of miss her."

25

Jane Fonda is not a cruel woman. She has a history of dumping people when they no longer were useful to her, and occasionally she did it with an appalling lack of adroitness, but sometimes—as in 1973—her own survival was at stake.

For her, 1973 was even worse than 1972. She had no work at all during the entire year; she was blacklisted by various studios and theater owners. She had to husband the money she had left over from *Klute* and *A Doll's House.* Tom Hayden's only income was from magazine articles, a few book royalties, and lecture fees. For Jane, a child of wealth and formerly a woman of independent means, it took a great deal of courage to adjust uncomplainingly to a totally different life-style.

Shortly after their marriage, she and Hayden had to move

out of her Laurel Canyon house and into the upper floor of a funky two-family Cape Cod in Venice, then a run-down, working-class, ex-hippie area of Santa Monica. They slept on a mattress on the bare floor and ate at a rickety kitchen table, painted yellow. The water-stained ceiling was similarly painted over by Jane in wild psychedelic colors. Henry Fonda loyally proclaimed that this manner of living was Jane's own choice, that "she has other commitments now and she must be able to identify with all the powerless people whose causes she champions." Also loyal, director Sydney Pollack said, "She could work if she wanted to, but she can't find a role with social relevance and artistic worth." He added that people were sending her scripts and she was reading them. He did not mention the strident boycott (against her ever working in films again) by Young Americans for Freedom and the Veterans of Foreign Wars.

Jane admitted that she had sold off all the jewelry willed her by her mother, but added, "I never liked to wear jewelry anyway."

Whether this period of poverty was self-enforced or induced by outside circumstances, it unquestionably exhibits a lot of steel and mettle in Jane Fonda's makeup.

But she showed even more guts in another vital decision she made in 1973. It all occurred in the last months of her pregnancy with Hayden's child (Troy, a son, was born on July 7, 1973). Jane seems to do a lot of serious thinking when she's pregnant. Just as she had decided to become a political activist while she was carrying Vanessa, now she was determined once and for all to rid herself of the monkey she had been carrying on her back for twenty-three years—her bulimia addiction.

Anyone who has been through the agony of withdrawal from alcohol or drug dependency knows what this would entail for Jane. She would have to endure cold sweats, insatiable cravings, feelings of hopelessness and despair. As previously noted, she took the crucial step because it was a matter of living or dying, because she realized her bulimia had caused her to do irrational things, and mostly because she felt the disease had made her a not-too-satisfactory mother to Vanessa, which she did not want to repeat with the as-yet-to-be-born Troy. With Vanessa, too easily shipped off to Vadim or to Hank and Shirlee Fonda, she had a lot of making up to do.

Jane knew she would die if she didn't rid herself, once and for all, of the bingeing and vomiting habit. The first doctor she went to told her that. He also told her that while an alcoholic, if successfully recovering from his addiction, can put alcohol out of his life, a bulimic can't divorce herself from food; she must eat. So the temptations to "slip" face her every day.

So far as is known, Jane did not slip. She went to a psychiatrist and later to support groups with other recovering bulimics. The techniques for such support groups are much the same as those for Alcoholics Anonymous—sharing the agonies of withdrawal, bolstering one another, taking recovery "one day at a time." As with alcoholics, there are side effects. For example, from being a desultory cigarette smoker, Jane now became a chain-smoker. But the struggle went on.

It is that struggle, along with other examples of her personal courage, that—in my view—has endeared Jane to millions of women. Bulimia is one of the most embarrassing of addictions, and its victims, in general, tend to have a great fear of embarrassment. Many of my acquaintances say, "Good Lord, what an awful and vulgar thing! How embarrassed she must have felt. Yet, Jane Fonda had the guts to conquer this terrible disease both physically and emotionally. And she bounced back more regally and more gracefully than ever. What incredible courage! Women can identify with that."

As previously noted, the bounce back from bulimia took more than a year for Jane. Finally, as she exulted to writer Leo Janos, she had that illuminating day in 1974, when she sat down to a normal meal with absolutely no urges to produce a high by vomiting. That's when she said to herself, "Thank God! . . . How much quality has been restored to my life! I'll never let it happen again."

So a new Jane emerged from this cocoon of recovery. She

became an exemplary mother to infant Troy and, belatedly, to Vanessa. Her marriage to Hayden became a true partnership, such as she never had had with Vadim or any of the other men in her life. They jointly founded the Indochina Peace Campaign (or IPC) and went around raising money to publicize events in Vietnam. U.S. interest in the war had waned with the withdrawal of most American troops in 1973, when a cease-fire and a peace agreement had been signed—but bitter hostilities continued between North and South Vietnam.

There was a much less shrill Jane on the lecture circuit at this time. She says, "One of the most important things Tom taught me—and which I put in practice to this day—is: 'Put aside what *should* be done in favor of what *could* be done.' "

That dictum—a far cry from Jane's thinking in her bulimic days—was to become the key factor in everything Jane *and* Hayden did in following years.

But the later transition to the mainstream of American politics had not yet been totally accomplished. When the American POWs were released in Vietnam and some came home with horror stories about how they had been tortured and brutalized by their captors, Jane called them "hypocrites and liars," thus causing another eruption of violent criticism against her. One congressman, Robert Steele of Connecticut, got up on the floor of the House of Representatives and said: "I would like to nominate Academy Award–winning actress Jane Fonda for a new award: the rottenest, most miserable performance by any one individual American in the history of our country."

But the anti-Jane fervor was not as great as it had been when she was in Vietnam, broadcasting on Hanoi Radio. Perhaps the American people were getting fatigued by the long-running conflict over the war. And perhaps, too, they were being distracted by the developing Watergate scandal, involving a president whom Jane had long been calling a criminal. Some people were saying, "Maybe she was right."

In April 1974, despite all the furor she had kicked up, Jane returned to North Vietnam. She was accompanied by

Tom, her nine-month-old son, Troy, and a distinguished Hollywood cinematographer, Haskell Wexler. They did a documentary film, *Introduction to the Enemy,* which was about the struggle of the North Vietnamese to rebuild their country after two decades of conflict. Leaving little Troy in the care of a doctor friend in Hanoi, Jane toured the country for twenty-four days with Hayden and Wexler, even venturing into Quang Tri Province in South Vietnam, which had been captured by the North.

It was a strangely moving film—despite its obvious political slant—with beautiful pastoral scenes and close-ups of hundreds of attractive and innocent children. Wexler showed bombed-out areas, but there was no grimness or horror. Jane looked radiant throughout the picture, as she narrated and conducted interviews.

In other times, the documentary might have been thought of as a possible masterpiece, but in 1974, it received practically no release in the United States. It thus became another in the string of films made by Jane since 1972 that most Americans have *not* seen.

The most interesting thing about *Introduction to the Enemy* was that it was labeled an "IPC Production." It was mostly made with money collected by the Haydens' Indochina Peace Campaign, and it was the first of many IPC films to come.

As the bulimia-free Jane soon was to expand her horizons into making her own films with her own film company, the initials IPC were changed to mean International Pictures Corporation.

From *this* IPC came such truly distinguished, award-winning Jane Fonda films as *Coming Home, The China Syndrome,* and *On Golden Pond.*

26

But if, like Robert Redford, you think of Jane Fonda's career as a phoenix constantly rising from the ashes, in late 1974 and early 1975, she was still up to her tailfeathers in ashes.

Despite Sydney Pollack's assertion that she could have worked in films anytime she wanted to, the only work she could get was little more than a bit part in the American-Soviet film *The Blue Bird,* shot mostly in Leningrad—quite a comedown for a recent Oscar-winner. Jane was onscreen for less than ten minutes. She says, "I could have phoned in the role from Santa Monica." Instead, she journeyed to Russia with Hayden, young Troy, and her mother-in-law.

It would be an understatement to say that *The Bluebird* was one of the great film fiascos of all time. Based on the fairy tale play by Maurice Maeterlinck, the film turned out to be a mish-mash of attempted American fantasy and stolid Soviet reliance on ballet techniques and flashy sets. The fine American director, George Cukor, was in charge, but the crew was mostly Russian—with inevitable foul-ups and breakdowns in production. The star was Elizabeth Taylor, and the picture nearly ruined her career for good. Many of the lines in the script were ridiculous ("I am the light that makes men see the radiance in reality"), and neither Jane, nor Ava Gardner, nor Cicely Tyson could do anything with them—let alone the hapless Taylor.

During her brief stay in the Soviet Union for her limited role, Jane attracted great curiosity and was well received by the Russians. They knew, of course, about her North Vietnam trip, and *They Shoot Horses, Don't They?* had been a big hit in Moscow and Leningrad, but *Pravda* made it very clear that "While Miss Fonda is a fine actress, she certainly cannot be considered to be a Communist or even a Socialist." That line, picked up by Reuters and reported in the United States, did not play well with Jane's enemies.

She was home many months before the picture was released (it took more than a year to complete). It was almost universally clobbered by the film critics, who blasted Jane, in her role of Night (a sort of Black Queen), as well as everyone else. Like all the other films in her ashes period, *The Bluebird* did not linger in the movie theaters for very long, if at all. The entire expensive experience came close to bankrupting Twentieth Century–Fox.

It was a financial boon, however, for Jane and Tom Hayden. With Jane having been well-paid for her brief role, they were able to move out of their rundown Venice home and into a considerably better, but still unpretentious, house on Alta Avenue, in a more upscale section of Santa Monica—where they continued to live for nearly fifteen years.

Their political fortunes, too, began to change for the better in 1975. The Watergate scandal now had brought down President Nixon, who was forced to resign, and many of the people who had put Jane on their "enemies list" (John Mitchell, Charles Colson, John Ehrlichman, H. R. Haldeman) were either in jail or on their way there. FBI surveillance of Jane was noticeably lifted.

When the North Vietnamese Army and the Vietcong overran Saigon in April 1975, forcing the surrender of the South Vietnamese and the hasty evacuation of the remaining Americans, the U.S. public overwhelmingly wanted to put the entire sad Indochinese conflict behind them. Jane and Hayden went along with the tide and formed a totally new organization, Campaign for Economic Democracy.

The CED, as it was called, was in sync with Hayden's realigned thinking, already imparted to Jane: "Put aside what *should* be done in favor of what *could* be done." Among CED's initial modest goals was legislation to promote solar energy and rent control, and to curb the political power of large corporations and monopolies. This was pretty much in the mainstream of thought in the liberal wing of the Democratic Party. In fact, the CED, unlike its predecessor, IPC, now was espousing many of the ideas of Hubert Humphrey, against whom Hayden had campaigned so furiously at the Democratic Convention in 1968.

It was quite a retreat from the extreme radicalism of the past, yet Hayden caused something of a shock wave when he announced, in 1975, that he was going to be a candidate the following year for the California U.S. Senate seat then held by popular Democrat John Tunney. Hayden filed to run against Tunney in the California Democratic primary.

Accused of enormous gall or chutzpah, he was given little chance to win, and Tunney did not take him very seriously as an opponent. But Hayden—with Jane at his side—put on an effective campaign. She was especially adroit, employing all the techniques she had learned as an antiwar crusader. She manned telephones twelve hours a day, she hit up her friends in the movie industry for campaign contributions, she made crisp speeches on the stump as frequently as Hayden did. "If anything," said the *Los Angeles Times*'s Robert Scheer, "she brought much more attention to Hayden's campaign than he would have received otherwise."

Hayden lost, but he did far better than anyone expected—save, possibly, for Jane. He got nearly 40 percent of the vote, much of it coming from students and ex-students (who remembered the antiwar speeches by both Tom and Jane) and from the Hispanic community, which until then had rarely been motivated to take much interest in statewide California elections. The Hispanics remembered Jane gratefully for her picketing of supermarkets in behalf of the United Farm Workers of Cesar Chavez. It did not hurt, either, that Jane had induced such fellow entertainment stars as Jon Voight and Linda Ronstadt to campaign openly and vigorously for Hayden.

In the general election, Tunney lost to Republican political unknown S. I. Hayakawa, who had been president of San Francisco State College.

Jane returned from Hayden's senatorial primary campaign to find that some interesting things had happened to her while she was engrossed in the exigencies of being on the hustings. For one thing, her mail miraculously had turned gentler and kinder, as opposed to the torrent of hate she previously had received. The public seemed to want to forget the bitterness engendered by the Vietnam war; they wanted to see her working again in films.

For another thing, there were several scripts for her to read, sent to her agent by various studios. They, too, apparently had gotten the message that the moviegoing public wanted Jane back on the screen. Jane was exhilarated, but said in an interview with my wife, Muriel: "I wasn't sure I wanted to go back to work after all the disappointments from *Tout va bien* to *The Blue Bird*, but I figured out that if Tom and I wanted to carry out our CED objectives, and if he wanted to continue with a political career, we would need money, *lots* of money. And the only way I knew how to make lots of money was by making films."

195

So she sat down and read all the scripts that had been sent to her. She finally focused more and more on a screenplay from Columbia Pictures. She said: "I liked it because it could be a hilarious comedy if it was done right, and I wanted to show people that I could still look pretty and still have a sense of humor. Also, I had promised myself that I would never again do anything without some sort of meaningful message in it, even though the message is disguised under a lot of entertainment values. This script had such a message. It was about a prime factor in society today: how people are carried away by materialism and consumerism and keeping up with the Joneses, so that they don't know how to deal with sudden poverty when it's all taken away. The way the people in the script handled it was itself a blow to our materialistic way of life."

And so Jane signed to do the film. It was called *Fun with Dick and Jane.* The phoenix indeed had finally risen from the ashes of the previous four years.

27

Jane had chosen well. *Fun with Dick and Jane* turned out to be an enormous comeback picture for her. People had forgotten her earlier comedies like *Cat Ballou,* and her reawakened sardonic wit delighted even the crew on the set (electricians, carpenters, et cetera, are notoriously blasé about what actors are doing before the camera).

The picture was a biting satire, with many hilarious moments. Jane (her character's name, too) is married to Dick (played by George Segal). They are a typical yuppie couple living in suburban luxury with all its cliché status symbols, up to and including membership in the Book-of-the-Month Club. Then Dick, an aerospace executive, loses his job because of troubles facing the company, brought on by political/financial hanky-panky by his boss (Ed McMahon). Suddenly stripped of income and having paid for everything on credit, Dick and

Jane have everything taken away from them, including the just-planted rolls of sod on their front lawn.

Dick tries to get a job, but can't. Jane does get jobs, but, having no experience except as a housewife, fails miserably (taking a tremendous pratfall, for example, when she is trying to be a model). They go on welfare. Finally they become robbers, as an ultimate expression of the free-enterprise system. They commit armed stick-ups of stores, supermarkets, even the telephone-company office. They end up by stealing the slush fund of Dick's former boss.

This may not sound too funny now, but it *was*—in the days when Ronald Reagan and others were trumpeting the virtues of untrammeled capitalism and upward mobility. For Jane Fonda—working before the camera in a Hollywood production for the first time in five years, and doing comedy again for the first time in more than a decade—the entire experience was, as she put it in the idiom of the time, "a gas."

She got along beautifully with director Ted Kotcheff, who initially worried that "she might have lost her comedic touch after all the heavy stuff she'd been doing," but soon said "she's even funnier than I remember her in *Cat Ballou.*" There was no rushing to the phone between scenes in furtherance of her causes, as in her more recent work, like *Klute.* There was not even a smidgeon of star/director conflict of the Fonda/Joe Losey variety. She only asked that there be no bared cleavage or other feminine-exploitive shots—and Kotcheff complied.

Co-star George Segal, too, had a "gas," working with Jane in this picture. He always had admired her as an actress, even before his own emergence as a star in *Who's Afraid of Virginia Woolf?,* and unlike others who had been considered for the part of Dick, he was not afraid of working with a woman who had stirred up so much political controversy. Segal said pretty much the same thing that others had said about her remarkable powers of concentration: "Jane was friendly and delightful, but she never did any kidding around on the set, like someone like Shirley MacLaine would. Also, she could be very somber, lost in her own thoughts, I guess. But when Ted Kotcheff called us out for a scene, there was an instant transformation. She'd be funny and outgoing, knowing her lines without making a single fluff, and doing and saying ridiculous things with the verve of a Lucille Ball. When the scene was over, she might go back to being somber and introspective again."

Perhaps the biggest surprise was the reaction of the crew, many of whom shared the hard-hat mentality that had so castigated Jane for her political activities. On the first day of shooting, many of the technicians came over and said, "Welcome back, Jane." Later, they openly applauded at some of her more adroit comedic moves, such as her spectacular falling down in the fashion-show scene.

Most surprising to me was a remark by one member of that crew, a man I know from other film productions on which I've worked. This man asked not to be identified because he, too, had been an antiwar activist, probably on a *more* activist scale than Jane. He told me: "When I went up to see Jane and welcomed her back into the industry, like the other guys did, a lot of wild thoughts went through my head: Why the fuck did the FBI pick on this lady? All she did was talk. They went after her like she was in the Weather Underground or the Red Brigades, or something. They fed out stuff like she was going to blow up a government building or something. If you gave her a bunch of ammonium nitrate and fuel oil, she wouldn't have the vaguest fuckin' idea how to make a bomb."

When *Fun with Dick and Jane* was released several months later, it was the first non-bomb Jane had made in several years. Columbia Pictures headed all its advertising with the slogan: "America Loves Jane Fonda Again." The critics certainly loved her. Vincent Canby, of *The New York Times,* for example, wrote: "I never have trouble remembering that Miss Fonda is a fine dramatic actress, but I'm surprised all over again every time I see her do comedy with the mixture of comic intelligence and abandon she shows here."

The public, wearied by Watergate and the Vietnam war,

loved her, too. As slight as *Fun with Dick and Jane* was, the film was a smash at the box office, outdoing Jane's weightier efforts, such as *Klute* and *They Shoot Horses, Don't They?*

The half-million dollars or so that she earned went mostly into the coffers of the Campaign for Economic Democracy, and into a ranch she and Hayden bought in the hills above Santa Barbara, California, to be used as a summer camp for underprivileged children. The ranch/camp, ironically, is not far from the Santa Barbara ranch of Ronald and Nancy Reagan.

But even before the money from *Fun with Dick and Jane* was put to work, there were so many movie offers for the once-shunned Jane, that she began instant preparations for a *much* weightier effort—a film called *Julia.*

A Twentieth Century–Fox project, *Julia* was taken by screenwriter Alvin Sargent from an autobiographical chapter in Lillian Hellman's book *Pentimento.* The rights had been acquired by producer Richard Roth. There still are some doubts about whether some of the facts in Hellman's account are true, but *Julia* is an arresting story. It's about Hellman and her long-lasting friendship with Julia, the daughter of an aristocratic European family, who meet again in pre–World War II Germany when Julia is with the anti-Nazi resistance. In the climactic sequences of the picture, Lillian smuggles $50,000 in funds for the resistance, which she carries across Germany, hidden in a large wool hat she is wearing. There are suggestions of lesbianism in the story, with one woman, Lillian, telling another woman, Julia, "I love you," for the first time in an American film.

After Jane was chosen to play Lillian, another politically sensitive actress, Vanessa Redgrave, was signed to play Julia. Redgrave already had made her Trotskyite views known and later ran for a seat in Britain's Parliament as the Workers Revolutionary Party candidate, garnering only a handful of votes. Since Miss Hellman also had been well-known for her leftist activities, the Hellman-Redgrave-Fonda combination immediately was dubbed by Jane's enemies as "Reds in Bed."

No matter. The political thrust of *Julia* was a popular one—anti-Naziism—and the public could not have cared less about the "Reds in Bed" barbs when the film was announced. They were only interested in seeing Jane again in a heavy dramatic role.

Jane herself seemed to take delight in exercising her feminist tendencies as a protest against the then-prevalent male-buddy film (Redford and Newman in *Butch Cassidy and the Sundance Kid,* for example). In a press release issued by the studio, Jane said: "Oh, to be able to play in scenes with another woman! People will see a movie about women who think and who care about each other. In every other movie I've ever done and in most movies I see where there's a woman, she's either falling in or out of love or worried that she's going to lose a man. She's always defined in a relationship to a man."

And so the new Jane kept emerging, another step back into the mainstream. She was still radical, by the standards of conservative America, but equality for women was one cause that was growing popular across the board. According to the Tom Hayden formula now instilled in her, it was something that *could* be accomplished.

In preparing for *Julia,* Jane was the old thorough Jane. She went to visit Lillian Hellman on Martha's Vineyard, sat out a hurricane with her, and learned all the Hellman mannerisms, such as sitting with legs akimbo and saying "Oy, vey" and crossing herself at the same time. Jane tactfully did not discuss *The Chase,* her movie disaster of a decade before, the script of which was credited to Lillian Hellman.

The filming of *Julia* was in England and France. Jane went without Tom and Troy, the first time she had been away from them for so long a period—three and a half months. She was still comparatively remote, but loneliness made her friendlier than usual with others in the cast—mainly Jason Robards (with whom she had done *Any Wednesday*) and a promising newcomer whose work she admired, Meryl Streep. She liked Vanessa Redgrave, whom she described as "the best performer I've ever worked with," but, significantly, made it clear that their political views did not jibe. "I'm a progressive Democrat," said Jane. "Vanessa's a Trotskyite and not too friendly to the State of Israel. So we avoid talking politics."

Julia was released in 1977, not long after *Fun with Dick and Jane,* which outdistanced it at the box office. The comedy was much more in keeping with the mood of the times; *Julia* was about a remote though popular war and the public had seen too much of war. Yet the box-office receipts for *Julia* were respectable and its reviews were good to excellent. Director Fred Zinnemann was singled out for praise, and almost without exception, Jane and Vanessa received top kudos.

As Jack Kroll wrote in *Newsweek*: "Fonda and Redgrave create a heart-breaking interplay of emotions, without a taint of sentimentality."

And with a shrewd hint of things to come for Jane and others, Kroll pointed out what he thought was the real significance of the film, which, remember, was only a little more than a decade ago: "*Julia* supposedly signals a new deal for women in films, in which they'll no longer be satellites to men but suns and stars in their own right."

This particular review gratified Jane immensely. This, indeed, was something that *could* be done—and she was doing it. But her next project—the third in her amazing one-year comeback—was her most startling accomplishment in this can-do category. Jane, the vehement anti–Vietnam war activist, was about to make the movie industry's first stateside film about the war itself, with a sympathetic view of the veterans who fought in the conflict and were killed or crippled by it.

The industry—excessively timid about even *mentioning* the Vietnam war—thought she was crazy.

28

The picture was *Coming Home.*
It was the first major production in which Jane had nearly total input—from the inception of the idea to its completion. It was the beginning of her career as an incredibly successful businesswoman. She did it through IPC Films, the company that had been born as the Indochina Peace Campaign, and which theretofore had only produced the barely seen documentary *Introduction to the Enemy,* about the North Vietnamese. She had taken on a partner in IPC, a young man named Bruce Gilbert, whom she had met while he was working in the Blue Fairyland day care center attended by her daughter, Vanessa.

Reaching back into the past again, Jane called in Nancy Dowd, the writer who had accompanied her to Norway for *A Doll's House,* and who was the cause of much of the controversy between Jane and director Joseph Losey over script differences. Even before Jane started on *Julia,* she put Ms. Dowd to work, developing a script for what later became the basic framework for *Coming Home,* and which earned the young woman "story credit" when the film was released.

Bruce Gilbert, too, contributed to the development, and the property soon was attractive enough to bring in producer Jerome Hellman, who hired screenwriters Waldo Salt and Robert C. Jones to do the final shooting script. Eventually, Hal Ashby was signed to be the director. Ashby had done *Shampoo,* and Salt had written *Midnight Cowboy,* two formidable box-office hits, but United Artists, which was to distribute the film, was nervous. The picture was basically about a paraplegic veteran, but the Pentagon and the Veterans Administration— still hating Jane Fonda vehemently—refused any cooperation whatsoever in the filming and would not allow use of any government hospital facility.

Casting was a problem, too. Jane, of course, was set as the female lead, Sally Hyde, but the role of Luke Martin, the embittered paraplegic vet, was turned down, in succession, by Al Pacino, Jack Nicholson, and Sylvester Stallone. Finally, Jane convinced the studio to take a chance with Jon Voight, an antiwar activist like Jane, who had fallen on evil days at the box office since his Oscar-nomination triumph in *Midnight Cowboy* in 1969. Voight originally was under consideration for the other important role, Sally Hyde's Army officer husband, Bob Hyde, but he begged for the Luke Martin part. So Bruce Dern ended up playing the husband.

The story was a basically simple one, heartrending but uplifting at the same time—and so typical of the post-Vietnam stresses of the day: Sally Hyde (Jane) begins as a typical military wife, unliberated, trying only to please her husband, who firmly believes that a woman's place is in the home. Her main objective is to make up and dress better than the other women on the base—"to look as much as possible like Jacqueline Kennedy."

Then, Sally's husband is sent to Vietnam. On her own for the first time, Sally goes to work as a volunteer in a hospital ward for disabled veterans, many of them paraplegics. One of the paraplegics is Luke Martin, extremely bitter and surly because he has lost the use of his legs in combat and is wheelchair-bound. He knows Sally because they were high school classmates. His bitterness subsides as he and Sally become friendly and they mutually support one another. Eventually, a romance develops and they make love, proving to Luke that he is not impotent because of his war injuries.

The denouement is when Sally's husband comes home. He finds out what's been going on, something snaps in *his* war-damaged brain, and in a dramatic scene, he nearly kills both Luke and Sally. To save her marriage, Sally promises not to see Luke anymore. Whereupon her husband—just as much a victim of the war as Luke—swims into the ocean and commits suicide (à la *A Star Is Born*).

Jane prepared thoroughly for the picture, as usual. She did days of research, talking to paraplegics in hospitals and taking copious notes and making many tapes. In fact, her research led to a hospital location for the film, which had been denied them by the army, the navy, the air force, the national guard, and the Veterans Administration. The filming ended up at a civilian hospital for spinal cord injuries in Downey, California.

Jane also did considerable research into her own role, investigating the looks and mores of military wives, much as she had done with call girls in *Klute*. She had other reasons, too, for her thoroughness, as she explained in an interview in the *Los Angeles Times*: "How does a woman like Sally Hyde move, dress, talk? That's what I want to know. The degree to which I can render that woman real has a whole political implication for me politically—because those are the kinds of people who hate me, who thought I was a traitor. Remember, there are still a lot of people out there who would like to see me dead."

Production began at last—at the civilian hospital in Downey. By speaking their language, learned in her research, Jane became an instant hit with the paraplegic patients. Not one harsh word was spoken about her radical days and "there was no one who would like to see me dead."

Director Ashby was kind and considerate and listened respectfully to Jane's advice. She was delighted to be reunited with Jon Voight and cinematographer Haskell Wexler, who had been her cameraman on her *Introduction to the Enemy* film in North Vietnam. As in that documentary, said Jane during the filming of *Coming Home,* he once again "came up with that wonderful sense of color and detail, with muted tones when the script called for it."

For all concerned, the only problem came with the filming of the ending of *Coming Home.* Jane said in an interview in *The New York Times:* "I always wanted the picture to end with great sympathy for everyone, especially the paraplegic, who gave hope of putting his life together again. But the way we did it was all wrong. Bob, my husband, went berserk, shot up the place, took hostages, and finally was in a church steeple with police cars and helicopters moving in on him. It destroyed the whole feeling of compassion and logical adjustment that we had been building up for all the rest of the picture."

Producer Jerome Hellman was even more specific: "It was all wrong for a film about the consequences of violence to end with violence. Finally we reached some conclusions. The paraplegic was going to survive; there was no question in our minds, particularly after we had met actual paraplegics. Also, Jane's character was a survivor. But we felt that Bruce Dern's character was so dedicated to one way of seeing things that if he could no longer depend on that value system, he couldn't live."

And so Bruce Dern walked into the ocean, in spite of the fact that it was reminiscent of the ending of *A Star Is Born.* But at least it was better than being reminiscent of the ending of *King Kong.* And that's how important movie decisions are made.

But the most crucial decisions about *Coming Home* were yet to be made. How to release it? Was the public ready to accept a film about Vietnam, even though it primarily was a love story? Would there be protests from veterans about Jane Fonda's participation in such a venture? Might there possibly be protests from people with handicaps over the way the subject was handled?

It was decided to open the film in Washington, D.C. A few weeks earlier, producer Hellman—not without considerable trepidation—set up a private screening of the film for representatives of veterans groups in Washington. Says Hellman: "I deliberately invited people who were not too well disposed toward Jane Fonda. I flew in from California for the screening and waited to see what the reaction would be. I could sense nothing but rapt attention while the film was running. When it was over, I got up and introduced myself and asked for opinions. I couldn't believe it. That toughest of audiences was overwhelmed. They remained behind, talking with me for more than an hour. Typical was one young man in a wheelchair who sobbed when he told me, 'The film really catches the experience of the paraplegic.' A paraplegic who had been in the marine corps in Vietnam asked me to send his good wishes to Jane Fonda. He said it grudgingly, but he said it."

A few days later, Hellman screened the film for a representative of the President's Committee on Employment of the Handicapped, who said it was the first time she had "seen a disabled person on the screen dealt with as a complete human being." The Veterans Administration and the armed forces remained noncommittal.

And so the picture opened, with Hellman and United Artists a bit more heartened, but still nervous. They needn't have worried. There were no pickets; the people rushed to see *Coming Home* from its opening day. The critics raved. In addition to heaping praise on the actors, the director, and the cameraman, *Time* wrote: "It reminds us of the choices everybody made during those harrowing war years—and of the price the nation paid thereafter." Some critics were impressed by the movie's musical score of loud rock music—a suggestion from Jane after having listened to Armed Forces Radio incessantly when she was in Hanoi. Nearly every Vietnam film and TV show since then has adopted the same technique of using a loud rock music backdrop, culminating with *Good Morning, Vietnam* and "China Beach."

As audiences lined up around the block at theaters all over the country, none of the critics noticed that with *Coming Home,* Jane had begun an entirely new career—as movie tycoon, as well as actress. The profits kept rolling in for her IPC Films. The production company's initials no longer stood for Indochina Peace Campaign. It had become International Pictures Corporation. Later, the initials would be dropped completely, and the company would be known as Fonda Films. Under whatever name, it was to become a force to be reckoned with in the movie industry, and Jane would make more money as a mogul than she did as a performer.

But first, she still had her commitments as a performer. She had agreed, in advance, to do a film called *Comes a Horseman* with her director from *Klute,* Alan Pakula; and soon after finishing work in *Coming Home,* she rushed off to Montana to play a dauntless ranch woman in the period just after World War II. She liked the idea because it involved one of her Campaign for Economic Democracy concepts—the ruthlessness of corrupt corporate interests (in this case, a cattle baron played by Jason Robards, his third picture with Jane). In all, however, the film was a dud. It was dull and draggy and did not come close to matching her other comeback pictures. Neither did her short role with Alan Alda in Neil Simon's *California Suite.* The structure of the movie was like three one-act plays, with Jane appearing in only one of them. Jane, in a frenzy of activity, making three films that year, played well with the sardonic Alda, but nobody can bat a thousand. Maggie Smith (in another segment with Michael Caine) stole the picture.

It may be that Jane's mind was on something else—the upcoming Academy Awards in March 1979. Another, totally different Vietnam war film, *The Deer Hunter,* had come out not long after *Coming Home* in 1978, and the two pictures seemed to be in a dead heat for the Oscars. Jane went to the presentations with husband Tom Hayden and was visibly nervous.

It was nail-biting time. She whooped with joy when her friend, Nancy Dowd, won the Best Original Screenplay Oscar for *Coming Home,* along with Waldo Salt and Robert C. Jones. She sagged when the tide seemed to be moving toward *The Deer Hunter,* which Jane had opposed publicly as being too hawkish and the ideological opposite of *her* film. Christopher Walken won Best Supporting Actor for his role in *The Deer Hunter,* and Michael Cimino won for Best Director. At the end of the evening, too, *The Deer Hunter* beat *Coming Home* for the Best Picture Award.

But first came the real drama—the awards for Best Actor and Best Actress. It was Jon Voight against Robert De Niro; Jane Fonda against the field, but also against her perceived reputation as a radical troublemaker, even with her changed attitudes in *Coming Home.*

Jane won. The audience erupted in unexpected sustained applause, led by an almost deliriously happy Shirley MacLaine. As she mounted the podium, the usually stoic Jane obviously was overcome by the reaction, speaking more haltingly than she had when she won her first Oscar for *Klute.*

She also did a touching thing, simultaneously delivering her acceptance speech in sign language. The sign language, she explained, was her way of acknowledging the millions of people in America who have handicaps.

When Jon Voight won, there was another uproar of applause in the auditorium. The major part of his speech was devoted to how important Jane Fonda was to him and to the success of *Coming Home.*

If there still was any question whether Jane Fonda was back in the eyes of the industry, it was dispelled that night.

29

In the meantime, Jane's personal life, too, had changed considerably. It now was five years since she had determined to rid herself of her bulimia addiction; four years since her months of self-torment and therapy had paid off in conquering the disease.

She was still recovering, however. Bulimics, like alcoholics, always refer to themselves as recovering, not recovered. The underlying factors that caused their problem may still be there—and constant vigilance must be practiced.

In Jane's case, there remained an obsessive fear of being fat. Even in the days when she was still bingeing and purging, she also went to dance classes "not to learn how to dance, because I was always a klutz, but just so that the exercise would burn off excess weight."

After she halted her bulimic tendencies, Jane felt she

needed the exercise even more, so she went regularly to a workout emporium run by Gilda Marx, one of the pioneers in the exercise-studio business. The more she jumped and pumped and sweated, the more Jane came to realize that jumping/pumping/sweating was something that millions of women wanted and needed, and that involvement in same could be a very profitable enterprise indeed.

So, in 1978 (even while making three films), she founded Jane Fonda's Workout, Inc.

It was a shrewd move—her second important business decision (the other being IPC Films). It erupted like a volcano in the midst of the previously quiet women's exercise field. The first Jane Fonda Workout studio still exists. Jane opened it on Wilshire Boulevard, later moved it to South Robertson Boulevard on the fringe of Beverly Hills. The neighborhood is not Beverly Hills chic. It is an area of stores and commercial establishments. Jane says: "I wanted it there so women could come in from their work, their shopping, from whatever they were doing, and do their exercise in a no-frills environment under skilled supervision. I got the best exercise instructors I could find. We use music to set the tempo of their aerobic dancing and other rhythmic unison exercise, but in no way is this just a plush gym-type salon to while away the time. Many of the women come in during their lunch hour, they do their exercise, and they leave."

There were complaints from Gilda Marx and others that Jane had simply mimicked their methods. That may be so, as uncopyrightable as exercise techniques may be. But Jane and her key colleague, Leni Cazden, apparently did it better. Women flocked to her salon—and not just because of her name. Soon she would branch out to reach millions more through her workout books and her workout tape cassettes. With that one smallish establishment on Robertson Boulevard in 1979, she had started another new business that would net many millions of dollars in the years to come.

But that enormous expansion had not yet started at the time she won her Oscar for *Coming Home.* In fact, she began with small expectations. Her main objective in founding Jane Fonda's Workout, she says, was to provide a steady source of income for Campaign for Economic Democracy, which was now taking up most of Tom Hayden's time. The way she incorporated her workout business, its sole owner was CED. For many years, it received nearly all of the vast profits.

Campaign for Economic Democracy was extremely active. It had an office near the Hayden-Fonda home in Santa Monica, and it was not unusual for Jane to be manning the telephone switchboard there at night. The CED now was concentrating on antinuclear issues, women's rights issues (with loud vocal support for the Equal Rights Amendment), and on a titanic battle for rent-control laws in Santa Monica.

The now toned down ex-radical giant, Hayden, was at his best in organizing for smaller, local controversies. A master analyst and strategist, he was uncannily proficient at collecting and galvanizing his troops. In the matter of Santa Monica rent control, the city had long been in the grip of a landlord-oriented mayor and city council. There are many renters in Santa Monica, an aberration from the overwhelming zest for home *ownership* that exists in much of the rest of Southern California.

When the city council wouldn't budge on rent control, Hayden was one of the prime movers (along with Jane) in getting the renters to coalesce into a formidable political force. In a matter of time, they voted the landlord-dominated group out of office and elected a much more liberal mayor and city council, which proceeded to institute one of the most stringent rent-control laws in the United States. A couple of years later, they also elected Tom Hayden to the first of his four terms as their assemblyman in the California State Legislature (the district also includes other liberal communities on the West Side of Los Angeles).

All this has impelled the right-wing opposition to post signs occasionally that read YOU ARE NOW ENTERING THE PEOPLE'S REPUBLIC OF SANTA MONICA. Although Hayden immediately became a surprisingly moderate slightly left-of-center legislator, old antagonisms die hard.

There were no antagonisms whatsoever toward another Hayden-Fonda pet project—the children's camp at their ranch in Santa Barbara. They called the camp Laurel Springs and it still gives a touch of the wilderness life every summer to some 250 kids, about a third of them from ghetto areas. The underprivileged youngsters are there on "scholarships" funded by the Campaign for Economic Democracy and they frolic with Jane's own children, Vanessa and Troy.

A visitor in 1981 described the camp as follows:

> There is grand space here—about 120 acres—but the Hayden-Fonda residence is a tiny, simple, almost ramshackle house. There is a mud room and a covered porch and the furnishings are Early Comfy— some old pine and oak, an overstuffed sofa, a potbelly stove, family photographs. . . . The house is one of a cluster of cottages overlooking the camp's main playing field. The place echoes with shouting, laughing children. Some are riding horses, which Jane says was her own favorite activity when she was their age. Troy is climbing a tree with friends; Vanessa has taken others on an overnight hike; Hayden has taken a group for a day of bass fishing at a nearby mountain lake. . . . It's all a far cry from Jane and Tom's city residence in Santa Monica, which has eight rooms, furnished smartly in chintzes by Jane, and is surrounded by shrubbery, fences and a security system—to keep out the few crazies who still send her death threats.

It was the same at Laurel Springs Camp two summers earlier, except that Jane had to take some time off from the kids and the horses to get her second major IPC film under way. She had been working on it for five years—ever since she was horrified by the story of Karen Silkwood in Oklahoma. Ms. Silkwood, a laboratory technician at the Kerr-McGee plant that manufactures plutonium rods for nuclear reactors, had discovered that she and seventy-three other Kerr-McGee workers had been contaminated by the radioactive material they worked with—a vitally serious health problem. She had collected a bulky file of documentation for the Nuclear Regulatory Commission and was driving her car to a meeting, at which she was to show the documentation to a *New York Times* reporter, when her auto mysteriously went off the road and she was killed. The documentation disappeared.

Jane had been trying for years to buy the motion picture rights to the Karen Silkwood story, but through a complicated series of circumstances, she had been unable to do so. However, worries about reckless use of nuclear energy continued to be high on the agenda of the Campaign for Economic Democracy—and also on her own personal agenda. So she kept looking for ways to translate these fears onto the screen with some sort of gripping dramatic story.

Unknown to her at the time, halfway across Los Angeles, some other people had the same idea in mind. They also had Jane Fonda and her Karen Silkwood efforts in mind. And so, before that year was out, she was to help produce and to star in the most important film she had made until that time: *The China Syndrome.*

30

The *China Syndrome* brought together the dynamic duo of Jane Fonda and Jack Lemmon for the first, and, so far, the only time. Lemmon had known Jane, on and off, since she was a teenager hanging around the production of *Mister Roberts,* watching her father at work. Lemmon, of course, was Ensign Pulver in that remarkable film, winning the Best Supporting Actor Oscar for it. He says: "Jane later told me she had a tremendous crush on me back then in 1955 and I said, 'Why didn't you tell me?' She said, 'Well, I was awfully young.' I said, 'I don't give a shit. You should have told me anyway.' " That's the outspoken Jack Lemmon for you.

He is just as outspoken in discussing his feelings about Jane as he watched and listened from afar during the height of her Vietnam war protest period. He is somewhat of an activist himself, mostly in the area of ecology and what he calls "the despoiling of the earth." Lemmon told me: "I had mixed emotions at first when Jane started her antiwar crusade. I admired the fact that she'd be willing to stand up and holler, but I also felt that from a practical point of view, she was going nowhere. I felt like saying to her, 'Thou protesteth too much, and you're turning people against you.' But then I began to appreciate her passion for her convictions. That's what makes her such a wonderful actress. She lives by her passions and is not afraid of expressing them—in life and on the screen. Besides, as it turned out, she was right about Vietnam.

"One of the things that made me come to admire her Vietnam stand was my own experience. I got to be very passionate about the bomb, pollution, building those fucking nuclear power plants—and I got a lot of flack, on a lesser level than what Jane was taking, of course. I made three TV documentaries about nuclear power, air pollution, and so forth, and I ended up getting called a son-of-a-bitch by a U.S. senator, George Murphy, who threatened to sue me. The power companies tried to wreck my career with nasty letters to the movie studios. One power company, Pacific Gas and Electric, sued Don Widener, my producer and collaborator, for the documentaries, but Don sued them back, and got millions of dollars in a settlement. But I kept getting letters: 'Go back to Russia, you Commie, pink, pervert fag bastard.' So it made me realize what Jane had put herself through in her passion for her convictions."

It was Lemmon's own passion about the dangers of nuclear power plants that got him involved in *The China Syndrome* project before Jane did. Michael Douglas, as a producer (he had previously produced *One Flew over the Cuckoo's Nest,* in which he did not act), had bought a screenplay about a potential disaster at a nuclear reactor, and had made a deal at Columbia Pictures to produce the film. But, as the outspoken Lemmon says, "the studio was scared shitless about going ahead with it." Nevertheless, Lemmon told me: "Michael went on with his preparations for the picture. The principal role of the engineer at the power plant was written as a thirty-two-year-old guy. The engineer is the man who discovers the potential disaster-in-the-making, and he blows the whistle on it, getting killed by a SWAT team for his efforts. He foresees a China Syndrome effect, meaning that if there is a meltdown of the nuclear core of the plant, the meltdown might continue until it reaches China, on the other side of the world.

"I knew very little about this project at first, except that Michael Douglas, another antinuclear activist, was involved in it. Because of my interest in the subject, I also knew, vaguely, that the same studio, Columbia, had also closed a deal with Jane Fonda and her IPC films to make the Karen Silkwood story, but that Jane was tied up in litigation over the rights to the Silkwood story."

One day, Michael Douglas came into the office of the William Morris Agency to discuss casting of the thirty-two-year-old engineer with Leonard Hirshan. Hirshan said, "Why does the guy have to be thirty-two years old? Wouldn't it be more effective if the engineer was an older man, more steeped in the ways of the power company he works for?" Douglas said, "Who do you have in mind?" Hirshan said, "Jack Lemmon." Douglas said, "Great. Can we get him?" It took a two-minute phone call to get Lemmon. The other principal role, a TV reporter who eventually sides with the power-company engineer, was to be played by Richard Dreyfuss. The TV reporter's sidekick, a cameraman, was to be played by Douglas himself.

The studio, Columbia Pictures, was still very hesitant about giving the final okay to the picture. Then Lemmon got another phone call from Hirshan, the gist of which is described by Lemmon as follows: "Lenny said to me, 'What if the Dreyfuss TV reporter role becomes a girl?' My first reaction was to get furious. I said, 'That's typical Hollywood bullshit for you—fucking up a worthwhile project by trying to jazz it up with a woman.' But then Lenny went on to finish the sentence I had interrupted: 'Jane Fonda.' I said, 'Holy shit. *Yes.*' So Jane came in. Columbia just combined elements of her Karen Silkwood project with ours, and we became a co-production of Jane's IPC company."

The film became a labor of love for Jane, Lemmon, and Douglas—three consummate professionals, as is James Bridges, the director. It took months to rewrite the TV reporter part to reflect the attitudes of a female rather than a male journalist, during which Jane—with her thorough research techniques—spent hours with Connie Chung and others in the TV-news field. She says: "I studied their attitudes, their resentments at being shoved off to do women's feature stories, instead of hard news. I watched how they had to rush to do their hair and makeup in a frenzy before rushing on the air for a fast-breaking story. Also, I came to realize that a lot of stuff they get sent out on is pretty thin indeed. Once we went out to cover a fashion show because First Lady Betty Ford was supposed to be there. No Betty Ford; no story. So in the picture, when my character, Kimberly, wants to pursue her nuclear reactor story and her boss says, 'Don't worry your pretty head about that,' I understood. It's hard for a pretty woman to be accepted on a level beyond or in contradiction to the stereotyped image of prettiness. It all helped to shape my performance."

The picture was shot in a remarkably accurate power-plant control room built at the Columbia studios—and at three actual power plants in the area. They were not allowed into nuclear facilities, so they used conventional power plants, which, aside from the radioactive cores, look much the same. Lemmon says: "It was at these power plants that we ran into trouble with the hard hats. They didn't know what we were up to—the script was kept secret—but they correctly assumed the worst. That's when they called Jane a Commie bitch and worse, and they called me and Michael Commie fag perverts and worse. It didn't seem to matter to them that Michael and I are both excessively masculine. It was tougher for Jane than it was for us. They brought up the Hanoi shit again, and they threw things at her. One guy let a wrench fall where she was standing. If it had hit her, it would have cracked her skull."

Jane did have an accident on the picture, but it was non-hard hat related. Near the end of the filming, she stumbled and suffered a hairline fracture of the ankle. She finished the picture in a small cast, hidden from the camera by her boots.

Before the movie opened, preparations for the publicity campaign were strenuous. Lemmon says: "They briefed us like they brief the President going into a press conference. A publicity executive named Chuck Ashman drew up a list of all the hard-ball questions a hostile press might ask, and we'd sit for hours while he threw the questions at us. It was like being in rehearsal for a play. But there were no surprises when we finally did meet the press. And the questions *were* tough when we came up against reporters of a right-wing bent. The power companies had bombarded them with all sorts of material about how fictitious our picture was, how inaccurate, and how such a nuclear meltdown in a power plant could never possibly happen. The hostile reaction from that part of the press lasted about two and a half weeks after the picture went into release. The accident they said never could happen, *did* happen—at Three Mile Island in Pennsylvania. They stopped calling us names, and they stopped knocking the picture. It happened overnight."

Never has the fate of a movie been so determined by an actual historic event. The Three Mile Island disaster occurred on March 28, 1979, just as *The China Syndrome* was opening in movie theaters in even the smallest towns in the United States. It was eerie how close the film came to depicting what actually happened in the nuclear plant in central Pennsylvania. The cooling system failed. The core began to melt, escaping radiation forced the evacuation of the civilian population for miles around. Ten years later, the fused radioactive core still was irretrievable in the earth beneath the now-abandoned power plant—just as in the "accident" at Chernobyl in Russia later on.

Attendance soared at theaters showing *The China Syn-*

drome, resulting in an eventual box-office gross of more than $60 million, which exceeded such previous movie blockbusters as Barbra Streisand's *Funny Girl.* The film earned no Oscars (that was the year of the *Kramer vs. Kramer* near sweep) but Jane got her fifth Best Actress nomination, her third in as many years.

And Jane now had a new predominant cause, which fit in perfectly with the agenda of Campaign for Economic Democracy. She spent $150,000 for a speaking tour of cities in the East and Midwest in which she and Hayden spoke out against the incipient dangers of nuclear power plants.

It was only between pictures, but the old fervor returned. And this time it proved to be an almost universally popular cause. It inspired hundreds of letters-to-the-editor in newspapers all over the country.

Several such letters pointed out that the conservative columnist George Will had written that in *The China Syndrome,* Jane Fonda "has invented nuclear fantasies about melting cores, in the interests of satisfying her own greed," and that the column had appeared just three days before Three Mile Island happened.

In a notable switch from previous Fonda-provoked letters-to-the-editor, a *Newsweek* reader, Robert Rodi, wrote, "Must we re-learn the hard lesson that Jane Fonda is usually right?"

Usually, but not always. In that year, 1979, Jane got into a hassle with some of her former confreres in the antiwar movement—notably Joan Baez—over the course events were taking in the now-unified Vietnam. Jane stubbornly refused to believe that the North Vietnamese were being repressive in their governing of what used to be South Vietnam.

That was the period of the Boat People, with thousands of refugees fleeing the country by sea in any ramshackle vessel they could find. Joan Baez visited them in their transit camps and raised money for them by singing in benefit performances in the United States.

Jane eventually backed off a bit, saying she "was not

going to be an apologist for North Vietnam," and she, too, helped organize a rally for the Boat People.

But the damage was done. Things were never quite the same again between Jane and Baez and some others in the peace movement.

31

It's surprising that Jane Fonda could find any time at *all* for causes during this period, since she was grinding out films at a rate even faster than her father when he was doing three a year in his early days at RKO. Soon after she finished *The China Syndrome* she began work on *The Electric Horseman,* and almost immediately thereafter, she was making *Nine to Five,* her fourth movie for her own company, IPC.

Both of these pictures were enormous money-makers and above-average lightweight entertainment, but neither was in the same prestige class as *The China Syndrome* and *Coming Home.* That seems to have been a pattern for Jane in those days—a report-card mixture of A's and B−'s, even C's. In a sense, she was still feeling her way as a tycoon and experimenting with what she thought was best for herself.

She did *The Electric Horseman* for several reasons: (1) She was offered her new rate of a million dollars to play the role; (2) she would work again with Robert Redford, whose Wildwood Company was the co-production entity with Columbia and Universal; (3) the director was Sydney Pollack, who had guided her so beautifully in *They Shoot Horses, Don't They?*; (4) she would join forces with another activist, Redford's main cause being environmental issues; and (5) the theme of the film coincided with two of her own concerns, the iniquities of big business and animal rights.

The picture was shot in and around St. George, Utah, not far from Redford's environmentally oriented resort and ski area, Sundance. It was an unlikely blending of love story and ecology. The plot concerned a once-great rodeo champion, Sonny Steele (played by Redford), who now is the boozing spokesman for a voracious breakfast cereal company and forced to wear a degrading electric-light-festooned jacket in his public appearances. He attracts the attention of TV newswoman Hallie Martin (Fonda), a part that is so close to her Kimberly Wells in *The China Syndrome,* with all its female-reporter plaints and ambitions, that it almost seems to be a sequel.

In this case, Sonny, after a foul-up in behalf of the cereal maker at a Las Vegas trade convention, finally kicks the traces and makes off with the company's prize stallion, Rising Star, who, he discovers, is being heavily drugged by the company's trainers. Hallie, always hot on the trail of a good story, goes into immediate pursuit of Sonny and the magnificent animal, soon learning that the motive of the crime is to turn the horse loose to live out his life with others of his kind in the wild.

The rest of the picture is a chase—sometimes ludicrous, as when Rising Star, with Sonny on his back, outruns an entire battalion of police cars. Sonny and Hallie team up, they end up in the sack (literally), Rising Star is released, Hallie gets her Big Story, and Sonny wanders off alone into the sunset.

Despite the fairy-tale self-righteousness of the story, it was effectively managed by director Pollack, and Jane had a wonderful time during filming. She endlessly discussed environmental issues with Redford, and she enjoyed being in the Utah wilderness. The wilderness sometimes is unrelenting to movie companies, however, and there were some ecological problems in production. For example, a procession of rolling thunderstorms kept interrupting a Redford-Fonda kissing scene, and it took forty-eight takes to complete the kiss.

Someone figured out that with all the retakes from different angles, the kiss cost the production company $280,000, and it was only on the screen for twenty seconds. Redford said later, when perusing the film's expenditures, "It would have been cheaper if I had kissed the horse, like in the old Gene Autry westerns."

The press had a lot of fun kidding the picture, for example:

Boy meets horse, boy gets horse,
boy meets girl, girl gets boy,
boy dumps horse, girl gets scoop . . .

With flashing teeth, blow-dried hair,
and the horse, Redford and Fonda make the
perfect Marlboro couple.

The ribs did nothing to hurt the box office. People wanted to see Jane—by now the number-one female star—in the same picture with reigning number-one male star Redford. And the story was pleasant enough in the old Spencer Tracy–Katharine Hepburn tradition. *The Electric Horseman* soon was one of the top-ten grossing films of the year.

It was a good learning experience in tycoonery for Jane, the budding tycoon. *The Electric Horseman* had shown her that with big names, you could make money with an average story and still get a message across to the public. So she immediately began thinking of big names for her next picture. This was to be *totally* an IPC production for the first time, with Jane completely in charge as the picture's sole boss.

Nine to Five had been in preparation for some months. While Jane was working on *The Electric Horseman,* her partner, Bruce Gilbert, had been doing exhaustive research into the plight of female office workers in America. Gilbert, a psychologist-in-training when Jane found him at the Blue Fairyland Day Care Center in Berkeley while she was making *Steelyard Blues,* had emerged as a fine movie executive, taking over many of the day-to-day operations of IPC from Jane. Because of his academic background, he also was an indefatigable investigator into subjects Jane found interesting. One of those subjects was exploitation of women workers, of course, and Jane had learned much about that through activities with Tom Hayden on behalf of a Los Angeles secretaries' group.

The original story for *Nine to Five* had been written by Patricia Resnick, who had gone undercover as a secretary in a large insurance company. Bruce Gilbert then took up the research. He spent a lot of time at the headquarters of the National Association of Office Workers in Cleveland. He spoke with dozens of secretaries about their bitter experiences with male chauvinist bosses. It was his suggestion, accepted by Jane, to make the film a comedy rather than a heavy message-laden drama. Gilbert, who like so many others, was to part company with Jane later on, said: "It all came about when, on a whim, I began asking the women if they ever had had fantasies about getting even with their bosses. The answers were so funny, and their fantasies were so bizarre, that we decided that the picture just *had* to be a comedy."

That decision having been made, Jane began to look in other directions for the big-name actresses she already felt she needed to get her prosecretary message across—and to make money. In the world of comedy, there was an obvious choice, Lily Tomlin, whose Ernestine, the telephone operator, routines she had always savored. Then she reached out into the world of country music for Dolly Parton, who never had made a movie before, but whose "outrageous boobs, outrageous clothes, and outrageous talk always had broken me up whenever I watched her on TV." So Jane signed Dolly. With Lily and Dolly in tow, Jane cast herself in the least important of three female secretary roles.

The eventual script that evolved was as uncomplicated as an old two-reel movie short. One critic, Gerald Nachman of the *San Francisco Examiner,* wrote: "This picture easily could have been called 'The Dead End Kids Meet Gloria Steinem.'" Judy Bernly (Jane) comes to work in a huge office as a secretary, her first job since becoming a divorced housewife. She soon joins up with Violet Newstead (Tomlin), the head of the secretarial pool, and with Doralee Rhodes (Parton), executive secretary to the boss. The boss, who is unspeakably horrible to all the women, is played by Dabney Coleman. Who else?

The three ladies, relaxing over a joint at home, begin to fantasize about taking revenge on the ogre, Coleman. The pot-inspired fantasies are played out on the screen and are quite funny. Then fantasy begins to become reality when the Tomlin character mistakenly puts rat poison in the boss's coffee. Soon they have kidnapped him, blackmailed him, and instituted revolutionary office reforms, which themselves are the feminist fantasy—job sharing, flexible hours, no making coffee, female advancement to the executive level, even a day-care center for secretaries' children.

Lily and Dolly stole the picture. That was fine with Jane, who deliberately underplayed her role, both in dress and demeanor. She tried to look and act as much as possible like Just Plain Jane—but didn't quite succeed. A little of Barbarella and Bree Daniel were still apparent behind the large horn-rimmed eyeglasses; she was not too convincing as a secretary.

But Jane, the tycoon, came out smelling like a rose. The picture, despite mixed reviews, made reams of money. It was seen by nearly every *real* nine-to-fiver in the country—along with millions who adored Lily, Dolly, and Jane.

Without even realizing he was paying Jane the tycoon one of the ultimate kudos, David Ansen of *Newsweek* wrote: "If Oscars were given out for the casting coup of the year, *Nine to Five* would win hands down."

Very few people knew that it was Jane and her IPC company who had put together that winning combination of Lily, Dolly, and herself. As for Jane the actress, it was not one of her biggies. Many critics echoed Ansen, who wrote: "Fonda has the least appealing role, playing straight woman to her antic cohorts."

Actresses being actresses, such comments were bound to bother her. But in this case, not too much. Because she already was involved in her next film, again for her IPC company, which she knew in her heart-of-hearts was going to be a *real* biggie.

That kid gave me trouble again a few years ago," .said Josh Logan in his very last interview with me in 1987. He still referred to Jane as "that kid," though she was nearly fifty at the time.

"It's not that she knew it," said Logan, "but she got in the way of a big production I had in mind." Logan continued: "I guess I shouldn't complain, though. She was smart enough to beat me to the punch. What happened was I went to see an off-Broadway play at the Hudson Guild. It was by a young writer named Ernest Thompson, and I loved it. I came home from the theater and immediately phoned Jimmy Stewart in California. I told Jimmy, 'This is a perfect movie for you and I want to produce and direct it. It's a touching story about a grumpy old man coming to terms with his wife and daughter in his last days.' Jimmy said 'Fine,' and the next morning I made calls about buying the film rights. Only I couldn't get them. Jane already had bought the property for her own company and was going to star Hank in the film. The play was *On Golden Pond.* When I called Jimmy to tell him what happened, he said, in his dry way, 'Wal, Josh, you can't win 'em all, especially when you've got a smart god-daughter who's a producer, too.' "

Her speedy acquisition of *On Golden Pond* was a further indication that Jane now was in high gear as a movie mogul. It didn't hurt, of course, that she knew playwright Thompson, who was a neighbor in Santa Monica, and that she was aware of the play when it was still in his typewriter. Why did she buy it—even before the good New York reviews came out? Her answer was a simple one, though her voice broke a bit while saying it, "I wanted to do this movie basically as a tribute to my father."

Hank Fonda was approaching his seventy-sixth year and was not doing well—either in health or career. In 1974—six years earlier—he had collapsed backstage at his Broadway one-man show, *Clarence Darrow for the Defense,* and was rushed to Lenox Hill Hospital. He had a wildly irregular heartbeat and a pacemaker had to be implanted in his chest to control the fluctuating aortic rhythms.

But it was a chronic form of heart disease, and Hank was back in the hospital eight times over the next seven years, eventually getting a new-type lithium pacemaker. He couldn't work very much, nor was he very much in demand. Even in the late 1960s, the great Henry Fonda had been playing mostly cameo roles in war films like *The Battle of the Bulge,* and now the movie roles were dwindling away almost completely. He was doing photography commercials on television, and an occasional TV drama, like David Rintels's *The Oldest Living Graduate.*

Jane felt very badly about her father's illness. There was guilt (as she confessed to friends) that she had been halfway across the world making *Introduction to the Enemy* in Vietnam and could not be at Hank's bedside after his first heart seizure in New York. Then came continuing mixed feelings. Hank had been her idol since childhood, and now the idol was crumbling—a common problem faced, in varying degrees, by millions of people with millions of ailing fathers. But Hank Fonda was not the average father, as it had become well known to Jane over the decades. She still could not connect with him emotionally, even while she sat with him in his many hospital stays. He was increasingly more proud of her, saying, on many occasions, "I am in awe of Jane," but his attitude, as analyzed by Brooke Hayward, continued to be like a gruff first sergeant in the army dealing with his troops.

A case in point is described by writer Howard Teichman in a visit made by Jane to Hank when he was in the hospital again the day after his seventy-sixth birthday. Hank's favorite beverage always had been root beer, spiked with ice cream. Teichman recalls that when Jane walked in, obviously terribly concerned, Hank greeted her with, "I thought at least you'd bring me a root beer float to celebrate."

It wasn't that Hank didn't recognize his shortcomings as a parent. He frequently confessed to them in public, even once when he was being honored with a Lifetime Achievement Award. At various times he said: "I don't like myself. I never have. I even need a script to be able to say thank you. . . . I don't think I've been a particularly good father, but I've been lucky in the quality of the kids I've spawned."

So there was more to it when Jane said she bought *On Golden Pond* and produced it as a tribute to her father. You don't have to be a psychiatrist to theorize that she still wanted to win the unconditional love of her father, that she felt guilty over the fact that she had won two Oscars and the brilliant Hank had not received even one; that she was hoping to restore her idol to one last display of old-time brilliance.

It also seems likely that she saw, in the Thompson play, a chance to communicate one-on-one with Hank for the first time—at least on the screen, something *he* had been unable to do in real life. She thought she might be able to do so because her situation with Hank was so much like that of Chelsea, the daughter in the play, with *her* father, Norman. Jane said, in an interview in *The New York Times,* "Here was this forty-three-year-old woman whose dad determined her life. And here *I* was: my father still evoked the same emotion in me as when I was young."

And so, as producers, Jane and Bruce Gilbert began to put the picture together. In Jane's now astute casting mind, there was only one actress to play Ethel, Norman's long-time wife, in their last days together on Golden Pond—Katharine Hepburn. From day one, Jane was determined that she herself would play the daughter, Chelsea—once again a selfless secondary part to the bravura alchemy of two genuine giants of the screen working together in a film for the first time.

Both Hepburn and Hank were delighted with the casting. Jane was overjoyed. She said: "I had admired Kate ever since I was a little girl. Now, I not only thought of her as possibly the most respected living actress, but to me, she had been the symbol of the emancipation of women ever since she had begun her movie career by standing up to Louis B. Mayer and out-foxing him, nearly fifty years before."

Hepburn said that Jane reminded her of exactly how she, Kate, had been as a younger woman. Extremely astute about human relationships, Kate soon caught all the nuances of the situation between Hank and Jane. Hepburn said, "They're both reaching for something they think they've missed."

How right she was.

Jane and Gilbert selected the respected Mark Rydell as the director, and the company went on location in New Hampshire, at a lake that closely resembled the Golden Pond described in Thompson's play. All the action took place at the lake, and it was still essentially a three-character play. The story was about Norman Thayer, crotchety, nearly eighty years old, senile at times, afraid of death; and his wife, Ethel, seventyish, brilliant, compassionate, loving. Norman and Ethel are on their annual summer sojourn in their cottage on

Golden Pond, where they have summered for years. It probably is their last time; Norman is still active but quite ill. The dialogue crackles as Norman and Ethel alternately squabble, love one another, and master life-threatening crises.

Into this environment comes Chelsea (Jane), who has long been estranged from her father. She brings with her nine-year-old Billy, the precocious son of the man she is planning to marry. Chelsea leaves Billy with her parents while she goes off to Europe with her intended, a dentist. An enormous fondness develops between Billy and Norman, who always had wanted a son but got Chelsea instead. They play together, fish together, and have a near-catastrophic accident on the lake.

An interesting thing about all this is that Hank, during the filming, developed a profound liking for Tom Hayden, who, like himself, was a devoted real-life fisherman. Their relations, prior to that, had always been pleasant but correct. Now, as they went off to fish for trout and bass on Hank's days off, a warm comradeship of the rod and reel developed. Jane was ecstatic. The wise Hepburn watched from the sidelines, and she was happy, too.

But Jane, at the same time, was exceedingly nervous. Her big rapprochement scene between Chelsea and Norman was coming up and, in a way, it could also be the big rapprochement scene between Jane and Hank. The key lines were:

CHELSEA (to Ethel): I can't talk to him. I've never been able to. Maybe some day we can try to be friends.

ETHEL: Chelsea, Norman is eighty years old. He has heart problems, and a problem remembering things. When exactly do you expect this friendship to begin?

It begins a couple of scenes later when Chelsea and Norman rehash old antagonisms between them, and Jane, genuine love glistening in her eyes, pleads: "I want to be your friend."

When the actual scene was done, Hank melted, Norman melted, Jane melted, Chelsea melted. It became one of the memorable scenes in the history of film, as underplayed as it was. When it was over, Jane wept, and Hank came over and hugged her, possibly for the first time in his life. Kate Hepburn cried, too. It reminded her of Spencer Tracy's declaration of love to her on the screen in their last picture together, *Guess Who's Coming to Dinner.*

Like Tracy, Hank Fonda had to struggle to finish *his* last picture. Production of *On Golden Pond* had to be halted at one point while he was taken to a hospital for a few days. He was ill when filming ended and soon back in the hospital again. Jane spent a lot of time with him, sharing visiting hours with Hank's wife, Shirlee.

Hank seemed to be all right for a while, and he exulted with Jane when the film opened to good reviews and healthy audiences. It was a hit—not as big a hit as some of Jane's others—but it did remarkably well at the box office for a picture about older people in a movie market dominated at the time by youth-film frenzy.

When Academy Award time came around, Hank, Kate, and Jane all were nominated—and so was the film. By now, Hank was haltingly calling Jane "honey" and "darling." He had softened considerably, but not all the way.

Hank didn't get to the Oscar ceremonies in March. He was back in bed again and watched on television with Shirlee. He won Best Actor, his first Oscar in all of his forty-seven years as an actor. A tearful Jane got up and accepted it for him. Then Kate Hepburn won Best Actress. Jane whooped with joy. After the movie lost the Best Picture Award (it went to *Chariots of Fire*), Jane and Hayden rushed off to Hank's house to celebrate with him and Shirlee. This time she brought root beer floats.

Five months later Hank Fonda was dead. He passed away in his sleep at Cedars-Sinai Hospital in Los Angeles on August 12, 1982. Jane and the rest of the family were at his bedside when he died.

A week later his will was filed for probate. He left nearly all of his considerable estate to Shirlee and to his daughter Amy, from his marriage to Susan Blanchard. A curmudgeon to the end, he left nothing to Jane, nor to Peter, because, as he specifically stated in his will, "in my opinion, they are financially independent."

33

Although it was not unexpected, the death of her father—and its aftermath—seems to have been quite a blow to Jane," says Tom Epstein, one of her colleagues in Campaign for Economic Democracy. The record bears out that assumption. Whereas she had ground out an incredible total of eight films from 1978 to 1981, her entire production for the next *six* years was only three movies.

It was sort of a semi-hiatus, at least insofar as her filmmaking activities were concerned. Some friends rationalize that she had reached a personal plateau when she helped Hank Fonda win his first Oscar with *On Golden Pond,* and that temporarily she was suffering a no-new-worlds-to-conquer syndrome. Also, they say, she was hurt by the terms of Hank's will—not from a materialistic point of view, about which she could care less, but from the realization that, as hard as she had tried, she had not been able to completely come to terms with her father.

Another opinion is that Jane simply was tired as the result of her frenetic three years of acting/producing. This weariness definitely had shown up in the last of her 1981 pictures, *Rollover.* It, too, was an IPC production, and Bruce Gilbert admits, "It was the first IPC film, excluding *Introduction to the Enemy,* of course, that was a financial failure."

Examining this film, in which she starred with Kris Kristofferson and once again was directed by Alan Pakula, one can find many signs that fatigue had set in. Missing were both Jane's flair as a producer and her fire as an actress. Gilbert indicates that the story probably never should have been bought in the first place, but in fairness to the writers—David Shaber, Howard Kohn, and David Weir—this also was the period when Jane was terribly distracted by her father's illness. It was a romantic thriller set in the world of international high finance—with greedy American bankers (a favorite Fonda theme) in contention with greedy Arab investors. Their manipulations can, and do, precipitate global economic catastrophe.

Jane gets to dress up in a lot of fancy clothes in this epic but, unusual for her, there is little warmth or credibility in her acting. It was almost a throwback to her French rich-lady pictures. The picture was demolished by the critics and did poorly at the box office—Jane's previous string of successes notwithstanding. For the industry, *Variety* headed its review "Not That Bankable," and ended with, "This is a cautionary tale to which there is no response except taking one's money out of the bank and stuffing it under a mattress." The only good thing to come out of this picture was that Jane got to know Hume Cronyn, who played one of the bankers and was to be a totally unexpected component of an important Jane Fonda triumph later on.

So, on a flat note, Jane's early-1980s hiatus began. She was not to go before the cameras again for another three years. For Jane, the producer rather than the actress, it was not really a hiatus. She was pursuing acquisition of two novels—one written a decade before, and the other still in the process of being written, as was the play, *On Golden Pond.* This acumen in rooting out obscure properties is the basic cause of Jane Fonda the producer being a power in the movie industry.

In the meantime, back then in the early 1980s, Jane had other fish to fry. Her workout studio in Beverly Hills was flourishing, leading her to open new studios in San Francisco and in Encino, in the San Fernando Valley area of Los Angeles. By 1982, the workout studios had become big business, with at least 3,000 women a week at $6.50 each. This was small change, however, compared with the income derived from the first *Jane Fonda's Workout Book.* The publishing world has rarely seen anything like it—1.8 million copies sold. Nearly as spectacular was Jane's second book in 1982, *Jane Fonda's Workout Book for Pregnancy, Birth and Recovery* by exercise expert Femmy DeLyser. At a royalty rate of $2.45 per copy, this amounted to more than $5 million pouring into the coffers of Jane Fonda's Workout, Inc.

But all *this* was small change, compared with what happened with the Jane Fonda video cassettes (along with corresponding audio cassettes and records). Her first workout video tape was released on April 25, 1982. It sold for $60 and immediately rocketed up to the very top of the charts, remaining there for years. So did the continuing procession of succeeding Fonda workout tapes.

Fortune magazine wrote: "Until Fonda made her hit, every videocassette winner had been a movie. Before Fonda, movies *were* the market. Movie rentals were eighty percent of most video shops' revenue. But people *bought* Fonda's cassettes instead of renting them. Now, everyone in the industry is wondering how to duplicate the act."

The secret of the success of Jane's tapes is a controversial matter. There is no question that her show-business savvy has a lot to do with it. The basic exercise routines are there—mostly aerobic dancing—but each tape is staged like a finely tuned Broadway show. There stands Jane, front-stage-center, clad in tight-fitting leotard, with a chorus of similarly attired attractive exercisers behind her. The music is stirring as breasts and buttocks fly in all directions.

Even the most avid critics of the sexiness of the tapes concede that they are valuable and instructional to millions of women who use them to keep in shape, but there have been mutterings that Jane's skimpy costumes are a throwback to *Barbarella.* One University of Southern California professor, Margaret Morse, in criticizing *all* exercise tapes—not only Jane's—published a study decrying them as encouraging "passive femininity." Ms. Morse deplored them as being "almost soft-porn, complete with heavy breathing, sexy stares and lingering shots on parts of the body not directly related to the exercises."

Concerning Jane specifically, Ms. Morse wrote: "I see Jane Fonda sitting on her buttocks with her legs raised in the air in a **V**. On the one hand, that looks powerful. But on the other, it completely immobilizes her and forces her into a submissive position. The message clearly is 'I'm powerful but I'm still a woman who needs men.' "

Such reasoning, provoking a one-word response from Jane—"Absurd!"—was a bit too arcane for the public and did not make a dent in Jane's tape sales. In fact, they may have *in*creased with purchases by certain voyeuristic males.

In any event, the money-making Workout empire was in full financial flower by mid-1982. Most of the income was still going to the Campaign for Economic Democracy, and, now, to Tom Hayden's first political campaign for his seat in the California State Assembly.

Hayden ran as a Democrat from his base in Santa Monica, though his 44th District would also cover some areas well inside the City of Los Angeles. His opponent was Republican Bill Hawkins, who campaigned almost solely on the charge that Hayden, despite his protestations of acquired moderation, was still a dangerous radical—as in his Chicago Seven days. It was a bitter contest, with Hawkins solidly backed by the landlord interests defeated in the rent-control fight. Hayden fought back with his long-perfected stump-speaking style and with Jane—also brilliant at rallies and shopping-mall appearances—as a very formidable campaign weapon.

It probably was the costliest race in California history for a lowly state assembly seat. Over $2 million was spent on both sides—more than it takes to win the governorship in neighboring, smaller western states. Hayden, with his monetary reserves from Jane's films and workout business—outspent his opponent, but not by much. Hawkins's billboards and commercials emphasized the dangers to the nation as a whole if the Fonda-Hayden wing of the Democratic Party took over.

On election day, 1982, it was no contest, however. Hayden won with 64,373 votes to 53,389 for Hawkins.

And so Jane settled down, for a while, to be the wife of an elected politician. With all her other activities, she worked from time to time in his Santa Monica office, and she hostessed political gatherings in their Alta Avenue home. These parties were nothing like the Beverly Hills and Bel Air shindigs with which Jane had grown up. In fact, she avoided most contact with her Hollywood celebrity friends. An interesting social comment comes from writer Andy Meisler, who went undercover as a parking attendant at movie-industry functions in order to do a magazine story on car ownership of the stars. Says Meisler, "I worked a party at Jane Fonda's house and I didn't park any of the Mercedes and Rolls and Jaguars that were *de rigueur* at the other parties. In fact, everybody was driving the same type of car up to Jane's gate—a Volvo. Now that's what I would call liberal chic."

On the whole, the Fonda-Hayden ménage was a rather unorthodox household. Having such a substantial war chest, Hayden—who hated being separated from his family—literally commuted from Santa Monica to Sacramento, the state capitol. This involved an approximate eight-hundred-mile round-trip by commercial airliner, an expense that the average legislator could not afford. Jane's attitude toward him bordered on idolatry, but, unlike the situation in her previous liaisons, the idolatry was reciprocated. Hayden had always been a movie buff and he admired everything Jane had done on the screen "since her awakening." He advised her with technical skill and was responsible, to some small degree, for her doing *The China Syndrome* and *Coming Home,* also suggesting some of the finer nuances of her performance in these and other films. For *her* part, Jane advised Hayden with technical skill on some of his political dealings in the legislature—such as a series of Hayden-sponsored bills in the area of employer-financed day-care centers, usually vetoed by Republican Governor George Deukmejian.

The good relationship of the couple was reflected in the attitudes of Jane's children. Troy, then nine, had Hayden's Irish face and was an inheritor of his father's love of sports. The child was an inveterate baseball player and doing very well in the Little League, with his mother frequently in attendance at his games. The fourteen-year-old Vanessa was now happily part of her mother's household, but her father, Roger Vadim, had deliberately taken a house nearby in Santa Monica so she could see him as often as she wished. Vanessa used to tease Jane with such snideties as, "Dad's cooking is better than yours," a premise that was more or less academic since both Jane and Vadim had servants, who presumably did most of the cooking.

Vanessa was entering puberty at the time, and Jane, unlike she had in earlier years, was taking her responsibilities as a mother very seriously. She said, in an interview in the *Los Angeles Times*:

> Remembering how I felt when my own mother died about the time I was Vanessa's age, and the lack of communication between us before that, I try very hard with Vanessa. She's so much like me. She's volatile and emotional, very dramatic, a person who, I think, because of certain feelings of insecurity about herself, goes too far, tries to command certain kinds of attention. . . . In a way, maybe, I'm a better pal than a mother. I'm real good to talk to about sex

and drugs and all that kind of stuff. And I do talk to her about it. She listens so hard. . . . I think Vanessa's going to be okay. Troy I don't worry about.

So those were the good years—Jane's hiatus from the frenzy of moviemaking. In 1983, she turned out another book (with Mignon McCarthy), *Women Coming of Age,* about how to cope with the problems of advancing into middle life. It was published in 1984 and became another best-seller, despite protestations about the originality of the book's ideas by others who had written on the same subject—notably Barbara Seaman, a guru in this field.

There was a lot of flack but no lawsuits, and, as with all of Jane's writings, *Women Coming of Age* went on to become a recording, an audio cassette, and a video tape.

So involved was Jane in these matters that in 1984, *Fortune* featured a full-length article about her, as one of the foremost businesswomen in the United States. The article was titled, "The Business Education of Jane Fonda." More intriguing was the subtitle: "Jane Fonda, who has spent the last decade proving that you don't have to like capitalists to be a successful one."

That February issue of *Fortune* sold out in the Los Angeles area. Film-industry people who had been wondering about Jane's absence from the movie scene for nearly three years, now knew at least one of the reasons why. A frequently asked question around town was With all these millions pouring in from other sources, would Jane Fonda ever make a picture again?

As usual, Jane, the mistress of the unexpected, confounded the show-business sages. She did make a picture again—in that same year, 1984—but it was for *television.* It was her first and only effort as a producer and star in that medium, and she hit the jackpot: the Emmy.

34

To my mind, at least, Jane Fonda's three-hour movie *The Dollmaker,* for the ABC television network, is the best work she has done.

There are many poignant aspects to her making of the film. For one thing, it reinforces my belief that even in death, her father continued to have a strong influence on her. Was she still trying to win his unqualified love? Was she still trying to emulate him? Remember that whenever she discussed her father's career in public, she almost always referred to his masterpiece as *The Grapes of Wrath.* There is much evidence—even from Roger Vadim—that she was searching for her own *Grapes of Wrath* for some years. *They Shoot Horses, Don't They?* came close, but it was not her own.

In 1971, when Jane was still heavily involved in the protest movements and was yet to be reviled as Hanoi Jane, she came across Harriette Arnow's novel *The Dollmaker.* She read and reread the book voraciously, and it was always in her duffle bag as she criss-crossed the country for her campus and GI Coffee House lectures. It became a perfect example of how, when Jane senses a potential movie project for herself, she never lets go until she sees it translated onto the screen. In this case, she didn't let go for an incredible thirteen years.

What attracted Jane to the novel was its principal character, Gertie Nevels, a woman of enormous courage, the mother of five children, who was uprooted from her home in rural Appalachia and forced to follow her husband to his World War II assembly-line job in Detroit. Jane said in an interview in the *Los Angeles Times*:

> She was so much like Tom Joad, the character my father played in *The Grapes of Wrath.* I loved Gertie's bravery and resourcefulness in the face of bone and soul-crushing experiences in Detroit, including the horrible death of a child under the wheels of a train. But here, too, was a woman who began to recognize that her talent for carving dolls and figures out of wood is a genuine artistic gift, and she begins to believe in her own abilities. I loved Gertie's humility and her capacity for mothering. It's very rare to find a project that shows a woman doing the things that women do—raising children, nurturing, serving as the backbone of the family—without condescension or false feminization.

Intrigued by the novel, she went out of her way to meet its author, Harriette Arnow, in 1974. That was when Jane was still in deep financial trouble. She had just finished *Introduction to the Enemy* in Vietnam, which made no money, and she was yet to go to Russia for her small part in *The Blue Bird.* Her first comeback picture, *Fun with Dick and Jane,* was still more than two years off. She had just finished the painful year she had devoted to kicking her bulimia habit.

Concerning her meeting with novelist Arnow, Jane said:

> I was on an antiwar junket in Michigan, and Harriette Arnow lives in Ann Arbor. While we were doing a rally there, at the University of Michigan, I called Harriette and asked if I could meet her and talk with her about *The Dollmaker.* We met, and the more we talked, the more I knew I wanted to option the book as a movie property. I couldn't do it at the time, but I acquired the rights as soon as some money came in to my company, IPC Films.

There is no better example of Jane's persistence when she feels avidly about a subject. "The Dollmaker" project languished for another ten years before she finally got it off the ground. At first, she thought of it only as a big-screen feature and hired a top-flight screenwriter, Millard Lampell, to condense the sprawling six-hundred-page novel into a two-hour movie. Lampell couldn't do it to her satisfaction, nor could other writers she subsequently assigned to the task.

In the meantime, Jane's career was blossoming with *Julia* and *Coming Home.* Finally, her partner, Bruce Gilbert, suggested tentatively that they should consider television, where long-form movies and multi-part miniseries were just beginning to get around the time constraints of theatrical films. At first, Jane vigorously resisted the idea:

> I guess I had had a somewhat elitist disdain for television for many years. And, after all, Joe Losey's *A Doll's House* had bombed when he couldn't get a movie release and it had appeared on TV a few years before. But then, in 1977, I watched "Roots" on television. It fascinated me night after night, and all my aversion to the medium disappeared. You could go through "Roots" and find a lot of parts that were

compromised artistically, but who cares? The impact that it had was extraordinary. It reached incredible masses of people.

So Jane and Gilbert decided to produce *The Dollmaker* for television. They signed up a distinguished TV director, Daniel Petrie (who had done such fine television movies as *Eleanor and Franklin* and *Sybil*), and they pulled a typically astute Jane Fonda stunt. She says, "The very next day after I had won my second Oscar for *Coming Home,* Bruce and I met with top executives at ABC. [She chuckles.] What were they going to say? I had just won my Academy Award, I wanted to do my first TV movie, and I had the great Dan Petrie in tow. They said yes."

Jane had her commitment from the network in April 1979, but she continued to be a long way from actual production. The script problems remained. Bruce Gilbert said at the time, "It's a very dense novel. It has a multitude of subplots and scores of characters. We could not seem to arrive at a satisfactory script that both pared down the book and still retained the spirit and essence of the story."

Another two years went by. Then, in 1981, producer Jane came up with another of her unexpected solutions to a problem. She then was making *Rollover,* her not-so-successful film about high international finance. In the cast, as an elderly banker, was the fine actor Hume Cronyn, then seventy years old. While he was acting in the movie, Cronyn simultaneously was at work writing his first play, with a collaborator, novelist Susan Cooper. The play, *Foxfire,* was about an elderly couple living in Appalachia.

Jane learned about the setting of the still unfinished Cronyn-Cooper play, which was similar to the background of the characters in *The Dollmaker,* and she asked Cronyn and Ms. Cooper to read the Harriette Arnow novel. They both fell in love with the heroine, Gertie Nevels, and enthused to such an extent (Ms. Cooper saying, "I strongly connected with the inner strength of this woman who has been subjugated by her husband but comes into her own in the face of tremendous adversity") that Jane took a tremendous gamble and asked them to take a crack at the script, which until then had seemed insoluble. It was a tremendous gamble because neither Cronyn nor Cooper had ever before written a teleplay.

Cronyn was terrified, saying, "Adapting six hundred pages of novel scared the hell out of me." Cooper was more sanguine. They went to work and, wonder of wonders, these two neophytes at TV writing came up with a suitable script for a film on which some of the most-accomplished best-known screenwriters had failed. It was one of Jane's most astute guesses as a producer. She even felt that Cronyn and Cooper had *improved* on the Arnow novel. They gave their teleplay a happy ending. The novel ends with Gertie staying in Detroit, resigned to a bleak future; but in the film, she manages to load the whole family in a truck and heads back to life on her own long-wanted farm in Kentucky.

Jane finally had a shooting script, in her hiatus period from filmmaking after her father's death. While the movie industry was wondering if she'd ever make a picture again, she was—unknown to them—assiduously preparing for *The Dollmaker,* along with conducting her burgeoning business enterprises.

As was her custom, she called on all of her known resources to prepare herself to act the role of Gertie Nevels. In this case, her best-known resource was Dolly Parton, whom she had befriended during *Nine to Five,* and who knows more than anyone about the patterns and speech of rural Southern women. Dolly recommended two families with whom Jane lived for days at a time. In the *Los Angeles Times* interview, Jane went on to say:

> I especially learned a lot from Lucy and Waco Johnson, a couple in their seventies living in the Ozarks. Lucy is an artist. She also makes dolls, in addition to working her farm. I'm in pretty good shape, but I spent one day doing what seventy-four-year-old Lucy

does every day—chopping wood, milking cows, churning butter—and at the end of the day, I couldn't move. . . . I also spent a good deal of time working with a great dialogue coach, Bob Easton. He knows every nuance of accents. He knows the subtle differences between Kentucky and Tennessee speech patterns. He taught me all the little rules and marked my script phonetically. From the time I got on the plane to go to the location, I spoke only in dialect, never in the way I talk naturally.

The locations were in the Smoky Mountains of Tennessee, and at an abandoned steel mill in Chicago, doubling for the factory and housing development in Detroit. Accustomed to the more leisurely pace of theatrical filmmaking, Jane was exhausted by the accelerated television shooting schedules, but director Petrie was kindly and patient with her. Petrie said, "She's such a superb actress that she doesn't need too much prodding from a director. Besides," he said, shrugging, "she also was my boss."

The story proceeded smoothly. It begins in rural Kentucky, where Gertie is living in abject poverty, rearing her five children, one of whom nearly dies of diphtheria in the opening scene. Gertie wants to stay in her mountain hamlet, hoping someday to own a farm, but her husband goes off to Detroit, where the wartime factory wages seem more practical for their survival. The husband later orders Gertie to follow with the children, and they settle in a squalid Detroit housing project. That's where most of the picture takes place, as Gertie interplays with an eclectic collection of neighbors, survives tragedy and near tragedy, watches her husband lose his job to a strike and become a fugitive from the police. In the meantime, she is perfecting her down-home skill at carving magnificent figures out of wood. She sells them, more and more frequently, to local art-collecting sources, takes over the destiny of the family, and eventually—in the Cronyn-Cooper version of the ending—earns enough money to take the entire family back to what should be a better life in their native village in Kentucky.

As usual in Fonda-produced pictures, the casting was startlingly good. The husband was played by Levon Helm, whom Jane had spotted as the father in *Coal Miner's Daughter*. Geraldine Page played Gertie's mother with her usual skill, and Studs Terkel, the writer, had a cameo part as a Detroit cab driver. Next to Jane herself, the collection of youngsters playing her children were the best thing in the film. They were all recruited in local talent searches in Tennessee.

In all, Jane was totally overwhelmed by this experience with *The Dollmaker*. She said, "The part of Gertie Nevels is as far from what *I* am as anything I'll ever play." Which is why *I* consider this her greatest performance. In almost everything else she's done, a little of Jane Fonda always shows through. Not here. With her baggy clothes, her skillfully made-up coarse-looking face, her unfailing Kentucky speech patterns, her literally *becoming* Gertie Nevels, it is almost impossible to believe that this is Jane Fonda of Brentwood, Vassar, and Paris.

So involved was she with the character of Gertie Nevels, that director Dan Petrie reports a remarkable occurrence. He says, "Jane was sitting behind me when I finished the last shot of the picture. She wasn't in that particular scene, but she couldn't bring herself to leave the set. When I said, 'That's the end of our work. It's a wrap,' Jane reached out and put her arms around me. She began to sob. She held me and sobbed for more than ten minutes.

"Finally she said, 'Forgive me for carrying on like this. But the end of the picture means that Gertie Nevels is gone and I'll never see her again, and I guess I'm mourning for her.'"

The critics did not mourn. They hailed *The Dollmaker* as one of the finest productions in the history of the TV long-form. In *The New York Times,* John J. O'Connor wrote: "This is an unabashed celebration of Gertie Nevels, her simple dignity and her determination. . . . Jane Fonda has shrewdly chosen a vehicle for the kind of bravura performance out of which awards are plucked."

It was a foregone conclusion that she would win the Best Actress Emmy that year—which, of course, she did.

35

The Dollmaker helped make 1984 a very good year for Jane—but there were some setbacks.

Among the good things: Hayden ran for reelection, and this time his victory total climbed to more than 62,000 votes, nearly 12,000 more than his Republican opponent, D. M. Shell. Tom was solidly ensconced in the state legislature now and soon was to become chairman of the assembly's important labor committee.

Among the setbacks: Jane was forced to close one of her three workout studios, the one in San Francisco. She no longer was used to failure, so it was a traumatic experience. It also was an embarrassing experience, because prior to the closing, three women instructors sued Jane for sex discrimination and violations of California labor law.

How could this happen to Jane Fonda, one of the world's most outspoken advocates of women's rights? It was almost like charging the Pope with discrimination against Catholics. Actually the suit against Jane was a minor matter that would have attracted no notice had it *not* involved Jane. The three female plaintiffs charged that they had been paid $6 an hour, while some men were paid $7. Jane, who had nothing to do with the actual operations of the San Francisco studio, replied that "the men were supervisors, and as such, were paid $1 an hour more. The discrimination in pay was legitimate and not discriminatory." She added, "Besides, all three of my *managers* are women." Nevertheless, the suit was settled by an after-the-fact payment to the women to compensate them for the $1 an hour wage differential.

But this was only a minor factor in the scuttling of the San Francisco operation. Jane's original idea was to franchise Jane Fonda Workout studios all over the United States—based on the fabulously successful Beverly Hills original. But with her first experience in San Francisco, the studio was poorly located and the building so poorly constructed that her aerobic-dancing programs caused it to vibrate up and down. This forced her to switch to weight-lifting exercises, which women didn't particularly like. So Jane, a pragmatist, just folded up in the City by the Bay.

She told Julia Vitullo-Martin of *Fortune*: "I learned a few lessons. I said, 'Whoa! If all these things could go wrong in a location that's just one hour away by plane, what could happen to me elsewhere?' The San Francisco experience taught me that I can't ride herd on all these things personally. I do not—and could not—run the daily operations of the business."

That was the end of Jane's ambitions to found a nationwide franchising operation. She soon closed down the Encino studio as well, which left only the Beverly Hills original, still in existence. This major move, however, made hardly a dent in the vast profitability of Workout, Inc. The money kept pouring in from the tapes, books, and records. Three new best-seller videotapes were issued in 1984 and 1985 alone, and the multimillionaire status of Jane Fonda, Businesswoman, continued to be confirmed.

The status of Jane Fonda, Mother and Wife, also continued to be confirmed. Twelve years into her marriage with Hayden everything seemed to be proceeding idyllically for a couple with such disparate careers. Their two children were growing up with none of the problems of drugs and alienation that affected so many other movie-industry kids in the mid-1980s. Both Vanessa and Troy were doing extremely well in school. Just as Jane had always wanted to emulate Hank, Vanessa wanted to emulate Jane. She wanted to go to Vassar, like her mother. Both Jane and Hayden talked her into making a try for one of the Ivy League universities in the East, once off-limits to women but now extremely accessible to the best and the brightest of them. Vanessa applied to Brown University, then rated by *Time* magazine as the most difficult to get into in the United States. Vanessa was accepted. A tearful Jane said, "That was just like seeing one of my family getting another Oscar."

But what about Jane's own pursuit of another Oscar, which had slowed down so dramatically over the preceding four years (her Emmy for *The Dollmaker* aside)?

Privately, she was hewing to her own personal agenda, which no one in the industry knew about. Through Hayden, she had met the distinguished Mexican writer Carlos Fuentes, and knew that he was writing a novel about the troubled Mexico-U.S. relations during the days of Pancho Villa and the Mexican Revolution of 1910. Fuentes was fascinated by the story of Ambrose Bierce, a great American author and journalist, somewhat eccentric in his ways, who disappeared without a trace into Northern Mexico in 1913 and was never seen again.

When Jane Fonda had first met Fuentes in 1981, he was fantasizing a story for a novel to be called *Old Gringo,* in which Bierce, living secretly in Mexico, gets tangled up in Pancho Villa's revolutionary operations, and also with an American schoolteacher in Mexico, Harriet Winslow. Jane was intrigued with the entire project and kept conferring with Fuentes about it. Eventually, she also put some money into it. Fuentes, for his part, was intrigued with Jane and kept building up the character of Harriet Winslow in his novel, with an eye toward Jane playing the role in a future movie based on the book. It was an interesting relationship—not unlike her involvement in the development of the play, *On Golden Pond,* and her after-publication interest in *The Dollmaker.* Again, her actual IPC movie production was still many years down the road, but she was carefully and sagaciously watching and waiting.

Publicly, it was announced in late 1984 that Jane was returning to the big screen to star in the Columbia Pictures movie *Agnes of God.* There were two reasons why she ended her long absence before the movie cameras since the death of her father. First of all, she would work for the first time with Anne Bancroft, whose brilliance as an actress she had discussed many times with Jack Lemmon while they were doing *The China Syndrome.* Second, *Agnes of God* had been a hit play in New York in 1982, "and the kind of philosophical exercise my dad would have delighted in."

Actually, its philosophical bent made it a very difficult project to transfer to the screen. It was about the discovery that a young nun had given birth to an infant at the isolated convent where she was stationed, and then had strangled the newborn infant. It was a mystery story, in a way, surfeited with a good deal of Catholic theology. How did young Sister Agnes get pregnant in her superprotective environment, and why did she strangle the baby? Jane's role was that of a court-appointed psychiatrist, Dr. Martha Livingston, whose job it was to find out if the young woman was fit to stand trial—putting the doctor in head-to-head conflict with the Mother Superior, Anne Bancroft.

Since this was not an IPC film, Jane did not have to face any of the multiple duties of the producer, and thus had plenty of time to prepare solely for her acting chores. Aside from delving into the intricacies of Catholic dogma, it was a fairly easy job for Jane because basically it was an extension of the many roles she had played before—the intelligent, modern woman investigator—except that this time, it was not a news reporter asking the questions, but a psychiatrist.

The filming took place, with Norman Jewison as the director, on locations in Quebec and Ontario. The country settings were lovely, and Jane enjoyed them, "even though I was painfully reminded of the fact that I had been journeying from Ontario when I was arrested by U.S. Customs in that dreadful experience in Cleveland."

Jane's verbal knock-down-drag-out scenes with Ms. Bancroft were monumental (they had both come from the Actors Studio in New York), and she interfaced effectively with young Meg Tilly, playing the accused neophyte nun. A visitor to this location noticed some subtle changes in Jane's demeanor. She no longer was standoffish and self-involved—as she frequently had been in the past—and went out of her way to be friendly with the other members of the cast and the crew. She explained her new attitude to Steve Jaffe, possibly not realizing that her previous attitude had been considered to be otherwise: "It's very important to me that everyone on the set *like* me. I have to be *popular.* I can't do anything, you know, if I'm scared shitless. So I have to feel love coming from everyone, *everyone,* the sound guys and the grips and the electricians. Even when I'm working in one of my own productions, my hands-on role as a producer stops the minute the camera starts rolling."

This warmness came through on the screen, especially in the great scenes at the end of the film, when the Mother Superior has revealed her own secular background to Jane's psychiatrist character, and the two women have reached some sort of understanding of one another. These scenes between Oscar-winners Fonda and Bancroft are pure dynamite.

Overall, however, there was a basic problem with Jane's role—probably not her fault but the fault of the writing. Her relentlessly probing, chain-smoking Dr. Livingston became annoying and tiresome. As the review in *Variety* pointed out,

"About eighty percent of Fonda's dialogue must consist of questions. Half-hearted attempts are made to flesh out the character with a senile mother and a barren personal life, but she remains a brittle cliché of a modern professional woman." The picture did well when it was released in August 1985, but it was not one of Jane's A+ efforts.

Neither was her next film, *The Morning After,* which she made a few months later. Again, Jane was captivated by a theme that interested her greatly. In this case it was alcoholism (possibly a reminder of the similarities to her own former bulimic affliction). The picture also was reminiscent of her first Oscar-winner, *Klute.*

Here, Jane is a washed-up actress who awakens from a drunken blackout to find a strange man dead in bed next to her, with a dagger in his heart. In fleeing from this trauma, Alex, the actress, encounters an ex-cop, Turner (played by Jeff Bridges), who attaches himself to her and helps her solve the mystery of how this happened and why she she was set up. There are many improbable twists and turns to this plot, but there are sparkling scenes between Jane and Bridges, whose characters fall in love despite an obvious age difference. Interesting, but not developed in the script, is the fact that Turner, too, is a recovering alcoholic. With all its shortcomings, *The Morning After* was a gripping thriller and Jane was good enough in it to receive another Oscar nomination.

Although this was not an IPC film (it was a Twentieth Century–Fox/Lorimar/American Filmworks production), Jane's long-time IPC partner, Bruce Gilbert, was the movie's producer. It was the last time they were to work together. Both Jane and Gilbert stolidly refuse to discuss the reasons for the breakup after twelve years. Gilbert simply says, "I wanted to pursue other interests." Jane says nothing.

Writer Ron Rosenbaum, who got fairly close to Jane, postulated his own theory of the break-up in a *Vanity Fair* article. He recalled that her association with Gilbert dated back to Jane's Red Family/Blue Fairyland days in Berkeley in her protest period, and he opined that what had become known as "the Bruce Gilbert Formula" for Jane Fonda films was subordinating Jane's acting choices in favor of getting a message across. Accordingly, a stereotypical Jane Fonda role had emerged—"the good-hearted but unsophisticated woman who gets exposed to injustice, gets wised up, and finds the courage to stand up for what she's come to believe."

I can't wholly agree with that theory—certainly not with *The Dollmaker* or even with *Agnes of God*—but Jane may have been stung by criticism that her roles had taken on a certain sameness, in the matter of the sometimes tiresome, chain-smoking investigative reporter/psychiatrist, for example. She was Gilbert's senior partner, however, and could have changed the formula any time she chose. So her shedding of Gilbert may simply have been a continuation of her life-long pattern of periodically wanting a change in her associations.

And change she did. Her next partner became a woman, Lois Bonfiglio, a sharp, witty New York producer with quite a reputation, over the years, for developing varied and viable movie and TV properties. Like Jane, Lois is a heavy smoker and dedicated exerciser. They work out together in a room across the hall from Jane's Santa Monica office. Strangely, it is equipped only with a treadmill and a stationary bicycle.

Perhaps the most significant change of all is that their company no longer is called IPC, which originally stood for Indochina Peace Campaign. In 1986, it became, simply, Fonda Films.

36

Fonda Films didn't make a picture for another two years, but everything was proceeding smoothly in Jane's life. So much so that trouble was brewing for her, but she didn't know it.

Tom Hayden ran a third and fourth time for his seat in the state assembly, swelling his margins of victory to the point where he won by landslide proportions of 60 percent of the vote in 1986 and 1988.

Jane Fonda's Workout, Inc., put out three new videotapes, one of which, *Start Up with Jane Fonda,* had an initial order of 781,659 units. According to Lorimar Home Video, her distributor, this pushed the total sales of Jane Fonda Workout tapes to well over 4 million. At Jane's usual royalty of about $21 per tape (less on *Start Up,* a cheaper item), that would put her total video income at more than $70 million.

It staggers the mind. No other video personality or movie has even come close to matching those figures.

In Jane's film career, her company fully acquired Carlos Fuentes's *Old Gringo* novel, and Luis Puenzo and Aida Bortnik were signed to write the screenplay. Sensing big bucks from this epic, Columbia Pictures negotiated a multi-picture deal with Fonda Films, making Jane's company one of the most powerful production entities at the studio. Shortly thereafter, M-G-M signed Jane, as an actress (not her company), to work in a film for them after she finished production on *Old Gringo.* The M-G-M picture then was called *Union Street.* It was being written by Oscar nominees (for *Hud*) Irving Ravetch and Harriet Frank, Jr. The studio was planning to shoot the film in a New England factory town, probably Waterbury, Connecticut.

It was now seventeen years after the "Hanoi Jane" hysteria, and the United States generally had forgotten all about the radical activities of Jane and Tom Hayden in the 1960s and early 1970s. Most people knew Jane only as a top-flight movie star and phenomenally successful exercise czarina. Without exception, almost every poll to name the most admired women in the United States had Jane no less than number four, and sometimes number one.

Her visible political activities had diminished to the point where only twice, in the late 1980s, did they attract headlines in the press. The first was her long and arduous campaign to free Soviet dissident Ida Nudel (described in detail earlier), which involved Jane's courageous flight into pre-Gorbachev Russia.

Her second burst of political activism came about because of her intense interest in environmental issues. In 1986, the voters of California were asked to vote on Proposition 65, which was meant to force the governor to list and eliminate all chemicals causing toxic wastes to contaminate the state. Assemblyman Tom Hayden and his Campaign California (the new name for his Campaign for Economic Democracy) was one of the prime movers in getting the initiative on the ballot.

According to Tom Epstein, campaign manager for the "Yes on 65" campaign, Jane Fonda was one of the key movers in getting the California electorate to vote for it. Epstein says: "We were up against formidable opposition from the oil companies, the chemical companies and agribusiness, which had poured millions of dollars into TV commercials to defeat Proposition 65. Our only chance against all that money was to generate a lot of hoopla through entertainment-industry celebrities who we knew were on our side. Jane and Tom Hayden already had assembled a lot of the younger stars—Whoopi Goldberg, Rob Lowe, Michael J. Fox, and many others—into an organization called Network. Network got into the thick of the fight, and then Jane—getting on the phone and making endless speeches as she had done in her antiwar days—brought in a lot of other people. We ended up with stars like Gregory Peck, Donna Mills, Chevy Chase, Morgan Fairchild, Robin Williams, and Ed Begley, Jr. I'd have to say that Jane was the glue that held the whole thing together."

Perhaps the key factor in the battle for "Yes on 65—Get Tough on Toxics!" as the campaign was called, was a three-day caravan, by bus, to important areas of the state, in which nearly forty celebrities rode the bus. Epstein says: "It was Jane who got up in the first meeting to discuss the caravan, made an impassioned plea to make our drinking water safe, and said, '*I'm* going to be there on the bus. How about the rest of you?' Following her lead, nearly everyone signed up. I doubt if many of them had been on a bus of any kind in years."

The bus caravan assembled at the Lorimar Studio and took off for speeches and fund-raisers in nine cities. It also was a voter-registration campaign. Jane went from seat to seat in the bus, encouraging the others. She made several of the speeches, personally signed up many new voters, and was the key figure in all the press conferences, along with Ed Begley, Jr., and Whoopi Goldberg. Most interesting of all was Jane's effect on the young actors and actresses who became known as "the Brat Pack" in California politics. They adored her and built up a legend about her past acts of courage, sitting at her feet as she detailed them. Many of the young women (Justine Bateman, for one) expressed ambitions of "someday becoming another Jane Fonda."

Concerning the bus caravan, Tom Epstein says: "In those three days, Jane helped us turn the whole thing around. We had been slipping badly in the polls with all that oil money against us, but after the caravan, we bounced right up again. To help us nail it down, Jane and Rob Lowe went up to the Bay Area and made appearances in a section of the state where we needed help. It all paid off. On election day, we won by a whopping 63 percent to 37 percent. At our victory party in Santa Monica, Jane introduced all the celebrities who had helped. . . . A few months later, when Governor Deukmejian was dragging his feet on implementing Proposition 65, Jane led another caravan of stars to Sacramento. It was her idea that they all wear sweatshirts printed with the telephone number of the governor's office, and the words 'Read Our Chest.' Deukmejian wouldn't see Jane and her group, but I guess a lot of people read their chests and began phoning the governor. He began to move slightly in naming a few more toxic chemicals to the list required by Proposition 65. Jane sure is persistent. It's no accident that everything she touches turns to gold."

So Jane was on the activist trail in public again, but for a popular cause—a good-government initiative. Only twice did Epstein see I Hate Fonda signs, alluding back to the Vietnam war. Demonstrations against Hayden also had almost totally disappeared. It was difficult to hold up signs like MURDERER and TRAITOR against an establishment-looking man in a three-piece suit, who was continually introducing bills in the legislature to help war veterans financially and to try to compensate them for the lingering effects on them and their children of Agent Orange.

What was to come a few months later, therefore, was something of a surprise. There were no signs of impending trouble when Jane went off to Mexico to begin production of *Old Gringo.* The director was Luis Puenzo, one of the film's co-writers, and the locations were to be in several difficult areas, such as the rugged mountains of Durango. The two principal characters in the screenplay, other than Jane's schoolteacher, Harriet Winslow, were a young general in Pancho Villa's revolutionary army, and Ambrose Bierce, the elderly American writer who, historically, had disappeared without a trace in Northern Mexico. Jimmy Smits (of the TV series "L.A. Law") was cast as the young Mexican general, and Burt Lancaster was signed to play Ambrose Bierce. The story revolves around Harriet Winslow, who is torn in her emotions between the two men.

There was an immediate problem, even before the $25 million production got under way. Burt Lancaster was seventy-five years old and had a history of heart problems. Columbia Pictures, which is the financier and distributor of Fonda Films, could not get insurance for Lancaster, who was to receive $1.5 million for playing the Ambrose Bierce role. The insurers thought he would be at risk working at high altitudes. Columbia dropped Lancaster from the cast and replaced him with seventy-two-year-old Gregory Peck. Lancaster sued. Jane, who is friendly with both Lancaster and Peck, stayed out of the legal squabble.

She refers to *Old Gringo* as "the biggest film I've ever done and one of the most difficult. There are no throwaway scenes. I went out on a limb with this one. It's very intense, very theatrical, and I play a virgin. It's been a long time since I knew what goes through the head of a virgin." She felt badly about Lancaster, but said, "I have an idea for another film I'll do with him." Peck was a delight for her to work with. They had appeared together on many rostrums for Democratic Party causes. An easygoing man, Peck understood her acting fanaticism completely. After she forced him to rehearse a kissing scene endlessly, deciding where heads and noses should go, writer Ron Rosenbaum asked him how it was working with someone exhibiting this kind of fanaticism. Peck replied, "Well, it's a benevolent fanaticism."

Jane was out of touch with the world during much of her

stay in Mexico (some of it was spent at the remote archaeologically important city of Zacatecas). By then, Hayden's press secretary, Steve Rivers, had come to work with her at Fonda Films. Rivers visited her one weekend and brought the disturbing news that M-G-M had announced Waterbury, Connecticut, as one of the locations for her next film, still called *Union Street,* and that some war veterans there were kicking up a fuss. The I'm Not Fonda Hanoi Jane posters and bumper stickers were beginning to appear.

Still engrossed in both her acting and producing chores (with Lois Bonfiglio) on *Old Gringo,* Jane waited for the flap to recede, as it pretty much had done over the preceding decade. The flap did not recede. By the time she got home from Mexico, it was worse. Although he still says the Connecticut veterans' outcry was never as serious or as widespread as the press made it out to be, Rivers decided to call a council of war with Hayden and Jane.

According to Rivers, they discussed the pros and cons of making a public apology for some of her actions in North Vietnam. She had done it before, as a side issue in many interviews—one as early as 1981, when she told the *Ladies' Home Journal*: "I totally empathize with the hostility of the men who fought the war, and their families. Their sacrifice was noble, even though the war was wrong. What I did was drastic and undiplomatic, but I was acting in the sincere belief that it was necessary for the country."

Having decided that Jane should make some sort of answer to the furor being stirred up in Waterbury and environs, the question now was: Should she do it piecemeal, with many interviews requested by the local press and TV stations in Connecticut, or should she do a single national TV news interview?

Rivers says they considered two minutes with Tom Brokaw on the "NBC Nightly News," but then decided it was better to go with fifteen minutes, on ABC's "20/20," with "the Mother Confessor of us all, Barbara Walters."

37

Steve Rivers says the decision to confess to Barbara Walters was unanimous, but Jane told Ron Rosenbaum for his *Vanity Fair* article that she and Hayden were "not of one mind on the question of the apology." She herself had some doubts: "What I had done in Hanoi was not all negative. After all, a week after I spoke about the bombing of the dikes, the bombing stopped. And maybe I even helped shorten the war. But over-riding all that was the fact that I owed something to the real guys out there, and their wives and their parents. They're the ones I'd been trying to help and they'd been led to believe that I was anti-GI. I was only anti what our Government had put them through."

So the deal was arranged with Barbara Walters. She knew Jane, but Walters's reputation is that she is toughest with people she knows, to avoid accusations of bias. That's why

Rivers had suggested her. The interview was to be taped at Jane's house in Santa Monica. ABC chose to air it the Friday night before filming commenced in Waterbury in June 1988.

The taping itself was done on May 31. Jane says: "I didn't sleep the night before. I was so tired. I'm afraid I was almost numb. One always wishes the inspiration will come, the words that will really say it. But they didn't."

The taping was done in Jane's living room with its traditional overstuffed furniture, striking antiques, and Oriental rugs. She wore a tailored shirt, pastel print skirt, and was not heavily made up. Walters wore a shortish blue dress and *was* heavily made up. Jane looked uptight and nervous and hesitated before answering nearly every question.

Some of the highlights of that memorable interview:

WALTERS: The famous picture of the anti-aircraft gun. *(After showing tape of Jane climbing into the gunner's mount near Hanoi.)*

FONDA: It was a thoughtless and careless thing to have done. Being in the communications business, and knowing the power of images, it was thoughtless and cruel. I take full responsibility for having gotten on the gun . . . I'm a strong woman. I'm naïve and I make mistakes, but I was a big girl and I should have said no.

WALTERS: In your radio talks in Hanoi, you told soldiers to disobey their officers' orders and referred to them as war criminals.

FONDA: I only recall saying the weapons were illegal and had been outlawed by the rules of warfare. I wanted to say to them, "Let's think about what we're doing." And when I said we, I meant all of us.

WALTERS: And the prisoners of war who heard your broadcasts while they were in prison in North Vietnam?

FONDA: I appreciate their point of view. But those of us who went to Hanoi and got documentary information that wasn't getting out, helped end the war. The POWs got out sooner. The killing stopped. So I feel we played a part in bringing them home . . . They, the POWs suffered enough. They didn't need to hear from me *(after a tape showing she said some of them lied about being tortured)*. I was angry that Nixon was using them to make the war look noble, trying to rewrite history. I shouldn't have done it.

WALTERS *(after showing a 1971 tape in which Fonda says she's a revolutionary woman)*: Are you still a revolutionary woman?

FONDA: I'm not a revolutionary woman today. In 1971, it was preposterous when I said that. I didn't know what a "revolutionary woman" meant . . . I didn't want to be thought of as some starlet. I used words and rhetoric I didn't understand. I'm not proud of it.

And then came the key statements in Jane's apologia:

JANE: I'm proud of most of what I did, and I'm very sorry for *some* of what I did . . . I'd like to say something not just to the veterans in Waterbury but to the men in Vietnam who I hurt, or whose pain I caused to deepen because of the things I said or did. I feel I owe them an apology. My intentions were never to hurt them or make their situation worse. It was the contrary. My intention was to help end the killing and the war. But there were times when I was thoughtless and careless about it, and I'm very sorry that I hurt them, and I want to apologize to them and their families.

Repetitious yes, but effective. The Walters broadcast helped quell the growing resentments against Jane, if, indeed, they actually had been growing, sixteen years after the fact. The hate-Jane hard core was still there and may *always* be there, but more than two-thirds of the Waterbury populace favored Jane in polls; and when production began, fans outnumbered protesters by about one hundred to one. Brent Layman of the Associated Press in Hartford, Connecticut, was the reporter whose story initially kicked off the flap. He later had to express regret that he had misread the facts when the anti-Jane protests first began in Connecticut.

Whatever quelling still had to be done after the Barbara Walters interview was accomplished by Steve Rivers—and by Jane herself. Her courageous face-to-face meeting with twenty-six hostile veterans at St. Michael's Episcopal Church in Naugatuck came just the day after the Walters show was aired. It lasted for more than four hours and was the real turning point. It is what sticks mostly in Jane's memory: "They all were guys with anti-Fonda buttons and bumper stickers, and for the first two-and-a-half hours, it was very tense emotional stuff. I told them my story—why I was antiwar and why I had gone to Vietnam. I listened to their gripes about what I had done. Gradually, we got to understand each other's point of view, and the hostility disappeared. Then came an incident which I'll never forget as long as I live."

The incident was this: After things had quieted down, she was talking about what she and Hayden had been doing for veterans' causes, notably compensation and treatment for GI victims of Agent Orange and their families. Suddenly, one of the veterans pulled a playing card out of his pocket. It was the ace of spades. He said, "This is what we'd leave on the bodies of the Vietcong." He implied that the card in his pocket had been meant to be placed on Jane's body. He said, "I don't need this anymore."

"And he tore it up," says Jane.

38

A few months after *Stanley and Iris* had completed filming in Toronto (entirely without incident), Steve Rivers made an announcement, on February 15, 1989, which shocked the show-business world and the non-show-business world alike. Rivers said, simply, "Jane Fonda and her husband, Assemblyman Tom Hayden, have decided to separate on a trial basis. Tom and Jane consider this separation a private matter and will have no public comment or statement on it." Rivers himself would not comment on it further.

The story made headlines all over the world. It was on page one of the staid *Los Angeles Times.*

It stunned close friends of both Hayden and Fonda, particularly since many of them had just taken down the Hayden-Fonda Christmas card from their mantles. The card, a zany one, said, "Enjoy the holidays and have a kinder, gentler New Year," and there was a photograph of Jane, Tom, Troy, Vanessa, and Hank Fonda's widow, Shirlee, in a loving pose over a food-cluttered table at Zucky's, a Jewish delicatessen in Santa Monica, near their home. There was no hint of estrangement or pending estrangement. The faces all radiated contentment and happiness.

So what happened? No one knew, but there were a lot of opinions. The *Los Angeles Times* quoted a "long-time friend of the couple": "I think it's been leading up to this for a long time. They have been trying to keep it together, but Jane went off to Mexico and Canada to make her pictures, and Tom was left here on his own. He's going through a mid-life crisis over his career, what he's doing and all that."

At the time of the separation, Hayden was leading in the polls naming possible candidates for the newly created statewide elective post of California Insurance Commissioner. He was also being mentioned as a possible candidate for Secretary of State of California, and for a seat in the U.S. Congress. A related factor—particularly galling to him—was the Barbara Howar TV documentary a few months before, in which Ms. Howar made a lengthy and absurd assumption that Jane Fonda wanted to be the next Jacqueline Kennedy, using her vast wealth to propel her husband into a U.S. Senate seat and eventually into the White House. Considering the increasingly conservative bent of U.S. national politics, this would be about as likely as Salman Rushdie ousting the Ayatollah in Iran.

Actually, Hayden was doing pretty well on his own, politically. He no longer was getting money from Jane's enterprises and had built a strong grass-roots organization of small contributors. Campaign California alone had more than 100,000 members.

Nevertheless, some friends say, Hayden had been undergoing a lot of introspection about his life and his career. Much of this was because of the book *Reunion,* which he wrote in 1988. It was a reminiscence about his activist days, mostly in the 1960s, and it may have induced in him a growing sense that his current life was devoid of change.

As for Jane, she too had a growing sense that things were not like they were. Her long absences on movie locations in 1988 were unavoidable, but she missed the fact that Hayden was not with her, as he almost always had been in the past. This, too, was unavoidable, considering his growing responsibilities in the legislature, as the chairman of two important committees. On the other side of the coin, Jane—still in production for *Stanley and Iris*—could not be with Hayden when he led a group of young Hollywood celebrities (the so-called Brat Pack she and Tom had organized in their Network organization) at the Democratic National Convention in Atlanta.

Only a year before, Jane and Tom had joyously led their annual Easter retreat, which brought together the young stars like Ally Sheedy and Rob Lowe with precinct workers and veterans of the antiwar movement. Jane dressed as the Easter Bunny, Hayden conducted religious Easter Sunday services, and the group sang old songs like "Puff the Magic Dragon." In 1989, that was no more. The Easter retreat had to be cancelled because of the separation.

The tabloid press was filled with gleeful speculation after Steve Rivers's startling announcement about the separation. There was one story that Hayden had had an affair with a speechwriter in the Dukakis presidential campaign, that Jane had found out about it, and eventually had kicked him out.

There was a story that Jane had tired of Hayden's heavy drinking habits. There was another story that Jane had tired of financially supporting Hayden's political ambitions. There was still another story that Jane had fallen in love with Rob Lowe, an idol of the country's teenagers. At twenty-five, Lowe, a member of the Brat Pack, is twenty-six years younger than Jane and, according to this report, the alleged affair had angered Hayden.

And so it went in the trash press. As a long-time Hollywood insider, I know how such unsubstantiated rumors get printed in the tabloids. A waiter in a restaurant gets paid if he provides a tip that two people are lunching together—even though the meeting might be an innocent political discussion. Other tipsters might be cleaning women, gardeners, or disgruntled hangers-on hungry for a buck. Under the current interpretation of the libel laws in the courts, it is virtually impossible to slander a public figure, such as Jane or Hayden.

My own investigation turned up nothing to confirm any of the above rumors. My opinion is that Jane and Hayden are undergoing mid-life crises, not unlike those that afflict millions of other couples in their late forties and early fifties, as they reflect on where they have been, where they are, and where they are going. Sometimes, such reevaluations bring the couple together again, sometimes not.

Apparently agreeing with me, the responsible press—such as *The New York Times,* the *Washington Post,* the *Los Angeles Times*—has more or less ignored the rumors spawned by the Hayden-Fonda breakup. This, in itself, is an enormous triumph for Jane. Fifteen years earlier they would not have been nearly as kind to her, had the same thing been happening then.

In fact, coverage in the nation's leading journals has reflected an overwhelming feeling of sadness. In *The New York Times,* Anne Taylor Fleming wrote, almost poetically, from Hollywood:

> In this town, certain things, certain states of being, have, over time, taken on a kind of talismanic quality. When Tom Hayden and Jane Fonda fall out of love and wedlock, people here feel imperiled, saddened. We like to think of our home turf—however glitzy—as somehow solid, survivable; we don't like casualties to wash up on the beach and prove otherwise. So there was no gloating here. Sure, there was the predictable tabloid buzz in the wake of the announcement . . . but mostly people felt bad for them, even people who had never been particularly keen on their politics. We had grown used to them to-

gether, that's all. We had watched, fascinated, as their haranguing passions of the 1960's and early 1970's gave way to bourgeois mainstream success— hers, of course, major and flashy, his, a dogged, conscientious tenure in the California State Assembly. He'd taken to campaigning as a family man and calling himself middle-of-the-road. . . . Along the way, they took genuine pride in each other's success. She gave him glamor and money to run for office; he gave her legitimacy as a political figure and counsel about her career. . . . Their union was one where the whole seemed so much bigger than the sum of its parts, an arresting, often-irritating quest-filled unit that has held our attention for over fifteen years. We're going to miss it.

But, basically, no one knew anything about the breakup. Except, possibly, Steve Rivers, who said to me, "Don't go out on the limb on this divorce thing. They might very well get together again." He was wrong.

39

It is mid-1990.

At fifty-two, Jane is pretty much alone, much as she started as a girl in Brentwood five decades ago—coming full circle, as it were.

She is still in the big Santa Monica house on Alta Avenue. Hayden is in an apartment he has rented in West Los Angeles. Troy is dividing his time between his mother and father. Vanessa has been on a leave of absence from Brown University, working as a production assistant on a film her father, Roger Vadim, is shooting in Africa.

Many things have happened that normally would cause great excitement in Jane—but not now.

She has signed a deal for Fonda Films to co-produce the movie version of *A Bright and Shining Lie,* Neil Sheehan's Pulitzer Prize–winning book about the Vietnam war. Her partners in this film? The Guber-Peters Company, which has won four Oscars for *Rain Man,* including Best Picture. It is another giant step up the movie-executive ladder for Jane. It will be the first time she will produce a film in which she will not act.

Her latest videotape, *Jane Fonda's Complete Workout,* has been released and is another smash hit. Jim Meigs, editor of *Video Review*, has called her "the biggest single success factor for the entire video business."

Jane has watched a "60 Minutes" segment on CBS, in which Morley Safer journeyed to Vietnam and interviewed, sympathetically, former North Vietnamese and Vietcong soldiers who had fought against us in the war. The TV show makes many of the points for which Jane has been labeled a traitor by some. No one calls Morley Safer or CBS traitors. Jane is quietly gratified.

Notwithstanding these successes, the *Los Angeles Times* reports: "Jane has worn a game face in public, 'but is just plowing through her days,' according to someone known to have her confidence."

Jane replies: "It would be dishonest to say that every day is joyous, but it's also dishonest to say I'm just plodding through my days. I'm somewhat on a roller coaster. Actually, I feel pretty good."

Hayden, too, sounds distraught. He says, "I'm thinking hard, sorting out my emotions, and I don't feel the need to resolve anything right now. Things in my personal life cannot be pushed, and I'm reluctant to give up on any of my legislative work."

All this sorting out is for naught. Jane and Hayden are divorced, amicably. Although their vast wealth was presumably divided in accordance with California's community property law, the terms of the settlement have not been publicly announced.

Apart from this, there have been some other bad days for Jane:

Her daughter, Vanessa, has been arrested in New York

City for interfering with police when they busted a boyfriend, Thomas Feegal, on drug charges. Vanessa was eventually sentenced to perform three days of community service.

Jane's son, Troy, was arrested for a boyish prank of vandalism with a can of spray paint in a parking lot. He was released into the custody of his mother.

Her movie *Old Gringo* opened to disappointing reviews and seems destined to become one of the few box-office losers in the history of Fonda Films.

All in all, Jane's life-style has changed noticeably. She is dating several men—among them, broadcast tycoon Ted Turner, who shares many of her liberal political views. Although she eschewed most movie-industry gatherings when she was with Hayden, she now seems to be present at nearly every Hollywood party and public event that comes along. Another throwback to her early days as Henry Fonda's daughter in the film colony?

She seems to have developed a lot of nostalgia for those early days, which, in fact, were not so happy for her. She was seen recently driving aimlessly around her old Brentwood neighborhood and stopping to stare at the spot where her old Tigertail Road house had stood.

Jane's father, Hank—dead for seven years now—also seems to be very much on her mind again. When asked why she still felt nostalgic about a man who had been such a son-of-a-bitch to her, she replied with the old Louis B. Mayer remark about Wallace Beery, "Well, he was *my* son-of-a-bitch."

Typical of Jane's stories about the old days was one that she told at a party recently, with a newly acquired dry sense of humor: "You want to know about my first introduction to sex? Well, my father liked to play at being a farmer and he ploughed the fields behind our house on Tigertail Road. For his plowing, he used a pair of mules named Pancho and Pedro. Pancho was a girl. One day, I was riding Pancho bareback and leading Pedro. Suddenly Pedro mounted Pancho and started screwing her, with me pinned between his chest and her back. It was an educational experience but pretty damned frightening.''

Considerably more poignant—and not funny at all—is a story Jane wistfully tells about her father's last illness: "I was sitting at his bed in the hospital, spelling Shirlee for a little while. Dad's feet were sticking out from the end of the bed. I looked at his feet and I remembered what heaven it was to have my own feet massaged. So I got some cream and began to massage Dad's feet. I must have massaged them for an hour. I really don't think he knew I was there. He didn't move; he hadn't said a word. Then suddenly I heard his voice, and it seemed to come from the deepest, darkest depths: 'Jane, that's *heaven*!' Then he wouldn't let me do it anymore. When Shirlee came in, I told her about the massaging. I said, 'You know, by Dad's old-fashioned midwest standards, you have to be a *wife* to touch him. He never even held me on his knee. This is the first chance I've ever had to give him physical pleasure.' " Jane always sobs a bit when she tells that story.

Whatever will happen to Jane in the future, that last memory of her father probably will always be with her—a mixture of love and resentment. It accounts for her strange dichotomy of still wanting to do things that would please him and, at the same time, still trying to out-do him. With this dual motivation, there seems little doubt that she will continue to succeed at most of the things she attempts—in many fields.

Hers is a resilient life. She is talented and tough—sometimes ruthless—and she keeps bouncing back to do better than she did before. Even emotional turmoil doesn't seem to stop her. So far, at least.

If Henry Fonda were still alive, he probably would say, again, "I'm in awe of that kid." That's what millions of other Americans say, though they do not regard her as a kid anymore. She has left an indelible mark on us—even those who have never particularly admired her politics.

The key words when referring to her continue to be courage, guts, mettle, steel, moxie. Generally considered to be masculine-type nouns, they apply specifically to this very feminine woman. All her life, even in the face of the worst adversity, she never quit, never ceased to fight back. She doesn't walk away from problems. In Waterbury, she exhibited the kind of courage that few people have. She didn't *have* to go into that room with all those hostile veterans. She didn't *have* to go on television with Barbara Walters. She didn't *have* to rub her dying father's feet, or bring him his favorite root beer float—in her lifelong pursuit of trying to win his love. It was almost more important that she *tried* rather than whether or not she succeeded.

These are the qualities that endear her to so many women, in particular. Women especially keep referring to her remarkable resilience. One female executive said, "She could have died of embarrassment at least a half-dozen times in her life, and what did she do? She bounced back—more of a heroine than ever."

A female phoenix who keeps rising from the ashes? Mythology never said a phoenix couldn't be a woman.

FILMOGRAPHY

Tall Story (Warner Bros., 1960). Director: Joshua Logan. Co-star: Anthony Perkins.

Walk on the Wild Side (Columbia, 1962). Director: Edward Dmytryk. Co-stars: Laurence Harvey, Capucine, Barbara Stanwyck.

The Chapman Report (Warner Bros., 1962). Director: George Cukor. Co-stars: Shelley Winters, Claire Bloom.

Period of Adjustment (M-G-M, 1962). Director: George Roy Hill. Co-stars: Tony Franciosa, Jim Hutton.

In the Cool of the Day (M-G-M, 1963). Director: Robert Stevens. Co-stars: Peter Finch, Angela Lansbury.

Sunday in New York (M-G-M/7 Arts, 1964). Director: Peter Tewksbury. Co-star: Cliff Robertson.

Joy House (M-G-M, 1964). Director: René Clément. Co-star: Alain Delon.

Circle of Love (La Ronde) (Walter Reade–Sterling, 1965). Director: Roger Vadim. Co-stars: Jean-Claude Brialy, Peter McEnery.

Cat Ballou (Columbia, 1965). Director: Elliot Silverstein. Co-stars: Lee Marvin, Dwayne Hickman.

The Chase (Columbia, 1966). Director: Arthur Penn. Co-stars: Marlon Brando, Robert Redford.

Any Wednesday (Warner Bros., 1966). Director: Robert Ellis Miller. Co-star: Jason Robards.

The Game Is Over (La Curée) (Royal-Marceau, 1966). Director: Roger Vadim. Co-star: Peter McEnery.

Hurry Sundown (Paramount, 1967). Director: Otto Preminger. Co-star: Michael Caine.

Barefoot in the Park (Paramount, 1967). Director: Gene Saks. Co-star: Robert Redford.

Barbarella (Paramount, 1968). Director: Roger Vadim. Co-star: John Philip Law.

Spirits of the Dead (American International, 1969). Director: Roger Vadim. Co-star: Peter Fonda.

They Shoot Horses, Don't They? (Cinerama, 1969). Director: Sydney Pollack. Co-stars: Michael Sarrazin, Gig Young, Red Buttons, Susannah York, Bonnie Bedelia.

Klute (Warner Bros., 1971). Director: Alan J. Pakula. Co-star: Donald Sutherland.

F.T.A. (American International, 1972). Director: Francine Parker. Co-stars: Donald Sutherland, Holly Near.

Steelyard Blues (Warner Bros., 1972). Director: Alan Myerson. Co-stars: Donald Sutherland, Peter Boyle.

Tout va bien (Everything's Okay) (New Yorker Films, 1973). Director: Jean-Luc Godard. Co-star: Yves Montand.

A Doll's House (Tomorrow Entertainment, 1973). Director: Joseph Losey. Co-star: David Warner.

Introduction to the Enemy (IPC Films, 1974). A documentary filmed collectively by Tom Hayden, Jane Fonda, Haskell Wexler, and others.

The Blue Bird (Twentieth Century–Fox, 1976). Director: George Cukor. Co-star: Elizabeth Taylor.

Fun with Dick and Jane (Columbia, 1977). Director: Ted Kotcheff. Co-star: George Segal.

Julia (Twentieth Century–Fox, 1977). Director: Fred Zinnemann. Co-stars: Vanessa Redgrave, Jason Robards.

Coming Home (United Artists–IPC Films, 1978). Director: Hal Ashby. Co-stars: Jon Voight, Bruce Dern.

Comes a Horseman (United Artists, 1978). Director: Alan J. Pakula. Co-star: James Caan.

California Suite (Columbia, 1978). Director: Herbert Ross. Co-star: Alan Alda.

The China Syndrome (Columbia–IPC Films, 1979). Director: James Bridges. Co-stars: Jack Lemmon, Michael Douglas.

The Electric Horseman (Columbia–Universal, 1979). Director: Sydney Pollack. Co-star: Robert Redford.

Nine to Five (Twentieth Century–Fox/IPC Films, 1980). Director: Colin Higgins. Co-stars: Lily Tomlin, Dolly Parton.

On Golden Pond (IPC Films/ITC, 1981). Director: Mark Rydell. Co-stars: Henry Fonda, Katharine Hepburn.

Rollover (Warner Bros., 1981). Director: Alan J. Pakula. Co-star: Kris Kristofferson.

The Dollmaker (IPC Films–ABC Television, 1984). Director: Daniel Petrie. Co-star: Levon Helm.

Agnes of God (Columbia, 1985). Director: Norman Jewison. Co-stars: Anne Bancroft, Meg Tilly.

The Morning After (Twentieth Century–Fox/Lorimar/American Filmworks, 1986). Director: Sidney Lumet. Co-stars: Jeff Bridges, Raul Julia.

Old Gringo (Fonda Films/Columbia, 1989). Director: Luis Puenzo. Co-stars: Gregory Peck, Jimmy Smits.

Stanley and Iris (M-G-M, 1990). Director: Martin Ritt. Co-star: Robert De Niro.

INDEX

285